Passing the Buck

Passing the Buck

Banks, Governments
and
Third World Debt

PHILIP A. WELLONS
Harvard Business School

HARVARD BUSINESS SCHOOL PRESS
Boston, Massachusetts

Library of Congress Cataloging-in-Publication Data

Wellons, Philip A.
  Passing the buck.

  Includes bibliographical references and index.
  1. Loans, foreign. 2. Banks and banking,
International. 3. Loans, Foreign—Developing countries.
4. Debts, External—Developing countries. I. Title.
HG3891.5.W46 1987   332.1'53   86-19508
ISBN 0-87587-146-5 (alk. paper)

The paper used in this publication meets the requirements of the American National
Standard for Permanence of Paper for Printed Library Materials Z39.49-1984.

Harvard Business School Press, Boston 02163

Printed in the United States of America
90 89 88 87 86   5 4 3 2 1

to my parents and my wife,
Alfred, Elizabeth, and Marilyn

Contents

Acknowledgments

Three colleagues at the Harvard Business School merit special thanks. The insights of Dwight Crane about banking, Bruce Scott about national strategies and debt, and Louis Wells about the book's broad conceptual sweep were all key. Reading the book in multiple drafts, they helped far above and beyond the call of duty.

Others also helped me with the entire book. Early on, Colyer Crum combined unique, challenging criticism with a poet's command of language. Norman Berg, Joseph Bower, and Richard Vietor all helped me sharpen my overall argument. Howard MacDonald, the chief executive officer of Dome Petroleum, and a banker who must remain nameless, both brought the practitioner's perspective to the book. Two reviewers made very constructive comments.

Many people contributed valuably to parts of the book. Here at Harvard were Joseph Auerbach, David Mullins, Michael Porter, Hal Scott, William White, and David Yoffie. I also received useful comments from participants in conferences at the Harvard Business School, the Harvard Center for International Affairs, the Council on Foreign Relations, the Lehrman Institute, and Middlebury College. Barbara Aguilera's contribution is rightly prominent.

Raymond Corey, Director of Research, supported me in ways that went far beyond the financial resources for the extensive travel and time that this project demanded. My able research assistants were Haluk Alacaklioglu, Odile Disch, Max Donner, Beate Klein, Robert

Lichtman, and Tamar Manuelyan Atinc. Their toil supplied much of the unique statistical data in this book. I am indebted to Nancy Macmillan for her editorial work over many months. Patricia Murphy, Leonie Morales, Alison Fennelly, Betti Tiner, Marion LeBer, and Jill Wierbicki know that their secretarial services greatly exceeded the typing of the manuscript.

I thank the hundreds of bankers and officials around the world who generously donated their valuable time and insights born of experience to make this book possible. In return for candor, I promised anonymity. Their willing contributions transformed my project into stimulating, exciting research.

Finally, I thank my wife, Marilyn, whose intellectual contribution to this book began many years before I started it and equalled her patience as I researched and wrote.

Boston, Massachusetts   Philip A. Wellons
September, 1986

Passing the Buck

Introduction

"The Buck Stops Here."
Harry S Truman

Passing the buck is, literally, the business of banks. During the 1970s
and early 1980s, banks from industrial countries passed billions of
dollars in credit to borrowers in the third world. To the extent the
money helped avoid a collapse of demand after the oil shock of 1974
and promoted economic development, the lending was of great significance.

Passing the buck has also been, figuratively, essential for all those
in the international financial system. In the mid-1970s, the governments of the major industrial countries faced big balance-of-trade
deficits; they needed buyers for their exports and most buyers needed
financing. Financing helped win export orders, shifting the pressure
for internal adjustment to competing countries. Unable or unwilling
to provide most finance themselves, the industrial governments passed
the buck to the banks who took much of the formal risk associated
with the financing. The banks, through such techniques as floating
interest rates, tried to pass much of this formal risk on to the borrowers. Borrowing countries, in turn, chose not to restructure their economies after the oil shock and relied on credit to finance trade and fiscal
deficits; instead of responsible action, they too passed the buck. Debt
crises followed.

The crises forced the industrial governments to act. The banks had
formally accepted the risk, but concluded that in fact the risk was

1

quite low. No matter how the borrowing country used the funds, the government in power would have to service the debt; to do otherwise would place the country outside the international trading system. In this sense the lenders played the system. The local elites also played the system, using foreign credit for their own purposes; their bad investments and capital flight assured that the remaining good investments would not earn sufficient returns to service the debt. This meant the middle and lower classes, and the next generation, would have to accept a continually lower standard of living to help service the debt in the future. But these groups had limited means and patience. If their countries were strategically important, or the banks greatly exposed, the buck then passed back to the banks' home governments and taxpayers.

What a far cry this is from President Truman's aphorism, "The buck stops here." Truman embraced the idea that leadership requires responsible and decisive action. True, the international finance community has no counterpart to a president. Responsibility must be elusive. Action must never stop. But it is clear that someone must pay the price of such a system and that the buck often stops beyond the parties to the loans. This happens because of political and economic interests in the major industrial countries and shapes the cost and direction of the banks' initial lending.

In the early 1970s, the banks' ties to their home nation allowed and even encouraged them to lend to countries otherwise not eligible for private credit. Until recently, it was obvious that these ties were crucial for the major banks of Japan, Europe, and the United States. The banks were not truly international; that is, they did not behave alike when faced with similar opportunities and problems. Everybody knew that nationality made a great deal of difference. A book to show this was simply not warranted at that time.

During the 1970s, however, the international environment changed, big banks spread abroad, and capital markets integrated. For many, this signalled a new era of "internationalization" in which nationality would have little impact on a bank's lending abroad. Some holding this view agreed that the home country's regulations fostered national differences among banks, but concluded that the regulators' power had eroded in the face of global economic forces. Others disagreed, arguing that, for reasons extending far beyond regulation, the behavior of the banks had simply not matched their geographic spread and the internationalization of markets.

2

The two conflicting descriptions lead to very different recommendations to bankers and government officials who address the major international issues that face banking today. I come down squarely on the side of those who argue that nationality still plays a central role. Banks must use nationality as a strategic tool to win competitive advantage. When public policymakers use nationality to steer through problems in the future, they must beware that their actions do not increase instability, as did their response to the oil shocks of the 1970s.

The impact of a bank's nationality on its international credit was obvious in the past because, twenty-five years ago, few banks competed actively across national boundaries.[1] Instead, correspondent relations linked banks in different countries. There were few substitutes or potential entrants to challenge the banks; suppliers' credits financed trade and banks often funded the supplier. Barriers to entry were still high in 1960. The Eurocurrency market, outside the ambit of national controls, was tiny. International banking was a stable, slow-growth market populated by cautious banks and investors.

By 1980, international banking had altered beyond recognition. Hundreds of new entrants had opened foreign offices, offering many of the same services provided by established banks. Many banks linked financial markets around the world, their increased competition integrating the financial markets of major industrial countries. Changes in the international monetary system hastened the shift toward integration: exchange rates floated and restraints on capital movements declined further. Changes in technology permitted fast worldwide communications and vast, rapid storage and retrieval of data. New borrowers from developing countries and Eastern Europe appeared.

The entire industry became more complex, more competitive, more integrated, and more public. All the participants—funding sources, intermediaries, borrowers—enjoyed a wider range of options in more financial markets than ever before. National boundaries seemed far less significant. World supply and demand, mediated by numerous competing institutions, seemed to reduce any single player—even a major national government—to impotence.

The change in banking also brought a change in ideas: Nationality was no longer perceived as a force of great significance. Free market ideology informs the concept of international finance held by many

1. Dwight B. Crane and Samuel L. Hayes, III, "The New Competition in World Banking," *Harvard Business Review*, July–August 1982, p. 88.

3

bankers, officials, politicians, even the press. Nowhere are these ideas stronger than in the United States. In 1979, a senior vice-president of Citicorp stated this relation between his bank and its home government:

> We don't look to the U.S. government for any guidance or help. If anyone from the Treasury phoned asking us to lend to a specific borrower, I'd hang up on him. If I began to hear that the State Department was happy with our lending, I'd start to worry that maybe we're making the wrong decisions. . . . If the [National Bank Examiners'] ranking of a particular country isn't justified by our own research, we follow our own analysis.[2]

Many people believe that Citicorp's executive is right in two senses. First, he accurately describes the behavior of banks. In a highly integrated, competitive market banks act independently of government and perhaps from a position of dominance. Second, he is morally right. Banks ought to be independent. But ideology can confuse the ideal with the reality. The more recent view of bank independence misstates the relation between banks and their home government in crisis and when banks initially lend. This truth has always been known by the chief executive officers of the big banks.

The broad issue discussed here is the existence and depth of economic nationalism in international lending by banks. Economic nationalism is not easy to define. According to Gilpin, it is "the priority of *national* economic and political objectives over considerations of global economic efficiency."[3] This economic nationalism is most visible today in the realm of trade (see chapter 2). As applied to international banking, it suggests a market with the players bound closely to their home country, subject to a dominant government. At its extreme, this view is consistent with a long line of neomercantilist argument and interpretation. In 1906, for example, the director of Germany's Dresdner Bank testified at a government hearing that

2. Quoted in Philip A. Wellons, *The Future of Eurocurrency Lending by Citicorp* (Boston: Harvard Business School, 1980), p. 10.
3. Robert Gilpin, *U.S. Power and the Multinational Corporation* (New York: Basic Books, 1975), p. 232. Chapter 4, below, describes both liberal and mercantilist views in detail. Both are complex.

the Foreign Office has frequently stimulated the German banks to enter into competition for Italian, Austro-Hungarian, Turkish, Roumanian, Serbian, Chinese, Japanese, and South American loans. Even when the banks are approached from other quarters, the first move made is to ask the consent of the Foreign Office for carrying on the negotiations. If the consent is given, then ministers, ambassadors, and consuls frequently support the representatives of the German banks by word and deed.[4]

Over half a century later, government policy is felt less directly but still powerfully: no government will abdicate control over money and each government uses its banks to national purpose.

It matters which view is correct. If one assumes that international banking is highly integrated, one can infer that banks play according to certain rules. Prescriptions for banks and governments derive from this view. Three examples present the activities of a bank strategist, a government official in a borrowing country, and an official in an industrial country, within the frame of the liberal view.

- The bank strategist analyzes competing banks. The analysis must, of course, consider the standard factors of competitor size and policy. The analyst need not, however, look for any major asymmetry in the impact that market forces would have on competitors by virtue of their nationality. That is, a U.S. banker need not consider whether a third oil shock would increase the market power of banks from the United Kingdom and weaken those from Japan (or the reverse).
- The official in a borrowing country makes portfolio choices about the mix of lenders. The analysis must consider the lender's size, skill, and reputation. The analyst need not, however, be concerned with the nationality of the lending bank. A Philippine central banker does not care whether his country borrows primarily from Japanese and U.S. banks or at random from banks from many home countries.
- The official in a major industrial nation weighs the external finances of a strategically important ally as part of a broader country analysis. The analysis must consider the ally's debt

4. Herbert Feis, *Europe: The World's Banker* (New York: W. W. Norton, 1965), p. 174.

profile in terms of maturity, growth, and size. The analyst need not, however, be concerned that the ally depends on banks with a particular nationality. A U.S. foreign service officer does not care if Israel and Egypt borrow solely from French banks, solely from U.S. banks, or at random from banks with different nationalities.

If one assumes instead that banks are closely tied to their home countries, then the banker, the official in the borrowing country, and the official in the industrial country must consider the nationality of the banks.

- The banker might conclude that another oil shock could change the competitive picture for banks from a particular country. British banks as a group could be much more aggressive, for example.
- The central banker might link his country's borrowing policy with other ties between his country and its main trading partners (or may deliberately cut the link).
- The foreign service officer could well be concerned about the Israeli and Egyptian debt to French banks, given France's policy toward the Arab boycott of Israel.

At the heart of both the integrationist or the nationalist view is the relation between the banks and their home government.

Banks and their home governments can have one of four relations. The integrationist view suggests a liberal relation: banks are strong and independent of their home government. The nationalist view suggests three possible relations: a mercantilist one in which the banks are weak and subject to the government or a negotiated relation in which neither banks nor their government is supreme and which may be adversarial or cooperative. Thus, banks and their home government may try to use each other without regard to the other's needs, playing the national system to maximum advantage. Or, government and banks may ally either formally or tacitly to achieve goals both sides want. The four relations may be termed liberal, mercantilist, playing-the-system, and alliance.

During the 1970s and early 1980s, some of the major industrial countries conformed most closely to the liberal type, others to the mercantilist. Yet neither pattern fully describes the actual relationship.

In many cases one party or another played the national system. Banks loaned in reliance on their home government's interests, even when those governments discouraged the loans (as the U.S. government discouraged loans to Indonesia in the early 1970s). Governments, without formally accepting any risk, wanted the banks to mediate between oil depositors and deficit countries in the mid-1970s. On the other hand, many cases reflect shared interests and suggest alliance. Banks and their home governments jointly promoted major projects for export, for example. According to the evidence, they played the system and they allied.

Overall, both big banks and their home governments played the national system in the 1970s, each passing the buck, but as they moved through the 1980s both needed to turn toward alliance. Several factors suggest a further shift toward alliance at home is possible in the future. First, the global system has been evolving in this direction for years. As U.S. hegemony ebbed and the Bretton Woods system collapsed, the five major industrial nations shared power, making each government even more significant to its own banks' international lending. Second, the debt crisis forced banks and their governments to cooperate. Third, the trade finance wars have forged national alliances. As long as the nation persists as the focal point of concerted economic activity, banks and their home governments can ally.

Embedded in this idea of economic nationalism is the notion that banks, as well as their home government, seek to promote national economic and political goals over global efficiency. Indeed, there are sound economic reasons for banks to remain close to their home countries (see chapter 4). In several countries examined here, the banks' corporate interests profitably lie in their role in the home country. These banks gain more by maintaining their home country links than by achieving a global scale, although they are major international lenders. For example, German banks have established lending priorities by which home companies take precedence over sovereign borrowers. Despite the entry of these major multinational banks into international markets, the banks remain bound to their home countries by many links—structural, cultural, even styles of management—that benefit them economically. Banks that can build and maintain an alliance with their home government win a competitive edge in international markets.

Public policymakers who strengthen the alliance of banks and their government at the national level can move beyond crisis management and give broader direction to the system. They can do so in their substantive policy and in the procedures for determining policy. This book examines both threads.

The first thread is a complex home policy that affects banks' international lending. Many government agencies set policy on (1) the safety and soundness of bank operations; (2) the structure of the financial system, including the nature of competition among banks and between them and other intermediaries; (3) the macroeconomic conditions at home, including output, the trade balance, and international capital flows; and (4) the national security. All these policies affect international lending by banks.

The second thread is the process or style of governance. I reject the simplistic view that the government is always dominant and its banks merely tools.[5] Banks are one of many interest groups that try to shape policy. Their power varies among the major industrial countries and on specific issues. Of course national objectives may take priority over global efficiency because some government agencies (or some other authority) use the banks. A home government may influence its banks' international lending directly by incentives or restraints, shaping the big banks' strategy, products, and geographical markets directly. It may act indirectly by shaping their environment through macroeconomic policy or through other players important to the banks, such as home corporations. In fact, the governments tend to work largely without direct commands about particular transactions. They may also, moreover, not act at all.

Other national factors that shape banks' lending abroad are less associated with government policy, such as home corporations' exports and investment, or the activity of rivals. Both banks and their government, even in pursuit of different interests, may seek a common goal. Here, rather than merely in the government's power to command, lies the strength of alliance. Alliance is grounded in self-interest as well as political power at home.

To some, it may seem that this is a "political" interpretation of banks' behavior that is designed to counter standard "economic" explanations. It is not. I reject the notion that in general either political

---

5. In that view, "the government uses the activities of business abroad to advance the interest of the state." C. Fred Bergsten, Thomas Horst, and Theodore H. Moran, *American Multinationals and American Interests* (Washington, D.C.: The Brookings Institution, 1978), p. 324.

or economic forces take precedence over the other. The world is too complex for such simple dichotomies. This book makes the case that to understand banks' international lending, one must understand both political and economic forces at work in the banks' home countries. The precise extent varies with the nature of the lending.

The impact of the home country is felt unequally in the various types of banks' international lending.[6] This unequal impact helps explain the prevalent view that banks in international markets act independently of government. A well-known activity of international banks happens to be outside government control: their interbank operations take place in one of the most integrated, deepest, and least regulated financial markets in the world. There is no home policy, since governments have other means to accomplish their objectives (they can, for example, manipulate domestic monetary policy). Many other major activities, however, are less free. Among these, a home country has its greatest impact where its interests are greatest, such as finance for trade in manufactures. Its impact is moderate where its interests are less strong.

The literature on international banks has mushroomed since the late 1970s, and I draw on it throughout. For readers who want a history of the Eurocurrency market or of banks' international expansion, or a guide to the techniques of banks' operations overseas, I refer them to the appropriate sources. I do not intend to duplicate here the numerous books that describe institutional developments. For this reason, the reader will not find here the IET, the VFCR, the Eastern European government that sired the Eurocurrency market, or a chronology of international banking in the 1970s and the debt crisis in 1982.

This is a comparative study of international lending by the biggest banks in the major industrial countries. The terrain is wide and deep. To limit the job, I make test borings at key spots, applying different tests to compare behavior. To map the activities of lead banks in the broad market for Eurocredit syndications, I use a quantitative approach (in chapter 5). For depth in analyzing the process of bank-

---

6. I seek to account for only international lending, an activity in which the bank acts as principal rather than broker or adviser. International lending is deceptively simple to define. Here I cast a wide net: lending is international when it involves two or more countries. If need be, to explain international lending, I also explore domestic activities.

government relations, I use case studies based on standard, carefully drawn questions (chapter 1 and elsewhere). I borrow from law the method of analyzing legislative history to interpret bank regulation in various countries (chapter 3). Each method used alone has drawbacks. Together, they reach below the surface of the terrain.

The big banks are the object of this study because they shape international lending. They are leaders in an industry with many followers. For reasons explored below, many smaller banks turn to a handful of big banks for help when deciding whether and to whom to lend. Already big lenders in their own right, the leaders thus shape the flow of credit worldwide not only by the way they place their own funds but also by pointing the way for the followers. The nine largest U.S. banks, for example, accounted for 35 percent of all syndications in 1982 but only 22 percent of all international assets. My narrow focus is on twenty-eight big banks that are at the center of the international banking industry. Although they are the ones whose officials I interviewed, no clear line distinguishes them from the other big banks of their home countries. There is no reason to think that those only slightly smaller would behave in a substantially different way.

I examine banks in the five major industrial countries: the United States, Japan, Germany, France, and the United Kingdom. These are the G-5 or Group of Five countries. They are the home countries of the biggest banks, and hence are the major intermediary nations. The G-5 governments' policies and performance drive much of the world economy. In international finance, their ministers of finance and central bank governors confer and, sometimes, act jointly. Yet differences among them in both style of governance and the aim or intent of their policies mean that each plays a different role in the international lending of its own big banks. As the following chapters show, that role is best understood in terms of what the home government is trying to accomplish—in a sense, its strategy.

I use different techniques at the four levels of analysis. Immediately guiding each bank's loans is its own business strategy; the tools for analyzing corporate strategy guide me at this level. Second, each bank's lending takes place in the international banking industry; here, the techniques of competitive and industry analysis are essential to understand the nature of rivalry among the banks themselves, and the relative power of the suppliers of funds and the users. Home government policies affect each of these forces. Third, the banks lend to many countries; to understand their behavior and the policies of the home country, I draw on a form of country analysis that uses the notion of national strategy. I examine the behavior of the governments with an eye for the overall direction that is greater than the sum of separate policies (see chapter 2). Finally, banks operate in a world economy beset with uncertainty. To think about the future, I use carefully constructed scenarios to present the implications of the study (see chapter 8).

Much of the data is from fieldwork that consisted of interviews in the G-5 countries and in Mexico. I interviewed bankers in both senior and middle management; government officials in regulatory agencies, central banks, export credit agencies, and ministries of finance, foreign affairs, foreign assistance, and commerce; and key Mexican government officials for the Sicartsa case (chapter 1) and for the debt restructuring (chapters 6 and 7). Since the interviews took place from 1979 to as late as 1985 in some cases, I was often able to meet the same person several times.

The book draws also on data gathered much earlier than 1979. This supplementary information comes from my earlier work. For the United Nations Center for Transnational Corporations, from 1977 to 1980 I worked on a study of transnational banks. For the Organization for Economic Cooperation and Development, from 1973 to 1975 I studied the strategies of major borrowing countries. For the government of Zambia, from 1971 to 1973 I negotiated with lending banks and began to gather data about them.

I first thought about this topic while living in Zambia in the early 1970s. At that time many people there knew their neighbor to the north, Zaire, as a country with a corrupt, undisciplined government. Yet we learned that foreign bankers were lending millions of dollars to Zaire. How could anyone expect to be repaid? Sure enough, Zaire soon reneged on its obligations. I began to wonder why the bankers loaned the money in the first place and why their regulators stood by and watched. One possible explanation was that U.S. bankers had gambled on the U.S. government's interests in Zaire as a friendly country near Angola, where Communist-backed insurgents opposed the colonial power, Portugal.

This book explains the role of economic nationalism in international banking and its implications. Each chapter documents its application. The chapters are arranged in four parts: first, the home government's policies and behavior (chapters 2 and 3); second, the banks' policies and behavior (chapters 4 and 5); third, the debt crisis (chapters 6 and 7); and finally, the implications of the study for policy on the part of public policymakers and banks (chapter 8).

Home governments play an active role in their banks' international lending far beyond the passive role of their macroeconomic policies. Their use of trade-related finance extends to policies on capital out-flows and the financial structure of the country. The competition among the industrial nations after the oil shocks placed prudential regulation in second place, after exports. And in one of the most important markets in the 1970s, Eurosyndications, a supposedly global market, I find evidence of strong national forces at work.

Even if a home government's trade policies and regulation were to be weakened, the home's role as lender of last resort would ensure its continuing importance to the banks, for in the international system of debt management, governments and their banks try to pass the buck, which leads to overlending and collapse. I believe that the chiefs of leading banks around the world clearly understood the system I describe and, acting accordingly, behaved rationally. The overall effect, however, was damaging.

A real case will help the reader understand the relationship between banks and their home governments. In chapter 1, I describe the financing of Sicartsa phase II, a multibillion-dollar steel project in Mexico and one of the most obvious cases of economic nationalism at work in the G-5 countries. Although one cannot generalize about all lending on the basis of one case, the Sicartsa project captures many of the problems in the recent episode of bank lending to developing countries.

1

Banks and the Export Credit Wars: Mixed Credits in the Sicartsa Financing

On February 17, 1983, Queen Elizabeth's royal yacht carried Her Majesty into the Rio de las Balsas on the west coast of Mexico. Sailing from Acapulco to California, the queen was to inspect Sicartsa, the integrated steel plant at Ciudad Lazaro Cardenas, near the town of Las Truchas.[1] One year earlier, the British firm of Davy McKee (Sheffield), Ltd., had won the largest part of the second phase of construction at Sicartsa. Davy's plate mill was expected to earn Britain $600 million in exports, almost one-third of the entire $2 billion expansion. Now, faced with a balance-of-payments crisis, the government of Mexico was considering canceling phase II.[2]

Milling in the crowd on the pier as the yacht docked were the agents of Davy McKee and Lloyds Bank International (LBI). The bank had done far more than simply arrange private finance for the plate mill; it had helped Davy win the bid in Mexico and official

1. Sicartsa is an acronym for Siderurgica Lazaro Cardenas-Las Truchas, S.A. It is part of Sidermex, a group of three Mexican integrated steel plants with sixty-nine affiliates. Public-sector agencies hold a majority of the shares in each firm. In 1980, compared to other groups in Mexico, Sidermex ranked second in sales (with $2.8 billion), third in assets ($4.7 billion). It accounted for 60 percent of Mexican steel output. See "Sidermex: A Description of the Sidermex Group of Companies," a prospectus prepared by Sidermex, Mexico City, 1981.

2. Interview, Mexico. Much of this chapter is drawn from interviews with executives in Sicartsa at the time of the negotiations and with executives in the major bidding firms and their banks, in Britain, France, Germany, Japan, and the United States.

support back home. Neither the supplier, its banker, nor the U.K. government intended to let the project slip away. Queen Elizabeth came to silence any murmurings of this possibility in Mexico or elsewhere.

To win the contract, the British had offered exceptional financing on top of a low bid for the plant. In a heated and sometimes Byzantine rivalry among national groups during late 1981, Britain beat Japanese, French, and German competitors. Davy's price was 25 percent below the average bid. The U.K. government offered to finance 10 percent of the price with a grant, free of interest or repayment. LBI would finance the remainder, half with a Eurocredit bearing interest 100 basis points (1 percent) below that offered by banks financing other bidders. The loan package would mature in twenty-one years.

This story of nation-based competition reveals an intense trade-finance war. By the late 1970s, the highly politicized conflict drew in several groups at home. Banks played an important part, in response to their home government's policies. No government coerced its banks. Instead, each changed the banks' cost and opportunities by manipulating the risk to the banks and the demand for their services. The banks responded of their own accord.

So intense was the rivalry among these national groups that a prospective buyer could play one exporting nation off another. In the case of Sicartsa, the Mexicans manipulated economic and political forces in several G-5 nations to their advantage. Without adequate home government aid, exporting companies would lose their bids, their employees could lose their jobs, and their banks would not lend. In projects worth hundreds of millions of dollars, the stakes were high. Exporters and their banks had an incentive to assure their own home government played the game. The governments had reason to act.

The trade wars opened opportunities for banks and their home firms to form national alliances when competing in world markets. By managing this process, banks could get an edge over banks from other countries. In Sicartsa, some did. For them, the key factor was their home government. In no instance was a government the pawn of the banks or the exporting firms. The home government pursued its own interests, with general policies for the export credit wars already in place. The banks and firms had to work together on indi-vidual transactions to elicit government support and to forge a bank-firm-government alliance that would win against similar groups from other countries.

This combative environment set the parameters for banks competing in global markets to finance big projects. When specific banks chose to enter, the play would depend on their home government's export credit policies, on the process of policymaking at home, and on the banks' ties to the exporting firms. Some, like Lloyds Bank, entered early. Others held back until the last minute. Each responded to its unique home environment. The same combative environment helps explain why developing countries were able to borrow massive amounts of money from banks for projects that, like Sicartsa phase II, did not make economic sense.

Garcia Torres Forges the Link Between Trade and Finance

At the center of Sicartsa's opportunistic and sometimes brilliant strategy was the second in command at Sidermex. Arturo Garcia Torres H., the chief financial officer, was trained as an economist. He brought to Sidermex fourteen years of experience in Mexico's central bank and two years in each of three parastatals, the bank Somex, the oil company Pemex, and the development bank Nafinsa. By the time he reached Sidermex, Garcia Torres had even negotiated the financing of a plant for another Mexican steel company, Ahmsa. The experience served him well. Prospective exporters and bankers from three continents credit him with the exceptional terms Sicartsa won for phase II.

Garcia Torres shaped opportunities for banks in this market. After opening the bids, he linked trade to finance irrevocably. The purchase would depend on financing terms, not merely on the quality of the equipment. He then set financial thresholds. Manipulating the players in each supplier country, he prodded exporters, their banks, and their home governments to go beyond terms offered by competitors from other nations. The process defined the banks' ability to finance one of the largest projects in the world. The home government's willingness and capacity to act determined a country's success in winning bids, in turn shaping the banks' costs and opportunities.

This was a buyer's market. In 1981, potential exporting countries suffered from serious balance-of-trade deficits. Further, few countries outside the oil-producing states had the need for and credit standing to undertake big projects. Still fewer wanted to erect steel mills in a world plagued with excess steel capacity. Mexico did. It was among the most creditworthy states, and the country used its economic muscle to approach the sellers, linking trade to finance.

The Trade-Finance Link

Sicartsa followed three steps in awarding a contract: first, a technical analysis to determine the type of product to be purchased; next, a tender to get bids on price; finally, negotiation about financing. When the bids were not technically identical, Sicartsa's engineers and technical consultants would homologize them, or make them comparable in value, after which the chief financial officer would negotiate terms. According to Garcia Torres, "I think of price and finance as two parts of the same thing."

This was the procedure for Sicartsa phase II. A negotiating link between purchase and financing may seem obvious, but it is not inevitable. In the late 1970s, Mexico's powerful agricultural parastatal Conasupo uncoupled finance from purchase. The ostensible reason was greater efficiency: the country should get the best price for the goods in the commodity market and the best price for the credit in the capital markets.[3] Mexican law prohibited changes in price after a bid was made, however, so a bidder could lower the overall cost only by offering good financial terms. The effect of this uncoupling was to prevent Conasupo from bargaining down the price by means of finance.

Sicartsa Phase II

Sicartsa phase II emerged at the end of the 1970s after a long, troubled gestation. From the early 1940s, former president Lázaro Cárdenas had wanted Mexico to exploit the iron ore deposits near the Pacific coast at Las Truchas, part of his political base. In 1969, a year before Lázaro Cárdenas died, President Díaz Ordaz set up a company to examine the feasibility of a new government steel plant for Mexico. Since the report was completed shortly before the end of his term, Díaz left the decision to his successor, President Echeverría. Unable

3. Another explanation for the policy of uncoupling was that the opportunities for graft grew with the number of transactions.

to decide on the merits of several sites, the new administration turned to the World Bank and the Inter-American Development Bank (IDB) for technical advice. The company hired British Steel Corporation as consultant.

By mid-1973, Mexico had a plan. Sicartsa would supply steel operations in other parts of Mexico. President Echeverría decreed the complex would be located at Ciudad Lazaro Cardenas (see Figure 1-1), and would rise in four stages, each phase to be built in the term of a different Mexican president. Phase I would create 1.3 million tons of steel capacity by 1976, which would be used to produce nonflat products such as reinforced bars and wire rods. Phase II would add flat steel, increasing capacity to 3.6 million tons by 1982. Phase III would increase capacity to 6.0 million tons by 1989, and phase IV, to 10.0 million tons by 1994.

The Sicartsa plan required a massive effort. The isolated location meant that everything would have to be built. There were no main roads linking the project to the rest of the country, no local infrastructure to support the plants, and no local population to run them; roads, houses, and services such as schools, shops, and utilities would have to be supplied. Workers and their families would have to be brought in; the population was to increase from 7,000 in 1970 to over 60,000 by 1976. Indeed, there wasn't even a port to bring in coal. That, too, would have to be built.

Then there was the plant itself. Phase I alone had many parts, and each component was technically complex. When they were combined, the scale of the project was immense. There were ten major components of phase I.

1. Deep-water port: dredging
2. Electric power generation: boilers, turboblowers, distribution system
3. Mining and iron ore concentration
4. Pelletizing plant for ore
5. Coke production (imported ore): dock, crushing equipment, conveyors
6. Blast furnaces to produce pig iron
7. Basic oxygen converter to produce steel: oxygen plant, lime plant, stockers, and reclaimers
8. Continuous casting plant for billets

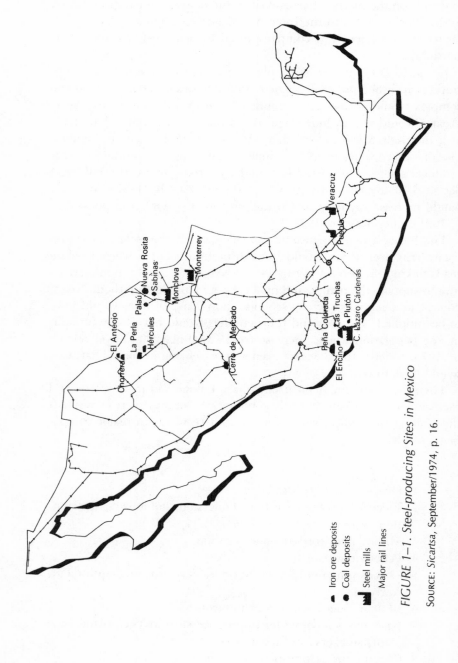

Iron ore deposits

Coal deposits

Steel mills

Major rail lines

FIGURE 1–1. Steel-producing Sites in Mexico

SOURCE: *Sicartsa*, September/1974, p. 16.

Charcas
El Anteojo
La Perla
Hércules
Palaú
Nueva Rosita
Sabinas
Monclova
Monterrey
Cerro de Mercado
Peña Colorada
El Encino
Las Truchas
Plutón
C. Lázaro Cárdenas
Veracruz
Puebla

9. Rolling mills (wire rods and bar, 50 percent; light sections, 50 percent): buildings, plants
10. Distribution system: rail line, locomotives, highway

On the advice of the IDB and the World Bank, Sicartsa's executives toured the industrial world for bilateral financing. With their major banks, the export agencies of Austria, France, Germany, Italy, Japan, and the United Kingdom made credit lines available. Mexico reportedly rejected an offer by the president of the U.S. Export-Import Bank to finance the entire project if Mexico would buy only U.S. equipment. Instead, Mexico chose to diversify its suppliers, largely by home country.

The diversification policy, in the words of one foreign observer, created a United Nations of suppliers. Each major supplier was an important firm at home. Fives Cail Babcock of France won the contract for the concentrator; Lurgi Chemie of Germany, with Head Wrightson of the United Kingdom, won the pelletizer; Nippon Kokan Kaisha of Japan, the coke production; Italimpianti of Italy, the blast furnaces; Voest-Alpine of Austria, the oxygen converter; Schloemann Concast of Germany and Canada, the continuous caster; and Davy Loewy of the United Kingdom, the rolling mills. In all, work outside Mexico would be done in eleven countries.

A United Nations of suppliers meant complicated financing. The IDB would lend $54 million, the World Bank $70 million, European banks $180 million, and nine industrial governments $170 million. Mexico provided the remaining finance. Cost overruns were high. With an estimated total cost of $560 million, phase I cost over $1 billion. The plant officially began to produce reinforced bars, wire rods, and light steel shapes on New Year's Day, 1977.

Phase II had a false start between 1975 and 1978. In October 1975, before phase I was completed, President Echeverría announced phase II. In May 1976, Sicartsa awarded a planning contract to British Steel Corporation, and there was talk of a $3 billion project. But during the economic troubles of 1976–1977, the steel sector encountered serious problems. Fundidora Monterrey Steel Company, after expanding too fast, was caught by the devaluation and recession. The government and foreign banks worked out a rescheduling during 1977. Then in February 1978, the public-sector steel companies reorganized under Sidermex. Two months later, Mexico abandoned the outstanding contracts and financial arrangements of the first part of phase II, including those with the World Bank and the IDB.

The second effort to initiate phase II began quietly in early 1979 in response to two internal forces. Within Mexico, support for the project revived as the economy recovered. By March, there was enough interest for the minister of industry to identify phase II, by function, as one of the priority industries eligible for tax incentives.[4] Forces outside Mexico promoted the revival too.

Promoters of Sicartsa found their project caught up in a Japanese initiative in economic diplomacy that seemed entirely extraneous to the development of Mexico's steel sector. In Japan, beginning in late 1978, a group led by the Industrial Bank of Japan tried to secure a long-term supply of one hundred thousand barrels a day of Mexican crude oil. To that end, after the second oil shock in mid-1979, the Japanese government opened direct talks with the Mexican government. In August 1979, Mexico agreed to supply the oil at market prices for ten years. In exchange, the Japanese government would make two loans. One, a $500 million loan for ten years, would support Pemex. The second was to be the yen equivalent of about $150 million, for twenty-five years at about 4 percent.[5] This loan ultimately financed Sicartsa, but in August 1979 the commitment could only be general; the project was far from the bidding stage.

Armed with concessional credit and an inside track, the Japanese saw their prize, the plate mill, in hand. Although it was the main plant, the plate mill was only one of eight major components in phase II:

1. Electric power generators
2. Mining and iron ore concentrators
3. Pelletizing plant for ore

4. See "Agreement Establishing Priority Industrial Activities," Art. 1.2.4, *Diario Oficial*, March 9, 1979, translated and reprinted in *Mexico: National Industrial Development Plan*, Vol. 2 (Mexico: Graham & Trotman, 1979), pp. 195-204.

5. Japan's Export-Import bank would provide 70 percent, Japanese banks the remainder. An unusual feature was the fixed interest rate, rare for private banks that normally fund dollar loans in the Eurocurrency market. Even more remarkable, the private banks' 8 percent rate was 2 percent below the market rate at the time. J. Andrew Spindler, *The Politics of International Credit* (Washington, D.C.: The Brookings Institution, 1984), pp. 172–173. Japan never received more than 22,000 barrels per day from Mexico.

4. Direct reduction sponge iron plant
5. Electric arc furnace to produce pig iron
6. Continuous casting plant for billets
7. Plate mill for flat steel
8. Casting and forging plant for large pipe

The Japanese expected difficult bargaining, not in Mexico, but in Japan, where several groups sought the right to sell the plate mill. The Japanese ignored the intense export competition among the industrial nations. The Mexicans did not.

Sicartsa's executives adopted a strategy that sought maximum leverage, which they used to shift as much risk as possible to foreign suppliers and lenders. Their strategy had five elements:

(a) solicit separate bids for each of the main components and negotiate serially (rejecting a turnkey project in which one company or consortium would supply the entire phase);
(b) seek a long grace period to allow adequate start-up time (in the tender documents Sicartsa requested five years of grace, then pushed for seven years in negotiations);
(c) seek maturities of twenty years, but not longer if to do so would reduce the share of costs to be financed;
(d) "overfinance" because Mexico in late 1981 was moving toward illiquidity; and
(e) do not weight future exchange rate fluctuations, which were too difficult to predict (thus rates were fixed on the day bids were opened).[6]

Garcia Torres relied on timing and secrecy, along with the link between purchase and finance. The absence of the link foiled his efforts to negotiate low-cost finance when President López Portillo selected two suppliers in September 1980. The president decided that the U.S. firm Dravo, which had built a similar plant for Ahmsa, would supply the pelletizer. The Mexican firm Hylsa would be the

6. Garcia Torres did not use forward rates or make any other attempt to modify an interest rate by taking into account anticipated changes in a currency's exchange rate.

source of direct-reduction technology for the sponge iron plant. Safely selected, the suppliers could be obdurate about terms for finance.[7]

Garcia Torres negotiated the other projects, however, with his own script. He bargained with bidding companies, their banks, and officials from their home government. The good terms for one component became the threshold for the next. Good offers from one country were used to bid down other countries in bilateral talks. Countries that lost on one component were goaded to bid lower on the next. Once they had lost the plate mill to the United Kingdom, Japan's firms and ministries regrouped to win both the continuous caster and the electric arc furnace. National competitiveness galvanized suppliers and their home governments.

Beginning in September 1981, Sicartsa awarded contracts; it seems to have rushed to complete the awards by June 1982. Compared to the original timetable, phase II had moved slowly. Building would have barely begun by the original completion date of 1982. Then, in August 1982, Mexico plunged into a financial crisis, derailing phase II once again.

Mexico's Opportunity in the Export Credit Wars

Garcia Torres helped make Sicartsa phase II a large battlefield in the trade war among industrial states. Since the big Mexican awards turned on the combination of price and financing, most bidding countries rolled out their full arsenal of trade support: official export credits, insurance, rediscounting, grants, soft aid loans, and guarantees for commercial bank loans. Some bidders, notably the British, offered credit in foreign currency, attracting the borrower whose export earnings were largely in currencies other than sterling and alleviating the burden of the British government, whose loans could be kept off budget and thus not seen to augment the deficit. Several governments offered mixed credits. Combined, these weapons might make high bidders into winners or block other nations from winning. Whether the weapons would help the country in a broader way is debatable.[8]

---

7. Thus for the pelletizer, Sicartsa could negotiate a loan only with a maturity of 18 years rather than 20 and with a grace period of less than 7 years.

8. The usefulness of export credit subsidies to the lending country has been challenged at two levels. First, some assert that cheap finance does not sway buyers, who are after low price and high quality. The second challenge is more

Circumstances in the 1970s and early 1980s helped big buyers like Sicartsa fuse trade and its finance to their advantage. The threat of greater unemployment and trade deficits haunted the governments of the industrial countries. The executives in Sicartsa saw that their company was ideally positioned: big, visible, with a long history during which it became known to virtually every major exporter and bank, in a country that seemed rich even to the banks that knew Mexico intimately, and in a world racked by recession and low demand for the exporter's product. The Mexicans exploited the competition among the industrial nations in phase I. The governments in the Organization for Economic Cooperation and Development (OECD) had tried since then to promote international cooperation to reduce financial competition among industrial states, but their efforts foundered repeatedly on national imperatives.

Banks have an incentive, because of the way official support works, to ally with potential exporters and their home government against similar groups from other countries. If a home government gives a guarantee to a bank, for example, the asset on the bank's books may fund a loan to Sicartsa, but the bank will treat it as exposure to the guarantor, which is much less risky than a Mexican credit. The bank prices the loan above the interest it would earn by lending to the home government, so its spread rises despite the lower risk. The official aid is important, however, not merely because it gives the banks more in interest and fees. The official subsidy will decide who actually wins the bid. Only with the subsidy does the bank lend.

The winning alliance of government, exporter, and bank changes the bank's portfolio. At the aggregate level, the home country's exports increase at the expense of nontraded domestic production. The bank's

---

complex. In this view, subsidies offer no help at the macroeconomic level. For example, Baron concludes that export credit cannot be justified to overcome capital market deficiencies, improve the balance of payments, stimulate employment, provide economic assistance, or support key industries. David P. Baron, *The Export-Import Bank: An Economic Analysis* (New York: Academic Press, 1983), p. 84. Baron adds, however, that a case may be made for government insurance or guarantees. He does not address the issue of intervention earlier in the production process. Though valid, these challenges oversimplify the impact of the export credit wars. Garcia Torres's negotiating strategy contradicts the argument that buyers are not sensitive to subsidized credit. His engineers, by making the bids equal in a technical sense, reduced the role of product quality as a factor. The cost of finance was extremely important to his decision.

assets shift in two ways: first, away from domestic to international business and, second, within international business to the supported activity, since banks limit overall lending. In the Sicartsa bidding, some alliances succeeded, and others never got off the ground.

The Big Banks, Exporters, and Their Home Governments

The way each country decides whether and how to compete affects its success in this market. Garcia Torres was able to work with the specific process in most countries, influencing the bids and awards. In this way, he shaped the demand for the banks' services. That he could do this is instructive. It points to an opportunity for banks and their client firms to build alliances that will help them win in the competition among nations.

The trade-finance link Sicartsa exploited is formed by many strands of public and private interests in exporting countries. The banks' interests tug in two directions. The banks contribute to a successful outcome if the pricing of their loans is competitive, but their loans, which are priced commercially, cannot alone ensure success. Others in the alliance determine if the bid will win. The banks depend upon this joint effort to win the competition among nations: if their home company loses, they do not lend. They have a stake in the success of their home country's thrust in the trade credit wars, but if they conclude the probability of failure is large, they have little incentive to build an alliance with their home government and clients.

Each government's stance toward export subsidies defines what the exporters and banks could expect from an alliance. In the Sicartsa case, the stances reflected government agendas extending well beyond the needs of the individual parties. In Japan, the government offered aid to Sicartsa in order to secure an interest in Mexican oil as part of a national goal of security in raw materials. The stances differed significantly among the G-5 countries, reflecting the various interests and varied processes of decision making embedded in a broader political mosaic at home.

Both strategy and process at home affected the banks' and exporters' efforts to build an alliance. In the three countries whose governments had a general policy of supporting exports—France, Japan, and the United Kingdom—the exporters' job was to mobilize the agencies that normally promoted this support, such as a ministry of trade and industry. In the two countries whose governments kept a formal distance from their firms—Germany and the United States—the exporters and their home banks adopted strategies that did not rely on official support. Germans limited their product and sourced as much as possible outside Germany. U.S. firms withdrew from most of the competition.

Garcia Torres used the nascent bank-exporter-government partnerships to Sicartsa's advantage in the negotiations over phase II. Manipulating the process in each country, he played off three nations—Britain, France, and Japan—against one another and others. He could not do the same with Germany or the United States.

Negotiating the Alliance in the United Kingdom, Japan, and France

On the face of it, the exporters and their bankers should have had a hard time getting government help for phase II. They had to persuade their home governments to give cheap loans and aid, violating the spirit if not the letter of intergovernment conventions. The aid was going to Mexico, which, as an oil exporter, was among the richest developing countries. It would finance new plants in the steel industry, already marked by vast overcapacity worldwide. Although a portion of the export finance would return to the home country,[9] the total aid sought could finance a range of exports with less dubious credentials. Under these circumstances, why should a government act? Export aid is usually a scarce resource. In the competition for it, the bidders were opposed at home by other firms and government agencies.

The governments of France, Japan, and the United Kingdom had the power to support exports for broad purposes. In each country, a firm and its bank won export aid in much the same way. They lobbied officials in the responsible government agencies—the trade ministry, the export credit agency, the treasury, and the foreign aid agency—and encouraged political allies to press those officials too. Their representatives met as a group either to set policy or to award support.

In none of these governments did the mixing of aid and export credits have unanimous support. The agencies had long since drawn their lines on the issue. One British official said:

9. See Heywood Fleisig and Catharine Hill, *The Benefits and Costs of Official Export Credit Programs of Industrialized Countries* (World Bank Staff Working Paper No. 659, Washington, D.C., 1984).

> We know in advance how most members will vote as a matter of policy. Treasury will oppose, as will the Bank of England. The [export credit agency] would rather not [extend help]. The Department of Industry, and the Defence Ministry if it is involved, will both urge aid, while the Foreign Office will say yes or no depending on the country.

Sure enough, Britain's Treasury, the Finance Ministry in Japan, and the Trésor in France opposed special help for bidders on phase II. How the exporters and banks won government support over this opposition affected the outcome of the bids in Mexico.

There seem to be many parallels in the way the various countries formally organized to allocate financial help for exports. The common stages and similar roles of agencies in the various countries might lead to the conclusion that the major industrial countries resolve issues of this sort in the same way. In fact, major differences affected the outcome. The United Kingdom won the most important contract, the $596 million plate mill, in a well-coordinated attack. Japan lost that contest, but regrouped to win two later bids, the $229 million electric arc furnace and the $225 million continuous caster. The French also lost the plate mill, then ultimately won the $126 million concentrator.

The United Kingdom

Britain won the plate mill, according to one of Sicartsa's senior officers, because it "had its act together." In fact, the key was the British grant equal to $57 million, or 10 percent of the entire cost. It was a gift that Mexico had neither to service nor to repay. To win the grant, the bidder, Davy McKee, "hammered away like hell," in the words of one government official. Davy attacked on two levels, civil servants and national politicians. Lloyds Bank worked with Davy.

At the civil service level, Davy and Lloyds drew on the Thatcher government's export drive, embodied in part in the Projects and Export Policy Division (PEP), in the Department of Trade and reporting to the Department of Industry. Set up in 1981, PEP was to coordinate all government support for major capital projects overseas. It was also, said one official, to "stop fractured U.K. industry from competing with each other."

The U.K. government offered exporters exceptional assistance through two agencies, the Export Credit Guarantee Department

(ECGD) and the Overseas Development Administration (ODA). Her Majesty's government distinguished between the ECGD's commercial support, which was to be self-funding, and its political support, which the government had helped fund. Each type of support had its own award process. For support judged by commercial criteria, a council of business representatives reviewed the ECGD's recommendations. For support judged by political criteria, the reviewing council was a Whitehall group called the Export Guarantee Committee, chaired by the Treasury and including the Bank of England, the ECGD, the Departments of Trade, Industry, and Defence, and the Foreign Office. Criteria for political support included the impact on employment in the United Kingdom, the benefits to a bidder whose survival depended on the export, and the political relations between the United Kingdom and the importing country.

The British government had also established in 1977 an Aid and Trade Program (ATP) that offered mixed credits. The ATP budget of £12.1 million in 1978–1979 had risen to £53 million in 1981–1982, and would be £66 million in 1983–1984.[10] The exporter applied to the PEP, which would recommend the application to the ODA. The ODA then decided whether the proposal met the government's criteria for aid. The Treasury decided whether the subsidy was within the OECD guidelines.

The PEP was a natural ally for Davy and Lloyds in their efforts to overcome the opposition of the Treasury and the ODA. The PEP's leverage came in its ability to time the flow of information. Passing Davy's application to the ODA in August 1981, hardly six weeks before bids were due, the PEP prevented the ODA from giving the project a full study, which might have uncovered flaws. This was the only manufacturing project the ODA had ever done without a quantitative cost-benefit analysis. It was also the largest project supported by the ODA. Yet with no inspection on site, no feasibility study, no solid estimates of Mexico's comparative advantage in steel, and no data about the rate of return on phase II, the ODA nevertheless determined the project could be good for Mexico. Davy, Lloyds, and the PEP had mobilized ministers at the cabinet level.

The political offensive was broad. Bureaucrats in the Department of Trade won the support of the secretary of state for trade, who

10. See House of Commons, 2d Report of the Foreign Affairs Committee, 1981–1982 Session, *Supply Estimates 1982–1983*, Class II, votes 10 and 11, July 5, 1982, and Government Response Command 8734, November 1982.

pressed his counterparts in the Treasury. Davy and a major subcontractor, the General Electric Corporation, sought the prime minister's support. Davy lobbied the leader of the Conservative party. At the same time, the acquisition of Davy, an important exporter, by an American firm was prevented by the government. The prime minister showed her support for the project by speaking in Parliament about the jobs phase II would create in the United Kingdom.

The Treasury's turnabout came only one week before bids were due. The interagency compromise addressed Treasury objections to the high cost of the support for phase II. The Department of Trade proposed a loan in deutschemarks, equal to $64 million, to finance the Mexican costs of the project and the goods sourced in other European Community countries. The loan eased pressure on the budget. Since the government subsidized interest rates above 7.75 percent, having the deutschemark interest rates below those for sterling lowered the immediate cost of the government's subsidy. To reduce the impact of the grant, the ODA would pay it in two different fiscal years.

Davy's bid of $596 million was the lowest. The French bid $773 million, and the Japanese bid a figure that surprised everyone in the room: $1,031 million. Prime Minister Margaret Thatcher informed Parliament that she had signed the memorandum of understanding with President López Portillo on October 24, 1981.

> We were delighted to get [the Sicartsa contract, which] . . . will contribute about 28,000 man years of work. It will help a great deal with Davy's . . . main manufacturing centre in Sheffield. It will also mean the provision of about 80,000 tonnes of British Steel Corporation steel . . . and a good deal of electrical work through GEC. . . . It is a very welcome contract and was won in the teeth of French, German and Japanese competition. We won it on price.[11]

Mrs. Thatcher was disingenuous. By its actions, Britain had taken a leaf from the Japanese book, just as the Japanese tripped on the plate mill bid.

11. Hansard, October 26, 1981, p. 562.

Japan

In the competition with the United Kingdom over the plate mill, "Japan did not have its act together," according to an officer of Sicartsa. "MITI [the Ministry of International Trade and Industry] had no clear rapport with the Ministry of Finance [MOF], and MOF had no clear direction from the prime minister." At this stage in the bidding, the Japanese export juggernaut was rolling off course; this explains in part the British victory and illustrates the slow process of decision making in Japan. That Japan quickly recovered its direction after the loss shows the country's resilience in matters of international trade.

Japan, like the United Kingdom, distinguished between extraordinary official export credit and aid while ensuring that the two were coordinated. The Export-Import Bank of Japan reported to both the Ministry of Finance and MITI. The aid program was administered by the Overseas Economic Cooperation Fund (OECF). Under the control of the Foreign Affairs Ministry, the OECF board included the Ministry of Finance, MITI, and the Economic Planning Agency. The OECF was funded through the Trust Fund Bureau, with its budget controlled by the Finance Ministry. Thus, both export support agencies—the Ex-Im Bank and the OECF—fit into a complicated administration coordinated by MITI. It initially decided the mix of export credit and aid a project would receive, then lobbied the Ministries of Finance and Foreign Affairs to build a consensus. In the case of Mexico, however, the prime minister had already committed Japan to supply Y 30 billion in aid.

Since Prime Minister Ohira had earmarked Y 30 billion of aid for Mexico in 1980, the competition in Japan had been over whose exports would receive that aid. As it became clear that Sicartsa would benefit, the struggle came to be among Japanese exporters. Unlike the United Kingdom, where Davy was the national champion in this sphere, Japan had several firms that could have built the plate mill. The problem was twofold: deciding who would build the plant and deciding who would market the project. In Japan, steel manufacturers left the marketing of their exports largely to trading companies.[12] In gen-

---

12. Alexander K. Young, *The Sogo Shosha: Japan's Multinational Trading Companies* (Boulder, Colo.: Westview Press, 1979), p. 130. Nippon Steel itself

eral, this specialization seems to have helped Japan export steel. In the bidding for Sicartsa phase II, however, it seems to have hindered Japan's performance. Japanese banks left the initial bureaucratic politicking to their trading companies. Compared to the active Lloyds Bank, the Japanese banks remained aloof from the fray.

Two trading companies had been preparing for Sicartsa phase II for years. The representative of Mitsui Bussan had lived in Mexico since 1967; Mitsubishi Shoji arrived in 1971. Mitsui Bussan was strong in this field; in 1981, for example, 29 percent of its sales were in iron and steel, and another 17 percent in heavy machinery.[13] Mitsubishi Shoji was also a natural choice, but for another reason. Although it was less strong in its own right (iron and steel were only 16 percent of its sales in 1981), its sister firm, Mitsubishi Heavy Industries, dominated the industry in Japan. The different sources of market power of the two trading companies explain in part Mitsubishi's success and Mitsui's loss of the right to bid.

The two trading companies competed first for the support of potential suppliers and then tried to hold the suppliers while competing for export support from the government. Mitsui Bussan courted Ishikawajima-Harima Heavy Industries (IHI), second only to Mitsubishi Heavy Industries in Japan. IHI had been part of the Mitsui *zaibatsu* before World War II. With several other firms, including Toyota and Toshiba, IHI kept apart from the Mitsui *keiretsu* after the war.* As a result, the Mitsui group was looser than Mitsubishi's. In persuading IHI to participate, Mitsui Bussan could not appeal to strong common group interests.

Mitsui Bussan was doubly disadvantaged when Sicartsa selected Nippon Steel as consultant for the plate mill. The largest steel producer in the world, Nippon Steel's corporate ties were closer to the Mitsubishi group than to Mitsui: Mitsubishi Bank was the consultant's ninth-largest shareholder.[14] Nippon Steel's corporate strategy also drew it closer to the Mitsubishi group. In recent years, with other Japanese steel producers, Nippon Steel had begun to shift from ex-

---

designated as wholesalers nine general trading companies and three other companies (p. 139).

13. Toyo Keizai, *Japan Company Handbook, 1st Half 1983* (Tokyo: Toyo Keizai Shinposha, 1983), p. 762.

14. *Ibid.*, p. 408.

* *Zaibatsu* were groups of companies that formed around a bank. The *keiretsu* are their post-war successors.

porting steel to exporting steel plants. In doing so, it cooperated with Japanese manufacturers of heavy machinery.[15] The leading manufacturer was Mitsubishi Heavy Industries, with assets of Y 2,818 billion. Mitsui Engineering and Shipbuilding, with assets of only Y 529 billion, had only 13 percent of its sales in industrial plant.[16] It is small wonder, then, that Nippon Steel encouraged IHI to cooperate with the Mitsubishi group, rather than Mitsui, in bidding.

The chairmen of IHI and Mitsubishi Heavy Industries personally negotiated the final structure of the Japanese bid. After "complicated" negotiations, they "talked and decided who would lead," then "finally shook hands," according to one observer.[17] IHI would be the technical leader, Mitsubishi Heavy Industries one of the main participants, and Mitsubishi Shoji the overall leader. In contrast to Mitsui Bussan, Mitsubishi's trading company never doubted its role if its sister corporation participated. A list of the major shareholders in the trading company is evidence of the group's close ties: Mitsubishi Bank was second, with 5.9 percent, and Mitsubishi Heavy Industries was sixth, with 3.9 percent.[18]

Before Mitsubishi Shoji won, both trading companies lobbied the government of Japan for export support. One officer reported visiting MITI and the OECF "almost daily" over a three-year period. Although this may be hyperbole, clearly the trading companies were the exporters' liaison with the government. Staff from the heavy industries unit would visit MITI and the OECF, and staff in the trading company's finance unit—if not in the sister bank—would visit the MOF. MITI lobbied other ministries. Despite the MOF's pro forma reluctance to allocate funds, government help appears not to have been in doubt. The competing exporters settled the issue of which would get the support by selecting one national champion. Compared with the tumultuous bureaucratic politics in the United Kingdom, the official process in Japan was uneventful.

In the abstract, the two Japanese trading companies could have led different consortia in bidding. The United States bidders competed against one another. But MITI discouraged this practice. Its goal was to coordinate firms as well as government agencies. It persuaded other potential Japanese bidders not to compete for the plate mill; instead,

15. Young, *The Sogo Shosha*, p. 222.
16. Toyo Keizai, *Handbook*, pp. 664 and 661.
17. Interview, corporate executive, Tokyo, May 1983.
18. Toyo Keizai, *Handbook*, p. 777.

it urged them to bid on later contracts in phase II. In this role, MITI became the model the British copied for the PEP in the Department of Trade. Before this, MITI had not been much of a leader.

The "queen's gift" galvanized Japan's government. In an attempt to eliminate the price differential between the Japanese bid and the others through creative financing, the government held the interest rate on its bilateral loan to 5 percent, below even France's low 5.58 percent rate.[19] The Japanese Ex-Im Bank offered a rate of 10.78 percent, far below the German KfW rate of 14.56 percent and the United States Ex-Im Bank rate of 16.04 percent.[20] Japan extended the maturity of the bilateral loan from 20.0 to 25.5 years,[21] which equaled the longest period offered, by the French. The Japanese bidders, reported to have tried to lower their bid, were thwarted by Mexican law.[22] Japan achieved the lowest average annual interest cost of all bidders: 14.84 percent, against 16.12 percent from the British and 20.24 percent from the French.[23] Low financing costs, however, could not bring the stratospheric bid back to earth.[24]

In later negotiations for other components of Sicartsa phase II, finance won the day for Japan. MITI made sure the initial bids were

19. Recall that Garcia Torres did not adjust these interest rates for antici-pated changes in exchange rates.

20. Interviews, Mexico, 1983. Somewhat like an export-import bank, Kre-diet für Wiederaufbau (KfW) supports German exports.

21. Interview, Tokyo.

22. Interview, Mexico.

23. The Italimpianti group offered to finance over 50 percent of their offer at 9.82 percent, which reduced their overall cost to 14.16 percent, but Sicartsa's managers appear to have excluded them from the real contest for technical reasons. Interviews, Mexico, 1983.

24. There were several reasons for Mitsubishi's extraordinarily high bid. Mitsubishi's $380 million for equipment costs roughly equaled Davy's $360 mil-lion. But Mitsubishi's $220 million bid for construction was double Davy's, while its $440 million bid for civil work exceeded Davy's by $300 million. The Japanese plant was to have been very sophisticated. Largely computerized and automated, it included safety features, like earthquake and seepage protection, that were not in the specifications but were common in Japanese plants. Davy's plant was traditional and much more labor intensive. The Japanese said they misunderstood Mexico's needs. "The Mexicans wanted a Volkswagen and we gave them a Cadillac" was a common phrase in interviews in Mexico and Japan. In addition, Mitsubishi chose an expensive local contractor. The fact that Nippon Steel as consultant drew the specifications seems to have lulled the Japanese bidders. Even the Sicartsa team was surprised that Japan's bid was so high.

competitive; after losing to Britain, MITI analyzed the plate mill bids in detail for deficiencies in the Mitsubishi bid in order to instruct later bidders. In the bids for neither the continuous caster nor the electric arc furnace, however, was the Japanese offer low. For the furnace, Voest-Alpine of Austria bid Ps 5,788 million, Ps 165 million below Nippon Kokan. Both offered the same interest rates: 4.25 percent for the bilateral loan, 7.75 percent for the Ex-Im Bank loan, and a 0.75 percent spread on the Eurocredit. The OECF kept the 25.5 year maturity for the bilateral loan, but Austria offered 27.5 years. Japan beat Austria by financing a larger portion with official credit: the Japanese government provided 72.0 percent of the financing, compared with 57.0 percent for Austria. This swung the bid to Japan. With a 10.32 percent average interest rate, the present value of the Japanese offer was Ps 3.5 billion; compared with an 11.26 percent average interest rate, the present value of the Austrian offer was Ps 3.8 billion.[25] Japan was not willing to be beaten a second time.[26]

France

France's Fives Cail Babcock lost the plate mill to Britain, lost the continuous caster to Japan, then won the concentrator from Austrian-German bidders. Before it bid, Fives Cail first had to win the support of the French government, and this carried the firm to the highest office in the land. In addition to support, the French government offered exceptional export credit and aid finance. The responsible department, or *direction* (DREE), framed commercial export credit policy, which two other government agencies, Coface and the Banque de France, then implemented. Coface provided guarantees and special finance for banks. The central bank could provide exceptional help such as prefinancing and financing for non-French parts of the project. Every two weeks, the Commission de Guarantie met to decide whether individual requests fit the rules. Chaired by the DREE, the

25. Interview, Mexico, 1983.

26. The competition for the continuous caster was more prosaic. The Japanese bid of Ps 5.9 billion barely fell short of the French Ps 6.0 billion. But because Japan could offer an average rate of 9.30 percent to France's 10.86 percent, the present value of Hitachi's bid was Ps 3.6 billion against Fives Cail Babcock's Ps 4.2 billion.

commission included officers from the Trésor (the most prestigious unit in the Finance Ministry), the Banque de France, Coface, and any technical ministry that might be involved.

The French government also set a budget each year for mixed credits. Like the British, the French had three goals: promotion of French exports; promotion of French political interests; and development for low-income countries.

A committee, chaired by the director of the Trésor, with representatives from the Ministries of Foreign Affairs, Trade, Industry, and Economic Development, set the standards and the annual budget envelope. The budget consisted of a list of projects likely to need funding during the year. Within this framework, the Trésor allocated the funds to specific projects as they took shape. In short, unlike the British Treasury, the Trésor played the central role. A finance ministry, responsible for the budget, is the least inclined of government agencies to add to government expenditure. By making the Trésor critical in awarding extraordinary export support, the French built into the process a greater check on the awards than did the United Kingdom or Japan.

In 1981, the new Socialist government in France had just taken office. Concern about poor economic performance at home and an expansionary fiscal policy prompted the Trésor to try to ease the pressure on expenditures. Big projects like Sicartsa phase II created special problems. According to one official, "They run up against budget constraints, and since it's hard to leave our firms in midstream, we have no control against budget overruns." In addition, the prospective aid recipient was atypical in several respects. Mexico was not poor. Latin America received only a small share of French mixed credits: in 1979, 31 percent went to the Maghreb, 24 percent to Asia, 16 percent to the Middle East, and only 4 percent to all of Latin America. And the government rarely financed capital equipment this way; in 1982, for example, exports received only 10 percent of all support, compared with 35 percent for infrastructure such as hospitals and 20 percent for telecommunications,

With the Trésor as an opponent, Fives Cail and its bank, Paribas, went up the political hierarchy. Located in Lille, the home of the prime minister, Fives Cail found that it had his support but that this alone could not overcome the Trésor. "We went right up to President Mitterrand's *chef du cabinet*," said one protagonist. "That the prime minister was not powerful enough to overcome the opposition of the Trésor shows how powerful the Trésor is." [27]

French aid failed to narrow the gap with Davy's bid on the plate mill[28] or Hitachi's bid for the continuous caster, but did lock in Fives Cail's low bid for the concentrator. A 3.5 percent mixed credit financed 15.0 percent of the cost and a 7.75 percent buyers' credit financed 60.0 percent. Despite a Eurocredit loan by banks for the rest, the average interest rate was 7.76 percent. The Austrian-German group offered only 10.02 percent.[29] Since the bidding on the plate mill, French aid had grown from 5.8 percent of the price to 15.0 percent and its cost had dropped from 5.58 percent to 3.5 percent. Like the Japanese, but somewhat slower, the French government seems to have learned from its early losses.

Summary

The capacity to overcome systemic shortcomings with extraordinary financial aid answers the conundrum posed by Sicartsa: in one of the biggest projects of the decade, how could the United Kingdom, notoriously uncompetitive, beat the Japanese in a realm—steel manufacturing—the Japanese dominated?

Official export support in Sicartsa phase II ensured that the low-price bidder stayed low; financing actually changed the rank of the bidders only for the electric arc furnace. Since finance played such an important role, access to it mattered to the exporters. Their access varied by country, despite the export promotion policies of each government.

27. Interview, Paris, June 1983.

28. France's bilateral loan protocol, though a cheap 5.58 percent, financed only 5.8 percent of the bid. Commercial sources and Mexican lenders financed much of the rest. As a result, the 20.24 percent overall interest rate on the French bid was the highest of all.

29. Interview, Mexico, 1983. There is some dispute about whether the U.S. Dravo Corporation was the lowest bidder. According to U.S. records, Dravo bid Ps 3,197 million, which was below the French bid of Ps 3,212 million. Mexicans assert that Dravo did not meet the specifications. Their technical adjustments had the effect of raising Dravo's bid to Ps 4,300 million.

- First, not all exporters had an ally within their government. In Britain, Davy and Lloyds had the Department of Trade, and in Japan, Mitsubishi had MITI to represent it in the inner councils of government; these two countries won the lion's share of phase II. Fives Cail and Paribas, lacking an equivalent ally, had to approach the president of the Republic.
- Second, Japan and France had a more hierarchical system of decision making than did the United Kingdom, which emerges as more flexible and aggressive. In Japan, a prior decision at the top favoring exporters to Mexico helped the bidders win support; the Finance Ministry's opposition was pro forma. The prior decision was itself part of a broader trade strategy that included securing raw materials. In France, the dominant ministry opposed aid and hindered the bidder; centralization forced the firm and its bank to go to the highest level in the government.
- Third, Japan's method of choosing its national champions allowed for substantial cooperation among firms and banks and between them and government. It also required time and resources without ensuring success. The British and French did not have to choose among competing domestic firms in this project. As discussed below, the U.S. government had multiple bidders without encouraging a national champion.
- Finally, even a country with a reputation as a juggernaut in world markets can be stopped. Even as a juggernaut, Japan was able to change course swiftly and effectively. After an embarrassing defeat, Japan won the next two largest units.

These conclusions support the school of thought that some countries set out to compete successfully in world trade and organize to that end.[30] According to this view, it is not surprising that Japanese firms allocate export opportunities among themselves, helped by MITI. Nor is the hierarchical structure in Japan and France surprising.

A common criticism of this school of thought is that the idea of a strategy ignores the clash of interest groups within a country by

30. See, for example, Bruce R. Scott and George C. Lodge, eds., *U.S. Competitiveness in the World Economy* (Boston: Harvard Business School Press, 1985).

suggesting that one small group imposes its program. Certainly that clash is evident in all three countries discussed above. In part, however, it is a clash among potential recipients of funds already committed by general policy. In each case, the eventual outcome was strong government support for the exporters despite groups within the government that opposed export help.

A second criticism is that this view suggests that certain countries are unbeatable. The weak Japanese performance on the plate mill bid reminds one that no strategy is foolproof. One cannot conclude from the history of the plate mill, however, that Japan lacked an export strategy and the means to implement it; the turnabout in later performance suggests the opposite.

Strong ties bound the exporting firms and their banks to their home countries, and these ties took precedence over international understandings about correct behavior in trade competition. Distrust among countries was rampant. Countries flouted the spirit if not the letter of the OECD convention on mixed credit by failing to notify in advance. A government using mixed credits must notify others at the time of the bid if its offer complies with the convention, otherwise in advance of the bid so the others can respond. Britain cut very close to the line in its bid on the plate mill. The stated policy of the Thatcher government was only to match mixed credits offered by other governments. Before the bids were opened on September 17, 1981, however, British officials had no hard evidence that others proposed to mix aid and credit. Undaunted, they guessed that others were negotiating aid protocols with Mexico for phase II, hence they could match. Their guess proved correct: France negotiated an agreement in September; Japan already had one.

When should the British government have notified the others? Mixed credits were supposed to include at least a 20 percent aid component. In calculating the overall subsidy, the Treasury considered the grant and the subsidy in the export credit. It set its interest rate assumptions high, assuming a market rate of 15 percent (based on long-term bond yields) for discount rates and the cost of ECGD finance. Against this assumed market rate, the fixed rate of 7.75 percent paid by the borrower created a large subsidy of 7.25 percent. The Treasury could then determine that the package was within the OECD guidelines and notify others of its aid on the day of the bid. The British government did not have to reveal its hand in advance.

This situation suggests that the OECD convention contributed to instability by its rules on notice, given the powerful national interests at stake.

Not all countries treated the OECD convention as cavalierly. The policies of the German and U.S. governments stand out in contrast to the three just examined. These two governments' policies underline a major point: In this market, without their home government's help, the exporting firms lose their bids and their banks lose the demand for their services.

The Government's Role in Germany and the United States: Arm's-Length or Adversarial Relations?

As a general policy, the governments of Germany and the United States opposed financial subsidies for manufactured exports. For example, as the negotiations on phase II progressed, the chairman of the U.S. Export-Import Bank and officials in the West German government campaigned to get fellow members of the OECD to reduce the subsidy in official credit and to remove development aid from the arsenal.

Unwilling to give exporters for phase II extraordinary aid, the German government made its views known at the highest level. On meeting a senior officer of Mannesman Demag, a Siemens subsidiary, at a charitable function, Count Lamsdorff, the minister for economics, said that Mexico was not even eligible for longer maturities. Its per capita income was above the legislated limit and Lamsdorff was not willing to try to change the law. Having expected such a response, the firm stopped seeking support. The result was that officials in the Ministries of Economics, Finance, and Economic Cooperation were unfamiliar with phase II of the Sicartsa project.[31] The only official help was diplomatic, and came from the German ambassador in Mexico.

Officials in the U.S. Export-Import Bank, in contrast, were well versed in the story of Sicartsa. Ex-Im Bank officials had participated in phase I, visited the Sicartsa site, and met Garcia Torres. Seven

31. Interviews, Bonn and Düsseldorf, 1983. The government does not veto all such projects. It supported bids for DM 10 billion in sales of tube to Russia as well as bids on an Indian steel mill, for example. The former was politically important, the latter economically poor.

U.S. firms won promises of regular Ex-Im Bank support. Unlike firms in Britain and France, these firms often competed against one another; thus both General Electric and Westinghouse sought the bank's help in bidding on the plate mill. Several firms asserted that winning would create many jobs. Arriving at an estimate remarkably like Davy McKee's in England, one U.S. bidder asserted that over two thousand people would be employed in Ohio and Pennsylvania.[32] The U.S. firm that won, Dravo Corporation, of Pittsburgh, was awarded the pelletizer plant before Garcia Torres made finance an issue. Of the $36.1 million price, the Ex-Im Bank loaned $26.4 million at 9.5 percent interest payable over 15 years and guaranteed a $3.52 million loan from Dravo on the same terms. Compared with the offers for other parts of phase II, the U.S. terms were not competitive. The United States opposed extraordinary aid for the project because it would add to already excess steel capacity worldwide. The bank staff was aware of this competitive disadvantage, having received notice from other export-import banks and learned of other offers of extraordinary support through newspaper stories or from the U.S. embassy in Mexico.

That the U.S. and German governments played by international rules they were trying to establish affected bidders from both countries. U.S. firms largely withdrew from the competition to lead bids; except for Dravo, the U.S. firms sought Ex-Im Bank help as subcontractors to suppliers from other nations. Mannesman Demag gradually changed its business strategy.[33] Once an exporter of a wide range of steel manufactures, it now limited itself to sophisticated parts and had increased its engineering capacity. This means that Mannesman Demag, like the U.S. firms, cooperates as a subcontractor with manufacturers from other countries who bid on a project like Sicartsa.[34]

32. Interviews, Washington, D.C., and New York, 1982.
33. Demag changed its strategy for various reasons, of course: the industry was maturing and costs in Germany were higher than elsewhere, among others.
34. Mannesman Demag's reputation for technological skill works to its advantage. The Sicartsa management wanted German technology with Japanese financing. It got both. Bidding on the continuous caster, Sicartsa's managers successfully pressed Hitachi to accept Demag as a subcontractor. The Japanese Export-Import Bank, which financed 75 percent of the cost, was able to provide subsidized credit to support third-country subcontractors like Demag. Japan subsidized the project to get the bulk of it. Germany gave no special support and a German firm exported a small part. Without confidential information, it is difficult to say which is better off.

These main contractors select their own banks to lead the financing. German and U.S. banks were not selected by the British, French, and Japanese contractors for Sicartsa.

Conclusion

In the history of the bidding for phase II, the G-5 governments took one of two stances, thereby shaping the competition among banks in this market. The first group actively helped its exporters, providing extraordinary finance. Even though exporting firms had to struggle to win this help, ultimately they and their government agencies cooperated. At the last minute, the British Treasury compromised to help Davy win the plate mill. In Japan, members of the staff of the OECF were as committed to winning the furnace and continuous caster as an official in MITI. Even in France, the consul in Mexico worked with representatives of Fives Cail and Paribas late into the night before the bid to get the best terms from home. In each country, all seemed to be members of the same team. The second group held help to a minimum; the underlying notion was that firms should act according to market forces, independent of their governments. These two approaches had important effects on the banks that considered financing phase II.

The Impact of Trade Finance on Banks

It is clear that banks play an important role in their home government's policy, but it is less clear how these policies affect the banks. The history of Sicartsa illustrates the impact of the trade-finance wars on banks.

In trade-finance wars, official export credit agencies never play alone. As insurers, they rely on financial intermediaries, including banks. As lenders financing part of the cost of the goods, the agencies generally expect banks to lend the rest. The bank share varies. In Sicartsa phase II, banks loaned 90 percent of the plate mill's financing and 85 percent of the concentrator's. Since the remainder was either a grant or a low-interest loan, the overall cost of the financing was low despite the high commercial portion. Banks loaned 28 percent for the electric arc furnace and 13 percent for the continuous caster, since the Japanese Export-Import Bank picked up the bulk of the finance on both items. For the pelletizer, the seller rather than a bank loaned Sicartsa 10 percent of the cost.

Banks pursue this business—which I call ex-im bank cofinancing—because of the fees and low risk. No bank would lend without its home country's involvement. In phase II, banks received a 0.75 percent spread over the London Interbank Offered Rate (LIBOR), a measure of the cost of funds to the banks. This was in line with the spread the Mexican government paid at the time. When the Export-Import Bank guaranteed the loan, the actual risk was more properly that of the bank's government, which, as one of the G-5, would incur less risk than Mexico. In addition, banks immediately received a flat fee of 0.75 percent of their loan, which effectively raised the return over the loan's ten-year life. Adjusted for risk, the return on ex-im bank cofinancing was good. The business could also be substantial. The ECGD estimated that it would need $1 billion of cofinancing each year in the late 1970s.[35]

Ex-im bank cofinancing radically changed the lead banks for this industry, to judge from earlier syndications. Banks knew Mexico's steel sector. They had syndicated nineteen Eurocredits totaling $1.3 billion to five steel manufacturers between 1972 and 1981. Most syndicate leaders were big banks from the G-5 countries: of the fifty-eight lead positions, 93 percent were G-5 banks, with 19 percent from the United Kingdom and almost half—48 percent—from the United States. Big French and big Japanese banks led syndicates only six times, and no German banks were leaders. If entry into the market segment for ex-im bank cofinancing were free, the banks financing Sicartsa should approximate this profile of lenders. In fact, the two profiles differ sharply. Among the banks financing Sicartsa, the leaders as well as most participants were from the country supplying the goods. Banks from the United States played a minimal role.

Lead Banks in the Sicartsa Cofinancings

As a general rule, the syndicate leaders in ex-im bank cofinancings are banks from the same country as the supplier and the official export financing agency. Lloyds faced two other British banks, not banks from Japan or the United States. As recently as 1976, this banking

35. William Hall, "ECGD Financing: International Banking's New Battleground," *Institutional Investor* (International Edition), October 1977, p. 53.

activity was completely protected in many countries. The British system was typical.

> British merchant and commercial banks could . . . make a comfortable income arranging and providing export finance for British companies. Through good times and bad, the demand for government-guaranteed export credits was British banking's Rock of Gibraltar, a safe haven that was immune—because of its sterling denomination—from the encroachments of the City's hungry foreign bankers.[36]

Since 1976, any bank with a branch in England has become eligible to participate. Foreign banks started to lead, in part because the government's use of nonsterling loans forced it to turn to banks with a deposit base in the other currency. According to a U.K. government official, however, most leaders are still British.[37] The economic nationalism that prompts the subsidies for trade carries over into the sphere of banking.

Within the home countries, banks won leadership in Sicartsa phase II ex-im bank cofinancings by different routes. In France and Japan, and in Germany to the extent that banks had a role, corporate ties to the exporter generally ensured a bank that it would lead. In France, Banque Paribas was a major shareholder of Fives Cail Babcock. In Japan, officials in Mitsubishi Bank were certain it would be selected to lead the plate mill financing after the chairmen of IHI and Mitsubishi Heavy Industries shook hands.[38] Deutsche Bank, as shareholder and leading *haus bank* to Siemens, the owner of Mannesman Demag, had the right of first refusal if Mannesman should win a bid. Though strong, the privilege of the house bank is not overriding, however, at least in Japan. When Hitachi Zosen decided that its lead bank, Sanwa Bank, was not skilled in joint export financings, it turned to the premier international bank in Japan, the Bank of Tokyo. A gentle-

36. Ibid.
37. Interview, London, 1982.
38. See Dodwell Marketing Consultants, *Industrial Groupings in Japan* (Tokyo: Dodwell, 1984), for the close connections within the Mitsubishi *keiretsu*.

man's agreement gave Sanwa the status of co-lead manager[39] without a substantive role as leader.[40]

In contrast to the privileged relationships of banks on the Continent and in Japan, Lloyds Bank International (LBI) pulled out the stops to get the lead in the plate mill financing. Its main competitors were Davy's lead bank, National Westminster Bank, and Lazard Frères. LBI had had offices in Mexico since 1869 and was the dominant British bank in Latin America. Its experience in Mexico and with ECGD financing displaced NatWest, a relative newcomer to international banking. Unlike Sanwa Bank, NatWest was given no honorary role as co-lead manager; it was just one more participant in the sterling loan. Lazard, the fiercer rival, had an Achilles' heel. As a merchant bank, it lacked a substantial deposit base. Reluctant to lend on its own account, it earned its revenues from fees rather than interest payments. LBI could waive fees Lazard needed and recoup on interest Lazard would not earn. Always cost conscious, Garcia Torres encouraged Davy to use LBI.

The precise jobs of a lead bank were far from uniform among countries. One might expect at the least that the leader would assemble partipating banks, but even this was not always so. In Japan, since Mitsui Bussan had already assembled banks to finance the continuous caster, the ostensible leader, Bank of Tokyo, did not even need to do this. Bank of Tokyo's job was to lobby the government to ensure that OECF funds would support the bid. Other banks lobbied their governments. LBI lobbied the British government. Mitsubishi Bank lobbied Japan's Finance Ministry. Paribas, however, appears not to have lobbied much in France even though its president had close ties with the Trésor. The supplier, Fives Cail, did the politicking.

Although one competitive advantage attributed to big banks is their world network, the presence of the lead banks in Mexico seems to have given no special benefit to the borrower or the financing. Some banks had long had local offices; Deutsche Bank, for example, had

39. See Tombstone, "Siderurgica Lazaro Cardenas, April 1982," *Euromoney*, July 1982.

40. Interviews, Tokyo, 1982 and 1983. Note that in Japan, the bank's tie is with the exporter and not the trading company that leads the project. Thus Mitsui Bussan does not bring in Mitsui Bank, which was deemed to be weak in Latin America (and, moreover, was part of a weak *keiretsu*). This appears to be an example of the competition between Japanese banks and trading companies.

opened its first Mexican office in 1880. The Japanese were much more recent; Bank of Tokyo had opened its Mexican office in 1958 to support Japanese cotton textile exports to Mexico. These local offices provided some information to the exporter about events in Mexico. They acted as a liaison between the buyer and the bank staff, who decided the credit terms. But local staff did not analyze the projects carefully. Normally, underwriters prepare a prospectus about the borrower, but the lead banks in phase II relied on the borrower's own prospectus. For judgments of Sicartsa's creditworthiness, at least some lead banks relied on others; Bank of Tokyo, for example, took the analysis of Mitsui Bussan. Others relied on the export credit agencies, which were assumed to have done an analysis. The faith of the banks was misplaced.

Syndicates in the Sicartsa Ex-Im Bank Cofinancings

In phase II, banks did not have equal access, among countries, to the few syndicates for ex-im bank cofinancings. In the two Japanese syndicates, only Japanese banks participated. Fuji Bank led a $130 million syndicate for the furnace. Of the eleven banks providing funds, six were city banks in either Tokyo or Osaka, four were specialized banks in international or project finance, and one was a trust bank.[41] Bank of Tokyo led the $100 million loan for the continuous caster. The twenty-one participants included all thirteen city banks, the three specialized banks, and five trust banks.[42]

In contrast to the all-Japan syndicates is LBI's £198 million syndicate for the plate mill. Although the lenders had to provide funds in sterling, which would give British banks a comparative advantage, the syndicate included only four banks from the United Kingdom. Three banks from France and one from Japan were present because of their participation in an earlier syndicate for another Mexican steel com-

41. The banks were Fuji, Dai-Ichi Kangyo, Mitsubishi, Daiwa, Tokai, and Taiyo Kobe; Industrial Bank of Japan, Bank of Tokyo, Long-term Credit Bank, and Nippon Credit; and Yasuda Trust and Banking. See Tombstone, "Siderurgica Lazaro Cardenas, April 1982," *Euromoney*, July 1982, p. 1.

42. The banks were those listed in note 41, plus Mitsui, Hokkaido Takushoku, Kyowa, Sanwa, and Saitama, and the trust and banking companies of Mitsui, Toyo, Sumitomo, Hokkaido Takushoku, and Mitsubishi. See Tombstone, "Siderurgica Lazaro Cardenas, April 1982," *Euromoney*, July 1982.

pany.[43] Since the margins were narrow (only 0.25 percent in one case), LBI had promised them a "juicy piece of the ECGD financing" in Sicartsa.[44] This sort of swap is not uncommon. In this case, however, these four non-British participants were criticized by their home customers. Having bid and lost to Davy, the home customers were reportedly angered that their banks were able to benefit anyway.[45] Their anger reflects the strength of national conventions tying the banks to their home customers.

The Impact of Home Ties on Banks in the Sicartsa Financing

The banks took part in, or stayed out of, the Sicartsa financings for reasons that varied by home country. The Sicartsa story suggests ways in which a bank's home country affects the structure of the market for ex-im bank cofinancings, hence competition among banks and the bank's strategies and structures.

In France, Germany, and Japan, the choice of bank flowed from the choice of exporter. That Sanwa Bank forfeited the actual lead does not really qualify this statement: the bank was part of a weak *keiretsu*. Even after it lost the lead, the bank kept an honorary role. House bank status has its limits, however. Trading companies cooperate with banks in the same group less than do manufacturers in the group. This is consistent with the competition between trading companies and banks in Japan today. Institutional ties between banks and exporters shaped the bargaining between banks and the users of their service in these three countries. In this sense, their market structure differs from that in the United Kingdom and the United States.

In the United Kingdom, the choice of banks did not flow automatically from the choice of supplier, despite a notion that the supplier had a number one bank. LBI won the plate mill financing for two reasons. First, it had positioned itself in the market, with its network and skills, to command information that National Westminster Bank, Davy's house bank, lacked. Second, it took advantage of the structure

43. The British banks were Lloyds, Barclays, Midland, and National Westminster. The French banks were Credit Lyonnais, Banque Nationale de Paris, and Banque de Paris et des Pays-Bas (Paribas). See Tombstone, "Siderurgica Lazaro Cardenas-Las Truchas, S.A., April 1982," *Institutional Investor*, (International Edition), 1982, p. 147.

44. Interview, Mexico, 1982.

45. Ibid.

of the home financial system, which distinguished between deposit-taking and investment banks; its position in that structure gave it a competitive advantage over its merchant bank competitor. The British system is closer to a competitive market at the national level, whereas the others could be called gentlemen's clubs.

The banks took different stances in the negotiations between exporter and buyer, depending on which market they were in. In Japan, France, and Germany, the banks were passive, waiting for their customer to win the bid. Mitsubishi Bank, for example, learned of its sister company's interest in phase II as early as 1979 but did not actively promote Mitsubishi Heavy Industries or Japanese interests before the bid was won. The stance of banks from these three countries differed vividly from that of LBI in the United Kingdom, which took an active role in the talks between Davy and Sicartsa, and from that of Deutsche Bank, which recognized that its customer had no chance to win. Thus the institutional structure at home was important for the banks' roles in international transactions.

One also finds different bank strategies associated with the different home market structures. In the market for ex-im bank cofinancings, the passive banks follow a low-cost, high-price strategy. They reduce costs in several ways: They lower overhead costs by doing little analysis of the borrower, little syndication, and little lobbying of the borrower or the home government. They reduce risk by relying on the group, which may include the home government, in case of debt problems. For this, the banks give up flexibility. German banks, with the right of first refusal, had some latitude to withdraw. The Japanese banks seem to have been the least flexible. Mitsubishi Bank decided it could not withdraw from the financing even though world financial markets lost confidence in Mexico in later 1981. The Industrial Bank of Japan could not stay out even though it concluded that the project was not feasible. Fuji Bank decided it had no choice except to enter, because of its ties to the exporter.

LBI's strategy matched its competitive home market. The bank took an active stance, treating ex-im bank cofinancing as a niche it could dominate. LBI estimated it had led 75 percent of the ECGD's cofinancings in 1981.[46] Since no other commercial banks were as active as LBI, its competitors were merchant banks. This was a market in which LBI had strengths it could exercise, including a deposit base

46. Interview, London, 1983.

46

and correspondent banking relationships that merchant banks could not duplicate.

Given the different strategies, one might expect the banks to adopt different administrative structures to match.[47] Indeed, the banks with a passive strategy tended to be more centralized than LBI. In general, more decisions were finally made at headquarters in Tokyo, Paris, or Frankfurt than in London. This is so partly because LBI's management style was more decentralized. Its headquarters was smaller and more collegial; its offices in Mexico were larger than those of other banks. This observation must be qualified. One cannot extrapolate an entire corporate organization from a specific market like ex-im bank cofinancings. All banks worked through representative offices, since that is all Mexican law allowed. All banks syndicated out of headquarters and financial centers like London.

An example of the roles played by headquarters will give a better view of the structural differences among the home countries. Garcia Torres had insisted on similar terms from all banks for loan pricing after the bids. As Mexico's economy faltered during 1981, financial markets began to tighten terms, raising spreads and shortening maturities. Alert to this trend, Tokyo and Frankfurt headquarters tried to raise spreads to Sicartsa at the end of 1981. Their local offices argued against such a move and ultimately won. LBI's headquarters did not try to raise spreads.

Overshadowing the specific differences between the two groups of banks is the government policy toward exports. At the most basic level, official export support helps determine which banks win share in this market because the support determines which supplier wins. No bank leads in this market if a firm from its home country does not win a contract. The U.S. banks were not significant in financing phase II because U.S. companies were not major suppliers. In the words of Garcia Torres, "We wanted U.S. technology . . . but ex-im finances were so bad we couldn't get it." German banks also concluded that their firms would not win contracts in phase II, given the German government's policy of noninvolvement. In circumstances like these, the banks leave the battle.

To observe that home government policy is important to a big bank's market position does not address the role of the bank in framing

47. See Alfred D. Chandler, Jr., *Strategy and Structure* (Cambridge, Mass.: MIT Press, 1962), and John M. Stopford and Louis T. Wells, Jr., *Managing the Multinational Enterprise* (New York: Basic Books, 1972).

that policy. Nor does it address the role of a policy of export support in the broader economic strategy of the government. A major German bank may prefer that its government appear to stay at arm's length from German firms, and therefore eschew a policy of export subsidies. Advocates of export promotion may recognize that export subsidies, one of the most obvious devices, are a blunt instrument. I address these issues below.

Sicartsa and Two Views of the Home Environment for International Banks

When public resources support private interests internationally, one issue is who helps whom. Has a weak government responded to powerful interest groups? Or, are firms marionettes of a government puppeteer? Although simplistically stated, the two questions project different views of business-government relations. Economists ask whether a public good is served by state intervention; if so, the state is not merely a vehicle for private lobbies. Political scientists ask whether firms extend "their own power at the expense of the power of" the state.[48] They ask whether regulated firms capture the regulating authority.[49] In the case of Sicartsa, there is no evidence of a weak home government's responding to powerful exporting firms, although firms did take the first steps on phase II. Indeed, some had followed the project from its inception under President Díaz; Mitsui Trading Company's representative had lived in Mexico since 1967, for example.

Which view is closer to reality is important to banks, buyers, and firms. Bankers must know which view is more accurate to anticipate

---

48. C. Fred Bergsten, Thomas Horst, and Theodore H. Moran, *American Multinationals and American Interests* (Washington, D.C.: The Brookings Institution, 1978), p. 314. The authors identify two models of business-government relations in which multinationals grow at the expense of the state and two models that "differ over how much narrow class interest predominates over the public interest . . . in the home state." The imperialist model assumes big business and government work hand in hand, while the neomercantilist model describes a government politically more powerful than its private firms.

49. For a review of the literature on the capture theory, see Douglas D. Anderson, *Regulatory Politics and Electric Utilities* (Boston: Auburn House, 1981), p. 7.

the firms' need for services. A buyer, like Garcia Torres, must know whom to press for good terms, the exporter or a government agency back home. Firms in global industries must know their competitors' business strategies. If a competitor can call on the help of its home government as it wishes, it has the advantage of flexibility. A competitor that marches to an official tune, however, has a strategy defined by the government's plan.

The home government's policies have long-term consequences that affect not only the outcome of the bid but also performance as the contract evolves. Suppose, for example, that the project encounters trouble midway through. A firm whose government provided little help at the bidding stage could expect much less diplomatic or financial help in the crisis than a firm whose government had a stake in the project. The British government, with the largest stake in Sicartsa phase II, sent Queen Elizabeth to Las Truchas early in 1983. If some exporters can rationally expect help, surely banks financing the firms can do the same.

Different environments affect banks' international lending in ways that extend beyond the standard analysis. It is common to observe that home regulations and macroeconomic policies encourage banks to lend abroad. This is true but it is only part of the story. This review of the Sicartsa financing shows governments actively promoting banks' lending to Mexico. When faced with the question of whether they should use finance to promote exports, the activist governments of France, Japan, and the United Kingdom were willing to do so; the governments of Germany and the United States were less willing. The second important factor was the banks' home companies. Here the constellations of G-5 countries shift. In the Sicartsa financing, institutional ties to home firms had a stronger effect on the market presence on banks from France, Japan, and Germany than banks from the United Kingdom. In Britain, competition played a greater role in determining which bank got lead status. U.S. banks are conspicuously absent from this part of the story because they played no lead role.

Some banks have a home environment in which institutional ties— between banks and governments or banks and firms or among banks— perform an important function in lending. These banks are part of a complex system that transcends the market and continues to be shaped by them. In the Sicartsa financing, British, French, and Japanese firms exercised their voice to direct home government policy. German and U.S. firms largely withdrew from the competition, drawing their banks with them.

The Relevance of Sicartsa for the World Financial System

The Sicartsa phase II financing seems an extreme case. One of the biggest projects, it is in the moribund steel sector. Rarely do queens, presidents, and prime ministers contest project finance. Yet the story is a microcosm of the issues of international lending. Some involve credit allocation. For example, what factors are important in a bank's decision to lend? What is the impact of massive lending on the borrowing country? Why do banks continue to lend when the recipient is in trouble? Another issue is responsibility for the debt crisis of the early 1980s. Today, debate rages over where to put the blame. Finally, the Sicartsa case raises questions about the structure of the international financial system. If national governments actively promote their own foreign trade, how free is the market for international banking?

The story of Sicartsa phase II only scratches the surface of the official factors that influence lending. The export credit wars affect trade flows and banks, but credit subsidies at the point of sale are probably the least effective way for a nation to compete in export markets. Many policies other than official green stamps are at work.

World Credit Allocation

Everyone agreed that Garcia Torres won exceptional financing for Mexico, but few defended the steel mill itself. It is remarkable that Sicartsa got twenty-five-year maturities with seven years before repayment began. But did Mexico need the mill? I will not attempt an economic analysis here. The important point is that neither the sellers, the lenders, nor the exporting government officials would assert that the mill made economic sense. They pursued the transaction, not because of Mexico's needs, but because of their own needs at home. This is rational behavior in the context of trade wars.

The mill is hard to defend. A defense cannot be based on demand outside Mexico. Worldwide overcapacity was high; in 1983, for example, Mannesman Demag closed two plate mills in Germany. Arguments for regional development—Las Truchas is remote, unpopulated, hard to reach—do not consider less costly alternatives.

Sicartsa was planned not for export but to meet internal demand. The steel complex grew from a dream of national independence in the early years of development economics, the vision of Mexico's president in the 1940s. Its best defense is that Mexico would protect its domestic steel industry as the economy grew, with the demand for steel fueled by Mexico's oil wealth. For this reason, runs the argument, the government might as well build a plate mill. The forecasters, however, seriously underestimated the effect of the boom-bust cycles in the Mexican economy. Following the August 1982 debt crisis, several years of recession, and the collapse of oil prices, the Mexican government put phase II on permanent hold and offered to sell phase I to private investors.

Few players carefully analyzed the economics of the mill. Participating banks relied on lead banks, which in turn relied on exporters for analysis. A Japanese banker said, "Sicartsa raised no special issue for us as bankers. This is one of hundreds of projects we are involved in. We have a big research department, but it was not needed to do any analysis of the project or the industry."[50] Exporters appear to have relied on the buyer. The same is true of the official lenders: Britain's aid agency had no time for an on-site inspection and the others did not make them. Even bidders who objected to the mill—as the wrong type, for example—bid anyway.

Consider the impact on the borrowing country when private and public foreign creditors lend with little regard for the underlying economics of the venture. Even foreign loans for specific productive purposes can hurt an economy. If the local government had had to finance the "good" project without the foreign loan, then a foreign loan would have freed funds for the government to use. To weigh the effect of a foreign loan, one must examine not merely the project but also government expenditures at the margin. Lenders that do not do this permit the borrower an economic indiscipline with potentially serious consequences.

The foreign loan may also affect local bureaucratic politics in a way that harms the borrowing country. Access to credit gives the borrower power. By strengthening the hands of entities like Sicartsa, the foreign lenders weaken the budget authorities. The finance ministry therefore, must fight to allocate resources elsewhere and enforce a financial discipline on the parastatal borrower, a discipline greatly needed for

50. Interview, Japan, September 1982.

large projects, which are notorious for cost overruns. Sicartsa phase I overran its $560 million estimate by about 80 percent. Overrun funds usually come from the government's general budget, and a politically strong parastatal borrower can seriously damage the country's economic health. In this instance, foreign lending distorts development programs by encouraging governments to pursue big projects that can disrupt budgets in other areas. An aid official described the process as "a kind of Empire Strikes Back."

By inference, the Sicartsa financing also points to a specific kind of credit allocation among borrowing countries. Although there is disagreement over the methods involved, banks set country limits on their exposure. For example, they may determine the limits solely by analyzing risk and return on the exposure in the context of their overall portfolio. In this case, official support changes both risk and return for the country. The change would then be accommodated elsewhere in the country portfolio, permitting a higher overall credit exposure by the bank. Or, banks may set country limits from the bottom up, aggregating available financings. In this case, the bank would allocate more exposure to Mexico, say, than otherwise. If the bank has an overall ceiling for the region or the type of country, such as developing countries, then other countries would get less.

Banks did not withdraw from the Sicartsa financing despite the writing on the wall in late 1981; the final agreements were not signed until May 1982. At the end of 1981, financial markets had begun to recognize Mexico's economic problems, raising spreads as the first sign of a general tightening. The banks that helped finance phase II nevertheless stood ready to lend at the earlier rates. One might dismiss this as merely honoring a commitment, but several bankers interviewed thought they had the legal power at least to raise the spreads. To do so, of course, could have radically changed Garcia Torres's present value calculations and possibly lost the home exporter its bid. The commitment of the banks suggests the importance of longer-term relationships for the banks: interests in the home companies' performance, in the borrowing country (where many had offices), and in the home governments' needs. Despite the liquidity of finance and the speed with which funds can be transferred, inertia plays a part in lending.

The Japanese bankers were apparently most sensitive to the rate changes, but they gave several reasons for not withdrawing. One said, "The suppliers and the trading companies wanted the funds for the project. It was also a national project, so Japan wanted to get closer relations with Mexico for its oil." This suggests the importance of the home customer and government. Another banker stressed good relations with Mexico. According to a local representative, "Headquarters . . . wanted to raise the spread . . . . We said we had promised [the lower spread] and they accepted this."[51]

Responsibility

Much of the recent literature about international debt grapples with the issue of responsibility for the crisis in 1982. The debate focuses on whether the problem resulted from bad economic management in the borrowing country or external shocks like the oil price rise, high interest rates, recession in the industrial countries, and the banks' excessive lending and abrupt withdrawal of funds to many countries, particularly in Latin America.[52] The debate identifies three important players: borrowing governments, for economic mismanagement; lending banks, for herd behavior; and the G-5 governments for harmful macroeconomic management. Each side argues that the critical player must change its behavior before the harm will stop.

Finger pointing is not useful. For example, would one characterize Garcia Torres as a Machiavellian financier or a victim of Mexico's grandiose goals and the export policies of industrial countries? Certainly he did a good job manipulating the trade competition among the OECD nations. Or one might reasonably conclude that the credit was being pushed on him and that given his job he could only accept it: a case of simultaneous push and pull.

The Sicartsa story suggests that the debate understates the active role of the G-5 governments. Their macroeconomic policies do shape aggregate supply and demand, but may be pursued for reasons entirely unrelated to world credit, creditors, and borrowers. Sicartsa suggests that several G-5 governments actively pushed credit on Mexico for a bad project and encouraged their banks to lend to the same end.

51. Interviews, Tokyo, May 1983, and Mexico, April 1983.
52. See for the latter view, for example, Carlos F. Diaz-Alejandro, "Latin American Debt: I Don't Think We Are in Kansas Anymore," *Brookings Papers on Economic Activity*, 2:1982, p. 335. Both sides were debated at the meeting of the American Economic Association in December 1984. See a brief report in the International Monetary Fund, *Survey* (Washington, D.C.: IMF, 1985).

Sicartsa may be one of the largest of such projects, but it is not an isolated case. Nor is the overt export credit the sole case of home government policy. One must dig deeper to see the full effect the G-5 economic strategies have on international loans by banks.

The Structure of the International System: Integration or Nationalism?

The Sicartsa financing also raises questions about the structure of the world economy and the international financial system. How integrated are national financial systems? How much do groups in one nation act in concert to achieve their national interests at the expense of other countries? The French minister of industry expressed a common view when he argued for support of phase II by saying, "If not us, then someone else will."[53]

The export credit wars testify to the potent mercantilist spirit abroad today. Britain is an example. The ECGD supports, in one form or another, 33 percent of British exports.[54] The law permits the ECGD to provide support for political as well as economic purposes. The Projects and Export Policy Division in the Trade Department is a step toward government coordination of a British trade offensive, and the Aid and Trade Program permits an increasingly activist government to support exports to what one British official called "dodgy markets."[55] The government silenced one internal effort to reverse this policy, a report named after its author, Ian Byatt, a Treasury economist. In 1983, the Byatt report argued that export subsidies provide no aggregate benefit to the economy.[56]

Mercantilist policies are not limited to Britain. More generally, the Sicartsa financing shows how the G-5 governments' broad policies, framed for domestic purposes, send mercantilist impulses through international banking. Japan's effort to secure its oil supply extended to the financing of phase II. Export subsidies took a roundtrip, from the home government to the borrower and then back to the home exporter, affecting the banks' foreign loans in the process. Even the German government, which held aloof from the competition in Mex-

53. Interview, Paris, June 1983.
54. Interview, London, May 1983.
55. Interview, London, September 1982.
56. Interview, London, May 1983.

ico, subsidized trade finance for Eastern Europe. Set against such potent trade promotion policies, international conventions wither. Several G-5 governments evaded the spirit of the OECD understanding about such subsidies, manipulating financial assumptions so they would not have to notify other bidders.

All this is important background to international banking. The question is not even whether neomercantilism is good or bad. Rather, one question is whether neomercantilism is a powerful impulse in the home economies of the international banks. Without suggesting Victoria's imperial monarchy, Queen Elizabeth's visit to Sicartsa is a powerful symbol of national interest in world trade and therefore finance.

In the financing of trade one sees the clearest example of a home country's impact on its banks' international lending. Sicartsa illustrates the reason: Banks are an important economic weapon. Neomercantilism affects competition and lending by international banks. The banks competed directly with other banks from their home countries, rather than with an array of banks of different nationalities. Banks had to be able to manage business-government relations at home as part of the competition. In decisions on credit, the link between trade and finance remains alive and strong. More generally, banks relied on home ties to justify long-term investments. One finds little recourse to analysis of the country, industry, or project, and heavy reliance on the exporting firms at home and the home government.

The willingness to let short-term factors shape long-term investments is not unique to banks. Garcia Torres did not forecast changes in exchange rates over twenty years in order to value the bids or the financing. Suppliers and their home governments ignored the long-term economic effects of export subsidies. The similar behavior of the various players united them and reinforced economic nationalism in the world financial system.

The Sicartsa case illustrates many of the themes of this book. The ties between trade and banks' lending extend far beyond subsidized export credits. Sicartsa reveals the way banks, their home government, and their home firms ally to win individual transactions. Much broader alliances thrive in the banks' home country. To promote competitiveness, the government uses the banks at many different points as the firms add value and sell their goods. To this end, during the 1970s, the regulatory policies of several governments toward the big banks' overseas lending were relaxed (see chapters 2 and 3). Obversely, as in the case of Sicartsa, the banks' own business strategies drew on their home country for aid and comfort in international markets. Many ties made the home such an important market for them that it affected much of their international lending. Trade finance is only one form of lending; the home's influence is palpable in other forms as well.

The Sicartsa loans funded a project that did not make economic sense for the borrower. A fair number of loans to borrowers in developing countries fit this description, setting the stage for the debt crisis. The Sicartsa story illustrates how the home government's regulatory and promotional policies encouraged loans for reasons that extended beyond the urging of exporters and banks. That official push does not explain all such lending, but it does add the home government to the list of those responsible for the ensuing debt problems. Banks could also anticipate that as debt problems appeared, the home government would intervene. Queen Elizabeth's tour of Ciudad Lazaro Cardenas is a symbol of that aid.

2

Trade, Finance, and National Strategies

The French Revolution marked a turning point in the history of European warfare. Until that time, cadres of professional soldiers fought one another according to certain conventions. With the Revolution, the French mobilized the civilian population to fight. From that moment, the entire nation became an instrument of war.

The G-5 nations are now caught in a trade war that mobilizes civilian institutions back home, including the banks. The export credit subsidies in Sicartsa are a weapon of the battlefield: Nations use them when competing head-on at the time of sale. The use of such subsidies represents the failure of many other economic weapons the country may have deployed long before bidding for the sale. These are often placed deep in the home economy. They include policies toward wages and prices, fiscal and monetary policies, even policies toward the structure of the economy. Financial institutions like banks play a key role. In this sense, the domestic economy can be mobilized for the trade war.

National strategies are a useful way to understand home policies as they affect banks. One example of national strategies at work is the G-5 governments' active use of their banks to promote exports after the oil price shocks of the 1970s. This example, described below, demonstrates that G-5 governments have been far more than permissive in their reliance on banks to promote exports. Home governments use the banks to stabilize the cost of inputs to manufacturing firms; promote capital-intensive firms by lowering the cost of capital; and channel financial flows to specific firms or industries engaged in trade.

Control at the border is a prerequisite for control at home. Although the degree may vary by country, the banks are integral to government trade policy at all stages.

The home government's strategy shapes the demand for the banks' international lending. It affects the export performance of the banks' corporate customers at home, changing their risks and opportunities systematically, much as the export subsidies changed the game for firms competing for Sicartsa. The strategy may also give the banks an edge against banks from other countries; if they can turn home government policy to their advantage, national strategies can be a competitive tool. Thus the banks are bound to their home in two ways: through their customers and through their role implementing policy.

Complex institutional ties link banks to their home government and to their home firms. For example, in Japan the *keiretsu* lower the cost of capital for certain manufacturing firms, which helps to explain their export performance and their demand for trade finance. The same interfirm ties help to explain the Japanese banks' international lending strategies (see chapters 4 and 5) and their behavior in debt crises (see chapter 7).

This chapter explores the link between the big banks and their home country's manufactured exports. Part of the link is a market relationship based on the traditional use of credit to grease the wheels of commerce. This chapter focuses on another part, the link forged by active home governments caught up in the trade war.

Home Governments' Use of Banks to Adjust to the Oil Shocks

International trade and lending grew hand in hand over the centuries as markets developed. There is clear evidence, however, that extra-market forces tighten the link between trade and finance. During the 1970s, G-5 governments actively used their banks to promote exports after the oil shocks. This is particularly important because many of the countries with debt problems in the 1980s went into debt in the mid-1970s.

It is now a commonplace to say that banks recycled petrodollars after the two oil price shocks of the 1970s. This view seems to place the responsibility for the shocks squarely on the Organization of Petroleum Exporting Countries (OPEC), which quadrupled the price of oil in 1973–1974 and doubled the price in 1979–1980. The view even suggests that the banks sustained the world economy through great trauma, allowing the deficit-ridden oil importers time to adjust to the new oil prices. The problem with this assessment is that it misses the important role played by the banks from G-5 countries in their own home country's adjustment.

From their homes' perspective, banks were important tools in the policy adjustment to the oil shocks. Of the five countries, four—France, Germany, Japan, and the United Kingdom—responded to the shocks in ways designed to improve their trade balances, increasing exports and slowing imports. The governments in three of these countries drew explicitly on their banks to help in the export drive, while the fourth—Germany—drew on banks implicitly. The United States took another route, inflating the dollar to erode the transfer of real resources to OPEC.

The combined effect of these adjustment strategies is clear. Much of the export drive aimed at sales to the developing countries, in effect shifting to them the G-5 trade deficits with OPEC and using bank credits to make the shift possible. The inflationary response of the United States made debt a sensible medium-term option for the developing countries and, creating liquidity, allowed the banks to lend. In this sense, G-5 policies directly related to trade set the necessary conditions for the growth of international lending in the 1970s.

The export-led counteroffensives of the four industrial countries differed sharply according to the willingness of each government to let the domestic economy adjust. Two adjusted quickly. German macroeconomic policy was contractionary: the government reduced the monetary base in 1974, then held growth to 2.9 percent in 1975. The economy slowed to 0.5 percent in 1974, then declined 2.1 percent in 1975. By 1976, inflation was below 4.0 percent, down from 6.8 percent in the previous two years. Japan, although somewhat less contractionary, nevertheless brought prices below even the preshock levels by 1976.[1]

Germany and Japan exported to different regional markets, so their sales relied on finance to different degrees. The two countries were able to compete successfully in exporting to the industrial world, where they established trade surpluses (see Table 2–1). Success in this

1. See OECD, *Historical Statistics, 1960–80* (Paris: OECD, 1982).

TABLE 2–1. Regional Trade Balances of the G-5 Countries

	Trade balance ($ billions)				
Year	Germany	Japan	France	U.K.	U.S.
1971	3.2	3.5	−1.0	−1.5	−6.6
1973	9.5	0.9	−1.2	−5.6	−5.6
1978	11.9	14.6	−3.7	−9.0	−20.3

SOURCE: International Monetary Fund, *International Financial Statistics Yearbook, 1984* (Washington, D.C.: IMF, 1985).

market was important for its sheer size: from 1972 to 1978, for example, industrial countries accounted for 73 percent of all imports.[2] With over 70 percent of its exports going to industrial countries during this period, Germany sold over 55 percent in Europe alone. Only 40 percent of Japanese exports went to industrial countries, most to the United States. Europe was much less important to Japan, accounting for barely 12 percent of exports. Asia received over 20 percent of all its exports, a far higher share than that of any other G-5 country. As seen above, importers in developing countries seek favorable financing much more than importers in industrial countries. Much more than for Germany, therefore, Japan's regional export focus made finance important.

The trade and adjustment strategies of France and the United Kingdom led of necessity to even greater reliance than Japan's on financing to win export sales. Compared with Germany, France and the United Kingdom relied more on developing than industrial countries as markets for their exports: both sold 14 percent of exports to developing countries by 1978, compared to 8 percent by Germany. With their products less competitive than those from Germany and Japan, France and the United Kingdom could use subsidized finance to win buyers in developing countries. Both had failed to bring domestic inflation back to pre-1973 levels. France did not accept austerity in 1974. The United Kingdom, burdened with stagflation, did not adequately tighten its macroeconomic policies until the International Monetary Fund (IMF) forced change in late 1976.

2. International Monetary Fund, *International Financial Statistics Yearbook, 1984* (Washington, D.C.: IMF, 1985), p. 109.

Even more than its distribution of exports, each country's regional trade balance suggests its need for credit subsidies. The ultimate concern of any country, of course, is its overall balance, since deficits with one region may be offset by surpluses elsewhere. During the first oil shock, however, the immense deficit with oil exporters was a given, forcing the G-5 countries to find offsetting surpluses. By 1978, the four countries had established solutions.

- For *Germany*, surpluses with industrial countries accounted for about 60 percent of surpluses totaling $23 billion. Eastern Europe and oil exporters made up the rest. Germany was in rough balance with the developing countries.
- For *Japan*, deficits of $14 billion with the raw material producers (oil as well as minerals from Australia) were offset by surpluses totaling $33 billion, of which 54 percent was from industrial countries, 28 percent from Asia, 10 percent from other developing countries, and 8 percent from Communist countries.
- *France* partially offset deficits of $8.8 billion (40 percent with industrial countries and 60 percent with oil exporters) by running surpluses of $4 billion, largely with developing countries (95 percent). Indeed, 55 percent was with former colonies in Africa.
- *Britain* resembled France; it could only partially offset its deficit of $13 billion with industrial countries (and $0.5 billion with Eastern Europe) by earning surpluses with developing countries, former colonies, and former economic partners in the European Free Trade Association (EFTA). Of surpluses totaling $5.3 billion, 41 percent was with developing countries, Australia, New Zealand, and South Africa, most former colonies. Another 42 percent was with oil exporters, and 17 percent with old EFTA countries.

The different patterns of trade surplus and deficits suggest different trade policies and financing. Germany competed effectively with manufacturers in other industrial countries, where it could rely less on financial subsidies to sell. Japan competed well in industrial markets, but also relied on markets in developing and Communist countries. This fits the evidence from the Sicartsa project that the German government would withhold subsidies, whereas the Japanese would at least match any other country.

Both France and the United Kingdom, like Japan, loaned money to buyers in developing countries who would take their exports. The former colonial powers relied much more on markets in countries they once ran. France is the extreme case. In 1973, before the oil shock, France reported a $500 million surplus with former African colonies. By 1978, the surplus was $2.2 billion, a growth rate of over 400 percent, which far exceeded the 200 percent growth of surpluses with other groups of developing countries. French banks financed much of this trade, rediscounting it with the central bank. In Britain the story was similar but, like the old British Empire, the surpluses were spread much more widely across the world map. [3]

The second oil shock brought a different response from many of the players. In comparison with the aftermath of the first shock, the home governments had different policies, home banks different port-folios, and borrowers different capacities to adjust.[4] These differences were largely the result of the response to the first oil shock. Still, microeconomic policies to promote trade drew on banks as some G-5 governments tried to offset more costly oil imports. Sicartsa illustrates the tenacity of the trade-finance wars even as some industrial countries tried to adjust at the aggregate level.

The governments' aggressive trade response shows that they pressed many more levers than simply such aggregate ones as the supply of money, encouraging exporters and banks to the excesses that followed. The conventional form of this familiar story usually neglects the role of G-5 microeconomic policy. The constellation of policies to right the economic imbalances included monetary and fiscal policy at the macroeconomic level, of course, but also trade-financing policies at the microeconomic level. The excesses that followed included the massive exposure of many big banks in countries that encountered debt problems in the early 1980s.

According to one view, the banks pursued their lending simply because they expected a bailout if problems occurred.[5] The home

---

3. After the first oil shock, the United States ran growing trade deficits, largely with Japan but also with the oil exporters and most developing countries. Surpluses with Europe and the Communist countries were small.

4. See IMF annual reports for 1980–1982, for example.

5. Staff, "International Debt, the Banks, and U.S. Foreign Policy," U.S.

governments' active role in promoting exports suggests that banks did more than calculate the risk. They responded to opportunities presented to them by their governments at home.

Home Governments' Broad Use of Banks to Promote Trade in Manufactures

It would be a mistake to see the G-5 governments' use of their banks to promote trade as a temporary response to the oil shocks. Home governments promote the link between trade and finance in many ways. Trade finance and demand management were just a part of each G-5 government's policies of growth and adjustment. To compare the five countries, it is necessary to move beyond simple contrasts of discrete policies and institutions and look at the whole range of policies. A concept that helps is the notion of national strategies.

National Strategies and International Lending

Many people speak of states as actors in the international arena. Some assert that the state is the only actor.[6] Others argue that there are complex cross-border ties among many institutions, but still accept that "states act coherently as units."[7] What, then, do states do when they act coherently? Students of international politics focus on the state's use of force. International economists focus on the role of the state in managing the flow of goods, services, and capital.[8] International lawyers ask whether the state complies with the law.[9] Students of multinational corporations see the state as embodying the varied

---

Senate Committee on Foreign Relations, Subcommittee on Foreign Economic Policy, 95th Congress, 1st Sess., August 1977, pp. 55–56.

6. See, for example, Kenneth Waltz, *Man, the State, and War* (New York: Columbia University Press, 1965).

7. Robert O. Keohane and Joseph S. Nye, *Power and Interdependence* (Boston: Little, Brown, 1977), p. 25. Stanley Hoffmann, *Primacy or World Order* (New York: McGraw-Hill, 1978).

8. See, for example, the annual report of the International Monetary Fund, which regularly describes adjustment policies by different industrial countries.

9. See, for example, Kenneth W. Dam, *The Rules of the Game* (Chicago: University of Chicago Press, 1982), and Louis Henkin, *How Nations Behave: Law and Foreign Policy*, 2d ed. (New York: Columbia University Press, 1979), p. 5. "My focus is on how nations (or states, or governments) behave in regard to law."

economic interests of nations.[10] Each group sees in state action the behavior of interest to its discipline. Yet each type of action could be important to international banks, and all would be subsumed in the state's strategy.

Although those who describe the strategy of industrial states approach the topic from different perspectives, there is remarkable agreement. All find a coherent set of policies the state has implemented consistently over time. They emphasize the goals that the policies support. Reviewing American national interests in markets for international raw materials, Krasner identified three objectives: "1) increase competition; 2) insure security of supply; 3) promote broad [foreign] policy objectives."[11] The comparison of the strategies of various states is more complex. Katzenstein, reviewing the foreign economic policies of the United States, the United Kingdom, Japan, Germany, Italy, and France, found "three distinct patterns." America and Britain subscribe "to the principles of a liberal international order." Japan aims "for a high rate of economic growth." The European states "mix elements of Anglo-Saxon liberalism and Japanese neo-mercantilism in a third, hybrid pattern."[12] Examining international competition, Scott describes a nation's goals as "the concept or 'vision' of how to compete."[13] Given his topic, Scott focuses on domestic policies that trade off work and economic security, savings and income redistribution, or investment and short-term consumption. He too distinguishes among the United States, certain European countries, and Japan, but concludes that all the North Atlantic countries emphasize distribution over development, whereas Japan does the reverse.[14]

The strategies of each of the G-5 states emerge from an analysis of this literature.[15] Over the decades since World War II, the strategy of

10. Robert Gilpin, *U.S. Power and the Multinational Corporation* (New York: Basic Books, 1975).

11. Stephen D. Krasner, *Defending the National Interest* (Princeton, N.J.: Princeton University Press, 1978), p. 14.

12. Peter J. Katzenstein, ed., *Between Power and Plenty* (Madison: University of Wisconsin Press, 1978), pp. 20–21.

13. Bruce R. Scott and George C. Lodge, eds., *U.S. Competitiveness in the World Economy* (Boston: Harvard Business School Press, 1985), p. 71.

14. Ibid., p. 127.

15. In addition to considering the substance of strategy, each author emphasizes that the process by which a national strategy is formulated also affects its content.

the United States has been to sustain a "liberal international economic order,"[16] taking the lead in security and not promoting its particular economic interests abroad,[17] while more actively distributing rather than creating income at home.[18] Japan has pursued a different strategy, designed to achieve autonomy by economic means; at home, development rather than the distribution of income has been central. Particularly since the first oil shock, Germany, France, and Britain have been increasingly "stuck in the middle," to borrow a phrase from corporate strategy.[19] Although Britain and Germany have been more concerned with the international economic order than France (or Japan),[20] all three have emphasized economic security, income redistribution, and short-term consumer benefits at home.[21]

The value of the concept of national strategy here is that it helps one see the relations among the home government policies that affect international lending by banks. It adds another dimension to the classic economic view that home corporate customers, through their trade, shape the banks' international lending. As its advocates admit, the notion "is obviously a simplification."[22] Its application depends on qualitative judgments rather than quantitative measures.[23]

The Impact of National Strategies on Banks

The theory of national strategies suggests the intricate web that binds banks to their home countries. Consciously using banks to achieve national goals, governments apply a mix of policies at the macroeconomic and microeconomic levels. The adjustment policies of

16. Katzenstein, *Between Power and Plenty*, p. 298.

17. Krasner, *Defending the National Interest*, p. 15, and Scott and Lodge, *U.S. Competitiveness*, pp. 125–131.

18. Scott and Lodge, *U.S. Competitiveness*, chap. 2.

19. Michael Porter describes as stuck in the middle a corporate strategy that is neither low cost nor differentiated. See Porter, *Competitive Strategy* (New York: Free Press, 1980).

20. Katzenstein, *Between Power and Plenty*, Table I, p. 302.

21. Scott and Lodge, *U.S. Competitiveness*, p. 127.

22. Ibid., p. 72.

23. John Zysman encountered the same problem of measurement and classification in his study of financial systems and the adjustment process. See *Governments, Markets, and Growth: Financial Systems and the Politics of Industrial Change* (Ithaca, N.Y.: Cornell University Press, 1983), p. 95n.

the mid-1970s are one example. The banks are tools, albeit willing, at every stage of the production process.

The full range of policies is broad, extending far beyond direct low-interest loans that finance the purchase or sale of exported goods. Governments act all along the chain of value added. Their methods of intervention are sometimes direct, but often broad and subtle. Precisely because this action is ubiquitous, a comprehensive OECD consensus that simply limits export subsidies is unworkable. Any response to government policies must consider three stages: input, production, and sale, as well as the role the banks play in implementing policy (see Figure 2–1).

FIGURE 2–1. Official Financial Policies Affecting Trade

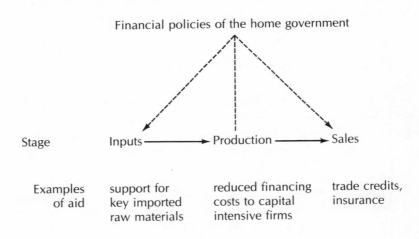

Stage	Inputs →	Production →	Sales
Examples of aid	support for key imported raw materials	reduced financing costs to capital intensive firms	trade credits, insurance

The government that uses the full range of tools as part of an export-oriented economic strategy changes the environment of international banking in this line of credit. In the following historical analysis, one finds that Japan's government was the most manipulative in the stages before export. This is a partial explanation for its modest subsidies at the export stage: having already shaped export prices in part through the financial system, it did not need to subsidize at the time of export.

In short, G-5 governments use their banks to stabilize the cost of inputs, reduce the cost of finance to capital-intensive firms, and channel finance to specific firms or industries engaged in trade. The following sections take these up in sequence.

Banks as Tools to Stabilize the Cost of Inputs

Among the G-5 governments, Japan is most active in using its banks to stabilize the cost of inputs for its manufacturers. Government policies shape the demand for the services of Japanese banks in two ways. First, the government changes the risk of financing certain imports. Second, the government increases the demand for export-related services from banks as manufacturers' sales abroad grow because of the cost advantage they receive from these policies. The Japanese Export-Import Bank, in its search for stable sources of essential commodities, lives up to its full name.[24] Official import finance has accompanied bank lending for projects by Japanese firms to tap resources around the world: oil in the Mideast and Indonesia, bauxite in Brazil, copper in central Africa, coal in western Canada, to name a few.[25] Japan is not alone; though less active, the German government

24. See Raymond Vernon, *Two Hungry Giants: The United States and Japan in the Quest for Oil and Ores* (Cambridge, Mass.: Harvard University Press, 1983).

25. In January 1984, the Japanese Ex-Im Bank extended the items eligible for low-interest import credits beyond natural resources to include "most manufactured goods and chemicals." The rate is fixed (it was 7.75 percent in early 1984) and the maturity varies from one to five years. Commercial banks supply up to 60 percent of the loan. In addition, the Ministry of International Trade and Industry was reported to be studying insurance for importers or creditor banks that, having paid in advance or invested in distribution facilities, are injured when "bankruptcy, fraud or political unrest prevent delivery." Euromoney, *Trade Finance Report*, February 1984, p. 10. The reported reason was that the government wants to encourage "imports to counter criticisms of its massive balance of payments surplus." One benefit is that it reduces the cost of key imports to firms, which then add value and may export.

guarantees private banks' foreign loans for raw material projects to support German industry.

In the wilds of the Canadian Rockies there is a partnership of firms, banks, and governments to exploit raw materials. The Quintette coal project in British Columbia was designed to ensure the supply of coking coal to Japan and, possibly, to France. The Can.$1.3 billion financial package included two international bank syndicates, a Can.$700 million nonrecourse loan and a Can.$250 million recourse loan.[26] The loans were arranged in January 1983 after more than ten years of relatively amicable negotiations that differed radically in tone from the Sicartsa contest.

A key player that drew only one paragraph in the prospectus was the government of Japan. For the project to be viable, nine Japanese firms—mainly steel producers—had to agree to buy 100 percent of the output. To make the promise convincing, the Canadian partners required the Japanese to buy 10 percent of the equity in Quintette (three other Japanese firms bought another 27.5 percent). All shareholders were to guarantee the Can.$250 million loan. In both the equity purchases and the loan guarantee, the Japanese government was key.

- The Japanese Export-Import Bank financed the Japanese 38.5 percent shareholding with a loan to each firm. The bank funded its loans at a rate of 7.3 percent,[27] but because this was an energy project, it priced the loans at less than cost. Although the shareholders did bear the exchange risk, they planned to import the coal into Japan, where they would earn yen to repay the loans.
- In addition to funding the Japanese firms' equity position in Quintette, Japan's government, through the New Energy Development Organization (NEDO), guaranteed the Japanese firms' own guarantee of 38.5 percent of the Can.$250 million recourse loan to the project. No such guarantee was made by the government of Canada, although the manager and 50 per-

26. See announcement, *Euromoney*, April 1983, p. 47.
27. The Export-Import Bank is funded through the trust fund from deposits in the post office savings bank.

cent shareholder in Quintette was Denison Mines, Ltd., of Canada.

Parties involved in the project said that without this official support, the project would not have gone forward.[28]

In Japan, official support for Quintette grew out of periodic consultations between steel makers and government. A five-year analysis of supply and demand led the firms to prepare a schedule of sources, planning which to tap for raw materials, including coking coal. The Japan Export-Import Bank prepared the feasibility study. Labor strikes in Australia suggested that Japan's major supplier was unstable, leading to a consensus that other sources should be investigated, hence Quintette. Japanese banks appear to have played no role in this decision, yet they benefited by financing a secure deal. The main beneficiaries were the steel makers, who—assured of a steadier supply of coking coal—have reduced their risk. Lower costs should affect their prices, thus improving their already strong competitive position in world markets and providing opportunities for the banks that finance them.

The Quintette case is not unique for Japan.[29] This form of government help benefits Japanese firms by reducing risk of several sorts. By ensuring a source for raw materials, it permits firms to maintain a shorter pipeline. This allows them to spend less on financing stockpiles, which reduces costs. It also permits greater efficiency, since with an assured supply the manufacturer can remove slack from the production process. To deal with the danger of oversupply, the Japanese enter joint ventures, shifting some of the risk to foreigners, and simply do not buy (sometimes despite contracts that require them to do so).

Government action to ensure supply benefits its banks in two ways. The more obvious is the transaction itself: the banks lend in a protected market, which enhances their fees. More important is the systemic effect. By reducing the firms' risk, the government action reduces their costs and increases their international competitiveness.

28. Interviews, New York, April 1983, Tokyo, May 1983, and Paris, June 1983.

29. See Vernon, *Two Hungry Giants*, and Katzenstein, *Between Power and Plenty*.

The firms' exports rise, creating more demand for the banks' trade-related lending and other services. A similar virtuous cycle results from government action to reduce the capital costs of its firms.

Banks as Tools to Reduce the Financing Costs of Capital-intensive Firms

Differences in capital costs appear to have affected competition in manufactured trade among the G-5 countries, and hence the demand for banks' services. Recent studies have shown that the cost of capital was lower in Japan and Germany during the 1970s than in other industrial countries and highest in the United States (see Table 2-2).[30] No single factor explains the differences in the cost of capital, or their evolution. The culture, institutions, government policy, and structure of the financial system all come into play. Although all are important, I focus on the role of the banks, as part of the financial system.

The big banks play an important role here too. Despite twenty years of reducing capital barriers, there were major differences in the financial systems of the G-5 countries, and their banks' roles, throughout the early 1980s. Japan's system contrasts most notably with those

TABLE 2–2. Average Weighted Cost of Capital to Industry (Percent)

Country	1971	1976	1981
United States	10.0%	11.3%	16.6%
France	8.5	9.4	14.3
West Germany	6.9	6.6	9.5
Japan	7.3	8.5	9.2

SOURCE: "A Historical Comparison of the Cost of Financial Capital," U.S. Department of Commerce, April 1983, p. 3.

30. See Chase Manhattan Bank, *U.S. and Japanese Semiconductor Industries: A Financial Comparison*, prepared for the Semiconductor Industry Association, June 9, 1980; M. Therese Flaherty and Hiroyki Itami, "Financial Systems and Capital Acquisitions," project on U.S.-Japanese Semiconductor Industry Competition, Stanford University, 1982; George N. Hatsopoulos, "High Cost of Capital," a study sponsored by the American Business Conference and Thermo Electron Corporation, April 26, 1983; and "A Historical Comparison of the Cost of Financial Capital," U.S. Department of Commerce, April 1983, p. 12.

of Europe and the United States. The biggest differences are in the financing of business, in the volume of funds, and apparently in their cost, the last two having important implications for firms' competitiveness and thus the banks' opportunities to lend to those customers abroad. The financial systems themselves play a role in creating the differences: an analysis of their structure—particularly the segmentation and the share held by intermediaries—reveals that funds can be channeled in Japan and France in a way not found in the other G-5 countries. That the channeling seems to have enhanced competitiveness in one country more than in the other is a function of national strategy. Much of what follows focuses on Japanese banks and financial markets, in contrast to the other G-5 countries.

THE BANKS' ROLE IN REDUCING THE RATES FOR OVERALL DEBT   In various ways, Japan induces its savers and intermediaries to accept real rates of return lower than they would have accepted without the inducements. The government promotes savings with devices that do not raise the cost of funds to the user. It lowers the risk of placing savings with particular institutions and limits the ability of the intermediaries to capture the value added in the flow of funds. Each of these policies has the effect of lowering the cost of capital. The following sections examine how this works.

Over the past twenty years, the country with the highest savings rate also offered investors the lowest returns. Japan's high net savings rate (21 percent of gross domestic product [GDP] from 1960 to 1980) stands in particularly vivid contrast to that of the United States (8 percent) and Great Britain (9 percent). It also exceeds Germany's (16 percent) and France's (15 percent). But Japan's investors reap no special rewards for their performance.[31] Government policy joined with the structure of domestic institutions to produce these results.

31. From 1960 to 1980, Japanese bondholders received a compound annual yield, adjusted for inflation, of only 0.23 percent, compared to about 1.00 percent in France, the U.K., and the U.S., and 3.00 percent in Germany. Roger G. Ibbotson, R. C. Carr, and A. W. Robinson, "International Equity and Bond Returns," *Financial Analysts Journal* (July–August 1982): 61. Although it is true that individual savers do not buy these bonds, the differences illustrate the returns to debt-holding savers. Obviously, tax differences will affect the impact on the issuers.

Japan's social organization and tax policies help promote savings and constrain consumption.[32] German policy also rewards savers,[33] whereas U.S. and U.K. policies encourage spending at the expense of saving.[34] In Japan, many dispersed small savers "bargain" with a few large banks. Like all governments, the government of Japan, through the Finance Ministry, sets rates for deposits directly, or through lender cartels indirectly. Given the dispersal of the savers and

32. The absence of full pension and social security systems, lump-sum payments at year end, and retirement at age fifty-five to sixty encourage workers to save. A worker who receives a large payment at the end of the year, rather than in small installments throughout the year, is more likely to save it. A worker with limited pension benefits is likely to save for the future. In a sense, such a structure forces the worker to save. Large down payments on mortgages and the absence of scholarships at private universities encourage savings. The social organization helps explain different patterns in the supply and demand for funds. Other things being equal, a large pool of savings ought to reduce the cost of capital and increase its availability. Tax policies exempt income on post office savings accounts up to a certain level (now the equivalent of about $13,000), after which savers simply open new accounts at other post offices. Chalmers Johnson, *MITI and the Japanese Miracle* (Stanford, Calif.: Stanford University Press, 1982). By law, the post offices also offer a rate slightly above that permitted to banks. Not surprisingly, the post offices command a higher share of household savings than do even the commercial banks.

33. In Germany, the taxpayer may not deduct interest paid on consumer loans or on mortgages for single-home dwellings (although favorable depreciation rates exist). Tax benefits, however,—including tax-free savings to DM 612 a year—provided a "general savings bonus" estimated by one study to equal 2.7 percent of all household savings during 1975–1978. In 1980, these "savings subsidies" began to wane. M. A. King and D. Fullerton, *The Taxation of Income from Capital* (Chicago: University of Chicago Press, 1984), p.334. Until 1981, Germany subsidized 40 to 50 percent of savings, giving premiums for savings in banks and for those contributed by employers. Economists Advisory Group, *The British and German Banking System* (London: Anglo-German Foundation, 1981).

34. Although the U.S. federal government exempts $100 in dividend income to each taxpayer, it exempts no interest income. It did offer special tax-free "all savers" accounts up to $2,000 at rates well below those offered on taxable government bonds, but with little success, since they appear to have encouraged switching accounts rather than saving more. By allowing unlimited deductions for consumer debt and mortgages, the government encourages consumption or investment in nonproductive activities. U.K. policies that allow only £70 in tax-free interest on savings accounts but do not even assess tax against pension funds do not increase savings but do affect their allocation among institutions (building societies benefit, for example).

the concentration of the banks,[35] it should not be surprising that the rates paid to savers are kept low. Since the big banks have always been cash short and have had to buy a substantial share of their resources from other financial intermediaries, they are vulnerable to these suppliers, not to the households whose rates are set by the Finance Ministry. When the cash-short big banks needed more funds, and the call market rates skyrocketed in times of tight money, the smaller source banks gained leverage. But a network of rules also limits the options of the smaller banks. The few big banks (only twelve account for over half of interbank uses) are not at the mercy of thousands of smaller ones. This balance of power proved important for the Japanese banks' international loan syndication and debt restructuring.

Two factors ensure that the big banks do not themselves capture all the value added in the financial system. First, Japanese intermediaries, which account for 80 percent of funding, lend in highly segmented markets. The big banks are twelve city banks, roughly equal in size, which alone account for over 30 percent of all intermediated credit and 40 percent of credit to business. Regulations hold them in relatively narrow service and geographic markets, within which there are enough banks to compete vigorously for share. The resulting competition prevents the big banks from retaining the value added. Second, the size and options of the large users give them further market power against the big banks. One large user is the government itself, which commands below-market interest rates.[36] Among firms, the large ones should be powerful. They are more concentrated, have more alternative sources, and may have close equity ties with the city banks, ties that could hinder or benefit the firms.[37]

Home governments reduce the risk to savers who place funds with the banks, thus reducing the cost of capital, since the premium de-

35. The structure of the Japanese financial system is discussed in detail later in this chapter.

36. Stephen Bronte, *Japanese Finance: Markets and Institutions* (London: Euromoney Publications, 1982).

37. Another study found that in the mid-1970s the biggest group "pays a third less for its debt capital than those with less than Y100 million in paid-in capital" and had done so for fifteen years. Richard E. Caves and Masu Uekusa, *Industrial Organization in Japan* (Washington, D.C.: The Brookings Institution, 1976), p. 37.

manded by savers is lower than it would be otherwise. All governments offer some form of deposit insurance and provide an implicit guarantee that no big bank will be allowed to fail, but in France and Japan that guarantee reaches much further than it does in Germany, the United Kingdom, or the United States. The effect on the capital structure of the banks, and hence on their costs, is striking. The French government implicitly guarantees the banks it owns. The Japanese government has permitted no bank to fail since World War II.[38] Moreover, the small number of big banks, with their large and pivotal role in the financial system, means that in a crisis a bank can be supported in a way that involves a relatively small number of players. Both the Japanese and French governments can do this because of their deep involvement in the financial system. This support has permitted equity: debt leveraging of as high as 1:100 in both countries, compared with ratios of 4:100 or 5:100 in Germany, the United Kingdom, and the United States. The higher leveraging permits French and Japanese banks to offer funds at lower rates, thus reducing the cost of capital to borrowers. Short of a crisis, no one bears any actual cost; in a crisis, the parties will negotiate.

In sum, the big banks can squeeze savers, who have limited options anyway, but cannot count on high margins from powerful big borrowers. This suggests that in Japan the low-cost funds can be passed along to industry without loss of profitability by the banks. Those who bear the cost are the savers, taxpayers, and, to the extent they pay higher prices, the consumers.[39]

38. In addition, in Japan, the government is the largest single intermediary. As the risk-free entity in the financial sector, the government in this role allows the saver to accept a lower return than would be required from a private intermediary. Thousands of post office outlets, all under the control of the post office itself, collect almost 16 percent of all savings and 25 percent of all household savings, channeling them to the government first and to business and home buyers second. In addition, thousands of private agricultural cooperatives collect rural savings (amounting to 12 percent of all savings) and channel them through the Norin Chukin Bank, which they own but which is under the authority of the Ministry of Agriculture.

39. Another factor is sometimes advanced to explain low capital costs in Japan: a perceived low level of demand for funds relative to supply in recent years. Certainly economic growth has slowed, but actual demand for credit has grown. Japan still invests much more than the others in machinery and equipment: 13.1 percent compared with a range of 7.3 percent (United States) to 9.7 percent (France), from 1960 to 1980. Japan does not lag behind other G-5 countries in

THE BANKS' ROLE IN REDUCING RISK IN LENDING TO
FIRMS   In several G-5 countries, the big banks help reduce the firms'
vulnerability to downturns in the business cycle or the cost of financial
distress should downturns occur. Banks lower the cost of capital in
advance of these events. Investors anticipate the reduced risk in their
initial lending. They may permit higher leveraging, more short-term
debt, or simply a lower risk premium. This allows firms to rely less
on expensive self-finance and on expensive equity finance. Firms in
Japan draw 70 percent of their funds externally, more than twice the
amount drawn externally by German firms (see Table 2–3). In Japan,
intermediaries—largely banks—provide over half of the external
funds; in the United States, they provide only about one-quarter and
public markets provide the rest.[40] When a few big banks provide the
external finance, they can manage the flow of credit. Administered
markets offer a much smaller number of players—including the big
banks—that can negotiate a coordinated response to a firm in financial
difficulty during a recession. In the G-5 countries, investors in the
public financial markets are too dispersed to do this. Yet in the United
States, 47 percent of total financial stock in 1980 passed through the

TABLE 2–3. External Funding of Business
(Percent Total Funds, Annual Average,
1970-1980)

Japan	70%
France	59
United Kingdom	58
United States	42
Germany	33

SOURCE: OECD, *Financial Statistics*, (Paris: OECD,
1982), Part III

---

demand for investment other than for plant and equipment. Perhaps relative to
the boom years of the Japanese economic miracle (up to 1973), demand for funds
in later years has been weak. In comparison with other industrial countries,
however, demand continues to be strong.

40. See Flaherty and Itami, "Financial Systems," citing Soichi Royama, "A
Perspective of Comparison of Financial Institutions," *Contemporary Economics*
(Summer 1981), in Japanese. Since 1973, some large, successful companies have
increased their dependence on self-finance in Japan.

public markets, compared to 29 percent in Germany and 22 percent in Japan (see Figure 2–2).

Of course, the banks must be able to administer, providing funds during a downturn that will enable the borrowers to weather the crisis. In the U.S financial system, there are too many players for easy administration: 14,000 commercial banks, over 4,500 savings and loan associations, almost 5,000 insurance companies. A firm may have scores of lenders, few of which see any advantage in providing new funds to a troubled firm. The contrast with Japan is vivid. Only twelve city banks account for 40 percent of the lending to business (and a larger share to big business). Highly competitive as the banks are, the incentive to cooperate in a crisis is reinforced by the means

FIGURE 2–2. Sources of funds for government, business, and households (stock outstanding, end 1980)

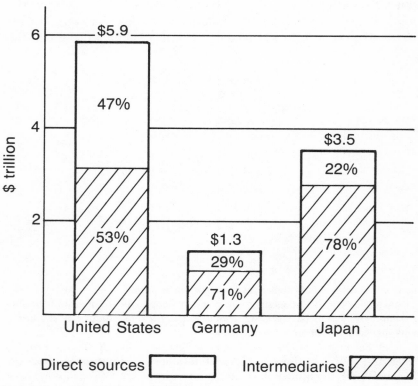

SOURCE: Central bank bulletins of each country.

to do so and conventions that guide the banks. One important factor is the equity the banks hold in the firms.

Commercial banks in Japan and Germany hold substantial equity interests in firms, whereas those in France, the United Kingdom, and the United States do not. In Japan, large industrial groups called *keiretsu* revolve around a major city bank and a trading company. Despite conflicting evidence,[41] several aspects of the *keiretsu* relation mean lower costs to the borrower: banks redeploy liquid assets within the group; bank board members with real power shape management decisions, thus reducing risk, and monitor performance.[42] A similar rationale guides banks in Germany. In a crisis, leadership among the banks in all five countries falls to the bank with the closest ties to the problem firm. But if banks are only lenders, their incentive is to place the burden of the loss on the shareholders. In Germany and Japan, where banks also hold equity, their dual interest induces the cooperation among debt holders and shareholders so often missing in the United States.

Since investors understand this process in advance, they are prepared to accept higher leveraging or shorter-term debt, both of which reduce the cost of capital. The high leveraging of Japanese and German firms is commonplace (although the amount is disputed).[43] At the aggregate level, Japan again stands out. The stock of business short-term debt in Japan was 110 percent of GDP in 1980, compared to a range of 25 to 40 percent in the other G-5 countries. All five had long-term debt in the range of 30 to 40 percent of GDP. Japanese firms could bear a much larger amount of short-term debt, and banks could lend it, because the administered system that supplied it recognized that the firms' vulnerability to economic cycles could be reduced by an ensured source of funding.

The same rationale governs firms actually in distress. Banks and other group members are expected, as shareholders, to help in times of crisis for their firm, thus reducing risk because there are fewer

41. Caves and Uekusa, *Industrial Organization*, p. 37. The authors found "no evidence that group membership raises a firm's rate of profit" and indeed that "group firms probably make higher average payments for borrowed capital than do independent companies" (pp. 77 and 82).

42. Flaherty and Itami, "Financial Systems," pp. 77 and 82.

43. Carl Kester, "Capital and Ownership and Structure: A Comparison of United States and Japanese Manufacturing Corporations," *Financial Management* (forthcoming 1986).

players with disparate interests.[44] In addition, the private sector in France, Japan, and the United Kingdom needs to deal with only one regulator of the financial system, the Finance Ministry and the central bank, rather than multiple regulators with conflicting interests, as in the United States. The government lending agencies, also under the control of the Finance Ministry, have a stake in the outcome. With fewer players on the official side, the chance of a misstep is further reduced and capital costs can reflect the benefit.

In short, the big banks play a central role in the ways in which capital costs can be reduced throughout the system in Japan, Germany, and to an extent France. When a subsidy goes to business, someone else must pay. Who pays will depend on the mechanism of the subsidy. The saver accepts lower returns in many cases but receives tax benefits in Japan for the use of certain institutions; in this case the taxpayer or higher-taxed consumer bears the cost. A regulatory system that segments the market so it can be administered will have costs as well, which may be shared within the financial system or across the economy. The big banks do not bear the full burden of the subsidy to business.

THE BANKS' ROLE IN CHANNELING FINANCIAL FLOWS TO FIRMS IN WORLD TRADE Governments also use banks to reduce the cost of capital for specific firms. The issue is whether in crucial areas of economic activity, which could be housing just as much as trade, the means (1) exist within the financial system and (2) are used to modify the mix of inputs to achieve a particular outcome. To maneuver the thousands of financial institutions toward national goals would require an explicit system of command or large, overt subsidies. Without the ability to command or reward, it would be impossible to "run things." Among the G-5, no government has so simple and obvious a system of command, not even France, where the government owns the banks, and all G-5 governments use explicit incentives to allocate credit, such as special interest ceilings or tax relief to encourage housing. A major question is whether a government could possibly target particular areas in a way not readily apparent. This requires an analysis of the structure of the financial market in each country.

44. Ibid.

THE JAPANESE FINANCIAL SYSTEM   The Japanese system differs strikingly from that of the other G-5 countries in ways that are important to trade. For example, a small number of banks allocate over half the intermediated funds, which account for almost 80 percent of all funds.[45] Japanese savings are transferred through two channels.

- Among private institutions, thousands of small banks collect savings from households and channel them, in part through interbank lending, to a small number of commercial banks (there are only thirteen city banks, if Bank of Tokyo is included). These banks, the preeminent international banks from Japan, lend to business, mainly large firms. The government is important in the loan market, since each group of intermediaries is required to invest in government securities.
- Among public intermediaries, thousands of post office outlets, all under the control of the post office itself, also collect household savings, channeling them to the government first and to business and home buyers second. Thousands of private agricultural cooperatives collect rural savings generated by government agricultural programs and channel them through the Norin Chukin Bank. Since rural demand for funds is limited, the Norin Chukin Bank deposits its excess funds with the city banks.

In Japan, the city banks are one of seven kinds of institutions that do most of the intermediating.[46] From 1976 to 1980, the seven pro-

45. Merely to know that a financial system is concentrated, of course, does not prove it is being managed. If in a country a small number of intermediaries raise a large share of funds or lend a large share, they could help frame or implement a national strategy without publicized directions from the government. Their small numbers might also augment their power in dealing with the government, leading either to a standoff or to their taking the lead. In either case, however, trade-offs among groups or their members could be negotiated in private. The management of the financial system can be quite subtle. Alternatively, if in a country each group had many members, no clear boundary on its services, and no large share of a segment, there would be big hurdles to using the financial system in any but the most overt manner.

46. They are city banks, long-term credit banks, trust banks, local banks, small business financing institutions, agricultural finance institutions, and the postal savings system. See Appendix for details. The intermediaries accounted for about 33 percent of the value traded in the industrial bond market and 33 to

vided 83 percent of the net industrial funds in the country. Within this complex financial system, three forces worked in tandem to target financial flows: private market power, official market power, and regulatory power.

Market power in Japan rests with the few city and specialized banks for three reasons: their small numbers compared to the thousands of savers (city banks, long-term credit banks, and trust banks number only twenty-three); proximity to the main borrowers (the *keiretsu* system described above); and control of about 40 percent of savings (many *keiretsu* firms keep their funds with their main banks). The banks do not compete head-on in all markets because of regulations that separate them by product and geography. Government policy is in part responsible for each of these factors.

The overall impact of the government exceeds its role as a direct lender but is closely tied to that role. Through its postal savings system, the government is the largest single player in the market for deposits, changing the game for banks and other intermediaries. The postal system enjoys regulatory advantages, including a slightly higher, tax-free interest rate, that make it a formidable competitor of the city banks in the deposit markets. Competition changes to cooperation, however, in the loan markets. Postal savings funds go through the Trust Fund first to government users, which include the Japan Development Bank (JDB) and the Japanese Export-Import Bank.[47]

---

40 percent of the number (not the value) of listed shares. *Industrial Bank of Japan Handbook* (Tokyo: IBJ, 1982), pp. 108–109, 204, and 298.

47. Some observers note that during the last twenty years much of the JDB's lending has financed shipping and electrical utilities, rather than the exposed industries; these observers have concluded that its impact on industrial policy must be small. Philip H. Trezise, "Industrial Policy Is Not the Major Reason for Japan's Success," *The Brookings Review* (Spring 1983): 13. Actually, JDB lending has gone through several phases since 1952, only the earliest of which concentrated on key heavy industries. In the fiscal year ending March 1981, however, 49 percent of JDB credit funded "energy resources and technology." "Japan's Strategy for the 80s," *Business Week*, December 14, 1981. In a study of the Trust Fund to 1977, although only about 7 percent financed "industrial development," about 17 percent financed trade and 40 percent financed small and medium industry. E. Sakakibara, E. Feldman, and Y. Harada, "The Japanese Financial System in Comparative Perspective," a study prepared for the use of the Joint Economic Committee, U.S. Congress, March 12, 1982, p. 44. The last category is important: "roughly 60 percent are subcontractors that contribute so much to Japan's competitiveness." "Japan's Strategy for the 80s," *Business Week*, December 14, 1981.

This direct lending, plus lending by the three specialized long-term credit banks, provided 18 percent of all outstanding loans to business in 1980 (see Appendix); if the net flow is considered, the percentage was higher. If 18 percent of outstanding credit seems small, the target is also small: Japanese exports are only about 15 percent of GDP. This lending also has an insurance function,[48] since private lenders in Japan treat it as a sign that the firm or project has government support, which reduces the risk of the credit. One cannot assume a harmony of interests between the Finance Ministry and the long-term credit banks (LTCBs),[49] but neither can one assume constant opposition. Thus, the 18 percent has a multiplier effect on private loans.

Finally, as in all countries, the government in Japan regulates innumerable facets of the financial system. It limits entry and expansion, shapes geographic and product markets, and controls pricing directly and indirectly through cartels of the intermediaries. For example, the Finance Ministry approves the long-term prime rate that three long-term credit banks set when acting as an official cartel,[50] and helps decide where, outside the agricultural cooperative, the Norin Chukin Bank can invest its funds. As planner, the government helps set priorities without actually lending money. The result is highly segmented markets. Competition across segments is limited, though not lost. Competition within a market segment can be severe, lowering capital costs to the borrowers.

Overall, the structure of the financial system—not simply the equity ties between banks and firms—should reduce the cost of capital in Japan, improving its firms' competitiveness. The point is not that the government gives all the orders, but that the government has put itself in a position to influence the flow of funds. For example, one of the targets of the Japanese financial system is the government itself. For each group to ensure its own protection, its members must buy an agreed share of new government bonds.

THE FINANCIAL SYSTEMS IN OTHER G-5 COUNTRIES
In the United States, where half of all financial stock is from public

---

48. Sakakibara, Feldman, and Harada, "The Japanese Financial System," p. 54. Participation of a long-term credit bank in a loan consortium gave a de facto government guarantee to the project involved, making it possible for the private corporation in the project to socialize the risk.

49. See, for example, J. Andrew Spindler, *The Politics of International Credit* (Washington, D.C.: The Brookings Institution, 1984).

50. Bronte, *Japanese Finance*, p. 39.

markets (see Figure 2–2) and the remaining funds are intermediated by thousands of institutions, one must look for overt signals. Most striking in the picture of the U.S. financial system is the enormous number of institutions in each group, nearly twenty-five thousand altogether (see Appendix). Within each group there is a hierarchy by size. But even a firm with $60 billion controls barely 1.8 percent of all assets in the system. Although the largest financial institutions in the world are in the United States, they are part of a system that dwarfs them. Depending on exchange rates, Bank of America and Citibank have been larger than any other bank in the world. But though the top ten banks in the United States command 22 percent of the assets of all commercial banks, this gives them only 8 percent of total assets in the intermediated system. Coupled with the proliferation of financial institutions and the assault on regulatory barriers among the segments, the plethora of intermediaries in the United States suggests that they cannot be used in a subtle way to help achieve a national strategy.

If the U.S. government wants to influence lending it must use broad, public measures, and it does. According to a recent study, the housing industry received far greater government assistance than did any other of fifteen major industries. The U.S. government, using the financial system, gave 78 percent of its industry assistance to housing, providing almost all its loans and guarantees to that industry.[51] This strategy uses the financial system in the most overt manner to promote housing, which is not an industry exposed to international competition.

Despite controversy in both Britain and Germany about the role of the financial system, there is little evidence to suggest channeling of the kind that may occur in Japan. Both countries have a few large deposit banks with close relations to major firms, but these banks are vastly outnumbered by the savings banks (called building societies in the United Kingdom), which have the dominant market share. An analysis of market segments in Germany suggests that the dominant practices result in the preservation of market share among the groups (see Appendix). A recent study of British and German banks concluded that the banks had little effect on savings, noting that since 1975 the high savings rate in Germany had fallen, and the low rate

51. Robert B. Reich, "Why the U.S. Needs an Industrial Policy," *Harvard Business Review*, January–February 1982, p. 78; author's calculations.

in the United Kingdom had risen, without change in the structure or behavior of the banking system.[52] The main point of critics in the United Kingdom and Germany is that the financial system favors the status quo. Given the distance the governments of both countries maintain from their financial institutions, and the nature of their own economic strategies, their recent use of the financial system does not appear to strengthen home firms in competition with others. To the extent government policy supports a status quo, it may endanger competitiveness.

The French banking system is nationalized, which falsely implies that the Banque de France and the Finance Ministry can direct the banks' operations almost as a puppeteer controls puppets. It is true that the line of official command is more overt and direct in France than in the other G-5 countries, especially since the Mitterrand government took office. In fact, however, the monetary authorities rely more on market mechanisms, such as credit ceilings, to manage the banking system. French firms that compete in world markets are helped mainly by subsidized finance at the point of sale.

Although both Japan and France could use their banks to channel financial flows, Japan is far better situated to do so in a way that reduces the cost of capital and improves its manufacturing firms' competitiveness. The Japanese regulators are in a better position to enforce such a strategy than are the other G-5 regulators. Unlike their counterparts in Germany and the United Kingdom, Japan's Finance Ministry and central bank are active. Unlike the United States, Japan has only two regulators; in the United States, the web of regulatory institutions almost defies unraveling. Unlike their colleagues in France, the Japanese authorities need not contend with a bank president appointed by the president of the nation.

Of course, the unequal or asymmetrical relations found in Japan exist elsewhere. In Europe and the United States, big banks dwarf other financial intermediaries. Big banks buy money from others. Government regulations create significant barriers between market segments, and the banks try to keep the barriers that sustain them while removing those that are costly. It is a matter of degree. In Japan, the distinctions seem more pronounced and the opportunity greater

---

52. Economists Advisory Group, *The British and German Banking System* (see note 33).

for guidance through administrative action as well as through the action of the government as player.

Although a nation's financial system can be described as managed, in an integrated world economy that management would fail in the face of powerful market forces. Savers forced to accept lower returns at home would merely turn to foreign forms of investment that offered market rates. Intermediaries constrained at home would go abroad to escape. An essential component of any system that seeks to manage financing costs and flows is control at the borders, yet the erosion of those controls has been the goal of major industrial states for at least the last twenty-five years. The dilemma is how the benefits of a system like Japan's could have survived in the increasingly integrated world of finance.

Control at the Border—Control at Home

Barriers block the free flow of capital from several of the G-5 countries. Until May 1985, the German queue for foreign bond issuers was managed by the large German banks. The French restricted franc loans to nonresidents, who could borrow francs only to finance the purchase of French exports. The Japanese went further: they controlled Samurai bonds, registered foreign currency loans by Japanese banks, controlled foreign banks' operations in the domestic yen markets, and limited the use of the yen even by foreign central banks. Neither the United Kingdom nor the United States had clean hands: the British exchange controls and the U.S. interest equalization tax ended only ten years ago. Since then, however, the two countries have become more open. These barriers affect the big banks' international operations and permit the government to manage its domestic financial system. Control at the border is prerequisite for the controls at home described earlier.

It is hard to quantify the impact of the protectionist policies, since other factors—relative exchange rates and interest rates, for example— also affect the flow of capital. One indicator is found in the extent to which nonbank residents of each country place deposits in international banks (Table 2–4). Japan emerges as the maverick. Compared to the G-5 average of 100, foreign currency deposits by Japanese residents were a mere one in 1980, far outside the range of 99 to 225

TABLE 2–4. Domestic Nonbanks' Use of International Banks: Deposits and Borrowing by Country*

	U.S.	U.K.	France	Germany	Japan	G-5 Average: Stock ÷ GDP
1980						
Deposits						
In domestic currency abroad	335	86	14	64	1	.734%
In foreign currency abroad	27	225	138	99	1	.564
at home**	—	245	37	19	—	1.250
Borrowing						
In domestic currency abroad	4	39	16	400	5	.95
In foreign currency abroad	22	160	148	82	87	.998
at home**	—	263	84	13	—	1.990
GDP ($ trillions)	$2.59	$0.43	$0.48	$0.66	$1.16	
1983						
Deposits						
In domestic currency abroad	405	37	10	47	1	1.002%
In foreign currency abroad	26	246	119	98	11	.614
at home**	—	263	27	11	—	2.000
Borrowing						
In domestic currency abroad	52	19	6	420	5	1.004
In foreign currency abroad	9	130	210	98	53	1.218
at home**	—	226	64	9	—	3.123
GDP ($ trillions)	$3.36	$0.46	$0.52	$0.65	$1.16	

*Each G-5 country's deposits with, and borrowing from, international banks are indexed against the average for all five countries. The average is 100.

** Three-country average.

SOURCE: Bank for International Settlements, "International Banking Developments," Basel, Switzerland, second quarter 1983 and second quarter 1984, Table 7.

for the other nondollar countries.[53] Japan also seems to have been most successful in preventing the yen from serving as a reserve currency: against the G-5 average of 100, Japan's domestic currency deposits abroad were also one and its domestic currency borrowing abroad was 5, both far outside the range for the other countries.[54] In vivid contrast, Japanese borrowers of foreign currency were well within the G-5 range.

Japanese residents have long been constrained in their ability to hold foreign currency deposits. There is no reason to suspect that Japanese residents require fewer foreign deposits than residents of the other industrial countries. Nor, given the strength and subsequent decline of the yen, can we assume that Japanese investors choose not to hold foreign currency deposits because of expectations about currency movements.

Several years after formally opening its borders, Japan was still the maverick. Although Japan's foreign-exchange laws were formally relaxed on December 1, 1980, informal constraints have continued. Before that date, residents wishing to export capital needed the approval of the Finance Ministry. After that date they were allowed to invest abroad if they notified the Ministry of Finance twenty days in advance. The twenty-day delay had the effect, of course, of dampening speculative movements. The Finance Ministry, moreover, retained the power to suspend or modify this more liberal rule if "the transaction might adversely affect (1) domestic and international money markets; (2) Japan's international reputation; (3) Japan's industrial activity or the smooth performance of the economy; and (4) implementation of Japan's international agreements, international peace and security, or the maintenance of public order."[55]

These new policies in Japan do not appear to have encouraged the flow of capital to the international banking system. The major outflows during this period, particularly to the United States, appear to have been made through financial intermediaries in Japan. If so, control over the behavior of the ultimate saver, at least, would appear to

53. Because of the role of the dollar as a banking currency, I exclude U.S. residents from the comparisons.

54. The low rate of French franc deposits abroad—nevertheless a multiple of the Japanese—reflects a prohibition against most uses of francs outside France.

55. International Monetary Fund, *Annual Report on Exchange Arrangements* (Washington, D.C.: IMF, 1982), p. 241.

remain strong. The question remains whether the behavior of the past is any indicator of the future.

National Strategies in the Future

Despite the view that barriers around national capital markets have been greatly eroded since at least the early 1970s, the collapse of these barriers is not imminent. Nor are governments likely to stop using their financial systems and big banks to promote exports. The link between trade and finance appears by aggregate measures to have grown stronger, not weaker, in the late 1970s. Certainly a large portion of trade is still financed. The deregulation that is sweeping through several countries' financial systems need not undercut national strategies that depend on financial systems to promote a link between trade and finance.

Historical Foundation

The practice of fusing purchase and finance was centuries old when Garcia Torres used it. Banking grew from commerce, international banking from foreign trade. As early as the twelfth century, bankers "spread through Europe" from northern Italy, financing trade among cities and at fairs like that at Champagne. Over time, people from other forms of business entered this market. The Fuggers, for example, traders of wool and silver from southern Germany, began lending in the sixteenth century.[56] Even in the twentieth century, the banks' initial motivation to expand abroad was to meet the commercial needs of their corporate customers at home. As Eurocurrency lending blossomed, the link between trade and credit persisted. The World Bank reported that 49 percent of the $57 billion in Eurocredits announced from 1974 to 1977 were for specific purposes and projects.[57]

56. Charles P. Kindleberger, *A Financial History of Western Europe* (London: George Allen & Unwin, 1984), p. 43 and chap. 3. See Fernand Braudel, *Civilization and Capitalism: 15th-18th Century*, Vol. II, *The Wheels of Commerce*, trans. by Sian Reynolds, (New York: Harper & Row, 1979), chap. 1.

57. See *Borrowing in International Capital Markets*, (Washington, D.C.: International Bank for Reconstruction and Development), Table 8, June 1977, and Table 12, July 1979. About 51 percent of publicized Eurocredits were either for general purposes or for financial institutions. Author's calculations based on World Bank data.

The question today, however, is whether the trade-finance link is still strong. Banks appear at first glance to have cut the cord to their commercial origins.[58] Their myriad financial services today suggest banks diversified far beyond their early role. Banks now engage in massive operations unrelated to trade, like deposits by one bank in another and loans to governments for general purposes.

Continuation of Trade Finance

At the aggregate level, one can test the strength of the trend away from trade-related finance, at least in the United States. If bank loans follow foreign trade, the regional distribution of U.S. banks' foreign claims (mainly loans) should correspond to that of U.S. exports, but this is not always the case (see Table 2–5). In 1983, for example, in the oil-exporting countries, the share of U.S. banks' claims and exports came closest to each other, with a ratio of 0.84. Orders of magnitude for bank claims and exports in most regions are about the same: a large share of both is with industrial countries (the Group of Ten) and a small share is with Eastern Europe and Africa.

Despite limitations imposed by the data, one can discern a trend for U.S. bank lending away from exports up to 1977 and toward exports thereafter. In 1977, U.S. banks seemed to be allocating their credit worldwide with increasing independence from the direction of U.S. exports. This is consistent with observations at the time that U.S. banks were lending more for balance-of-payments purposes. From 1977 to 1983, however, there is a closer association between lending and exports. This is also consistent with the reported slow-down in balance-of-payments lending by U.S. banks at the end of the 1970s.

In short, the regional congruence of U.S. bank loans and trade is approximate, not precise. It is increasing in many groups of countries: the G-10, other developed, and Eastern Europe. It is steady in the oil-exporting countries and Asia. The congruence is weakening in the regions hardest hit by the debt crisis, Latin America and Africa, to which presumably exports drop as involuntary lending grows. In the

58. R. M. Pecchioli, *The Internationalization of Banking* (Paris: OECD, 1983).

TABLE 2–5. Comparative Distribution of U.S. Exports and Claims on Foreign Countries by U.S. Banks (end of period)

Region**	Ratio* of each region's share of U.S. banks' foreign claims to its share of U.S. exports				1983 Distribution	
	1975	1977	1977	1983***	U.S. banks' foreign claims	U.S. exports
G-10 countries	.92	.81	.70	.80	46.8%	58.4%
Other developed	1.40	1.45	1.70	1.29	11.6	9.0
Oil exporters	.60	.87	.84	.84	8.4	10.0
Non-oil-developing						
Latin America	1.65	1.73	1.98	2.51	22.1	8.8
Asia	.72	.87	.84	.81	7.9	9.7
Africa	.55	.50	.64	.52	1.2	2.3
Eastern Europe	1.09	1.54	1.92	1.11	2.0	1.8
Total					100.0%	100.0%
U.S. $ billions					$298.1	$177.6

* The closer the ratio is to 1.00, the closer the region's share of U.S. bank claims (mainly loans) is to its share of U.S. exports. If the ratio exceeds 1.00, its share of the bank claims is greater than its share of exports. For example, in 1983 46.8 percent of all U.S. banks' foreign claims were in G-10 countries while 58.4 percent of all U.S. exports were there. The ratio is given by 46.8/58.4 or .80.

** Offshore banking centers are not included: the United Kingdom, Switzerland, Bahamas, Bermuda, British West Indies, Netherland Antilles, Lebanon, Liberia, Hong Kong, and Singapore.

*** As of June 1983.

SOURCES: IMF Direction of Trade; Federal Financial Institutions Examination Council, *Statistical Release E.16*, "Country Exposure Lending Survey," various issues. The series changes in 1977.

United States, one cannot yet dismiss the tie between trade and bank lending as a relic of the past.[59]

Financing home country trade is much more important to banks from France, Japan, and Germany than to U.S. banks. Unfortunately, the data do not permit a comparison of trade and credit similar to that for the United States. Other evidence is necessary. In France, export credits exceeded 12 percent of all domestic credits by the end of the 1970s. In Japan, the banks support trade in two ways: directly, as creditors to buyers and suppliers, and indirectly, as the major source of finance for the trading firms, which in turn lend to finance trade.[60] In Germany, bankers note that about one-third of their balance sheet is international and assert that a "good portion" goes to finance exports and imports. For banks in Europe and Japan, however, third-country trade finance, involving two countries other than the home, appears to be much less important than it is for U.S. banks, which seem to be more independent of their home country in this regard.[61]

The greater importance of home trade finance to the banks of France, Germany, and Japan parallels these countries' greater reliance on exports. In 1983, for example, exports and imports were 62 percent of the gross national product (GNP) in Germany, 45 percent in France, and 31 percent in Japan, compared to 17 percent in the United States.[62] Japan appears closer to the United States, but Japan exports a much higher proportion of its industrial product.[63] Manufactured goods, which require more complex financing than agricultural exports, call for longer-term involvement by banks.

59. This congruence does not necessarily entail a causal relation. Both trade and credit could be a function of relative demand, for example.

60. Richard T. Murphy, "Administrative Guidance Abroad: Regulation of Japanese International Banking," unpublished paper, Harvard Business School, January 1981. E. Sakakibara, E. Feldman, and Y. Harada, "The Japanese Financial System in Comparative Perspective," a study prepared for the use of the Joint Economic Committee, U.S. Congress, March 12, 1982.

61. Interviews in Tokyo, Europe, the United States, and Mexico.

62. International Monetary Fund, *International Financial Statistics Yearbook, 1984* (Washington, D.C.: IMF, 1985).

63. In 1977, for example, from an economy half the size of that of the United States, Japanese-manufactured exports of $78 billion were the third largest in the world, close behind those of the United States ($85 billion) and further behind Germany's ($104 billion). *World Development Report, 1980* (Washington, D.C.: World Bank, 1980), Table 12, p. 133.

One might expect British banks, as part of a world financial center, to be the most independent of trade flows, and indeed, using the same ratio as that for U.S. banks, one finds this is true (see Table 2–6). Yet even these recent trends toward independence from trade must be interpreted with caution. Of the five largest British banks, three were born and grew in different parts of the British Empire: Barclays Bank in Africa, Lloyds Bank International in Latin America, and Standard Chartered Bank in Africa and Asia. Only in the late 1960s did these banks shift from decentralized operations based on their foreign networks to operations in world money and capital markets based at headquarters in London.[64] Moreover, British exports have performed particularly poorly at least since the end of World War II, forcing British banks to uncouple their growth from British trade, to prevent the erosion of their own international operations. In short, despite the advent of many new banking activities, banks have not abandoned trade finance as an important operation.

The Role of Bank Finance in Trade

The continuing participation of banks in financing trade raises the question of the importance of their role. No one knows the full dimensions of trade finance.[65] One cannot simply estimate the banks' trade finance from a country's exports. Credit funds a fraction of trade that varies by country of origin and destination. Export credit may

64. See *Transnational Banks: Operations, Strategies, and Their Effects in Developing Countries* (New York: U.N. Centre on Transnational Corporations, 1981) and Derek F. Channon, *British Banking Strategy and the International Challenge* (London: Macmillan, 1977).

65. A recent BIS/OECD compilation, for example, excludes, for nonbanks, suppliers' credits without official guarantee and foreign aid related to trade; for banks, lending outside the fifteen BIS reporting countries; and for multilateral institutions like the World Bank, all loans. Moreover, to the extent that short-term export finance is liquidated in less than a year, these data understate the financing. Bank for International Settlements (BIS) and Organization for Economic Cooperation and Development (OECD), "Statistics on External Indebtedness: Bank and Trade-related Non-Bank External Claims on Individual Borrowing Countries and Territories," at end-1982, end-June 1983, and end-1983 (Paris and Basel, April and July 1984).

TABLE 2–6. Comparative Distribution of U.K. Exports and Claims on Foreign Countries by U.K. Banks

Region	Ratio of each region's share of U.K. banks' foreign claims to its share of U.K. exports					1983 Distribution	
	1979	1980	1981	1982	1983	U.K. banks' foreign claims	U.K. exports
G-10 countries	.68	.71	.74	.71	.67	41.8%	51.8%
Other developed	.75	.85	.81	.90	.92	18.3	19.9
Oil exporters	1.24	.88	.67	.68	.75	10.5	8.5
Non-oil-developing							
Latin America	6.33	7.25	8.95	12.92	21.50	17.2	0.8
Asia	1.26	1.59	1.62	1.55	1.69	6.6	3.9
Africa	.86	.79	1.00	1.05	1.38	1.8	1.3
Eastern Europe	2.94	3.13	3.00	3.58	4.06	6.5	1.6
Total						100.0%	100.0%

Sources: IMF *Direction of Trade Statistics Yearbook, 1985* (Washington, D.C.: IMF, 1985), p. 396; "U.K.-registered Monetary Sector Institutions and Their Branches and Subsidiaries Worldwide," *Bank of England Quarterly Report*, Table 15, various editions.

take diverse forms, further complicating measurement.[66] Though data for other G-5 countries are not comprehensive,[67] one broad study of U.S. exports in 1982 found that, of the exports analyzed, 30 percent were financed.[68] The share was higher for importers in developing countries (36 percent) than in industrial countries (18 percent), as one would expect. In 1982, of all net financial flows to developing countries, at least 33.5 percent was tied to imports: 12.5 percent was tied to aid, 9.0 percent to suppliers' credits, 9.0 percent to official export credits,[69] and perhaps 3.0 percent trade-related official guarantees of bank loans.[70] This excludes another 25.0 percent from banks, some of which financed trade, as in Sicartsa.

There is a wide range in export financing solely by governments. In 1981, for example, the United States gave official support to 5 percent of its exports; Germany, 9 percent; the United Kingdom, 31 percent; France, 32 percent; and Japan, 55 percent.[71] The U.S. Export-Import Bank provided only about 10 to 20 percent of all U.S. trade finance.[72] At the other extreme is France, where "virtually all medium- and long-term export [credits] are eligible for either redis-

66. See Charles J. Gmur, ed., *Trade Financing* (London: Euromoney Publications, 1981).

67. For example, the Banque de France reports in *La Balance des Paiements de la France, 1981* (Paris: Banque de France, 1982) that exports of Fr. 665 billion were financed by long- and short-term commercial export credits totaling only Fr. 61 billion, or less than 10 percent of exports (pp. 6–7). Total foreign loans by French banks amount to another Fr. 37 billion, and though franc loans to non-residents must support exports, only Fr. 5 billion was in francs (the rest in foreign currency).

68. "1982 Export Finance Survey," unpublished report, U.S. Export-Import Bank, January 26, 1983.

69. OECD DAC Report for 1983, Table A1, p. 179. These figures understate the size of trade finance by excluding credit for military goods and for less than one year, much of which is usually assumed to finance trade.

70. The *stock* of bank loans to these countries, $56 billion or 10 percent of outstanding bank credit, carried a trade-related guarantee or insurance from an official agency in 1982. I extrapolated a similar share for the flow. "1982 Export Finance Survey," U.S. Export-Import Bank, January 26, 1983.

71. U.S. Export-Import Bank, *Report to the U.S. Congress on Export Credit Competition and the Export-Import Bank of the United States* (Washington, D.C., 1982), Country Appendices. Similar data are not available for 1982.

72. The 1982 study (note 71) shows 9 percent for that year, whereas the 1975 study shows 20 percent during the third quarter of 1975.

count or direct financing support for 85 percent of the contract value."[73]

An estimate that at least one-third of all G-5 exports are financed probably understates the volume of trade finance. Yet even at that size, the volume is immense. The nominal value of G-5 exports in 1982 was $768 billion.[74] If one-third of this was financed, the loans amounted to $256 billion. Since most financing goes through banks, the volume is substantial, if indeterminate.

Trade finance persists as an important activity for banks, and financing remains important to trade. The home governments' ability to manipulate the trade-finance link, however, is threatened by the integration of national capital markets. As barriers fall, home governments—particularly the Japanese government—will be less able to limit the options of savers, hold down capital costs, and guide the flow of funds.

The Continued Effect of National Strategies on World Capital Markets

In Japan, Britain, and the United States, the financial systems went through major changes during the early 1980s.[75] The dramatic changes in Japan led many to welcome a new era of deregulation there, both externally and internally. During 1982, largely in response to high interest rates in the United States, net capital outflows were $12 billion, against annual average net inflows of $2 billion from 1976 to 1981. Since $12 billion is 1 percent of GDP, the swing was not trivial, but one would expect it, since Japan had moved into current-account surplus. In 1983 and 1984, when capital outflows exceeded the cur-

73. U.S. Export-Import Bank, *Report to Congress* (1982), p. 1.

74. International Monetary Fund, *International Financial Statistics Yearbook*, *1984*.

75. The changes in France and Germany are less dramatic, but also important. For example, in April 1985 the German government decided to end its practice of restricting the underwriting of deutschemark bond issues to German banks. Disbanding the capital markets subcommittee, which included the six leading German banks and set the calendar of bond issues, the government allowed foreign banks' subsidiaries to lead the issues beginning May 1. John Davies, "West Germans Open Bond Sector to Foreign Managers," *Financial Times*, April 13, 1985, p. 19. Since the subsidiaries lack the deutschemark-placing capacity of the big German banks, however, it is not clear how they can become a major force in the market even with the restriction lifted.

rent-account surplus, domestic savings were being exported. Apparently the old constraints are breaking down. Does this mean that Japan's complex, administered financial system is becoming obsolete? To answer this, one must first answer two more basic questions.

The first question is whether the *external* barriers are down permanently. The aggregate data do not indicate a secular change (see Table 2–4); there was no substantial narrowing of the gap between Japan and the other G-5 countries by the end of 1983. The outflows of domestic private savings have not been excessive in view of the size of Japan's current-account surplus. A crude measure is the relative shifts in the major components of the country's balance of payments. The current-account surplus is by definition offset by changes in the capital account and reserves. Japanese private savers are reinvesting abroad only the current surplus; the capital-account deficit will equal the current-account surplus and official reserves will not change. If private savers decide to invest some of the current surplus in Japan, the capital deficit will fall short of the current surplus, and reserves will rise. If, however, private savers export some domestic savings in addition to the current surplus, then the capital outflow will exceed the current surplus, and official reserves will fall. In 1983, the $21.32 billion capital-account deficit barely exceeded the $20.80 billion current-account surplus. In 1984, the gap was not much larger: the capital account's $37 billion surplus was only $2 billion more than the current-account deficit.[76] Little of Japan's large pool of private savings appears to have flowed out of the country in the years after the external barriers were supposed to have been lifted. The real test will come when there is a threat to current-account surplus.

The consensual behavior typical of Japan's historical strategy persists on the microeconomic level. For example, trust banks have been a major vehicle for the outflow of funds. Late in 1983, the Ministry of Finance became concerned about their foreign lending. It was soon announced that "Japan's trust banks are to voluntarily curb the investment of pension funds in foreign securities and bonds so as to check capital outflows from Japan in line with the government's efforts to stem the further decline of the yen."[77]

76. International Monetary Fund, *International Financial Statistics* (Washington, D.C.: IMF, April 1985). Twenty-five percent of the $50 billion in long-term outflows was offset by short-term inflows of $13 billion.

77. Yoko Shibata, "Japan's Trust Banks to Curb Investment in Foreign Securities," *Financial Times*, November 24, 1983, p. 22.

For countries to which trade is important, the disincentive to integrate their financial market with the rest of the world is strong. The governments of Japan, Germany, and France have made it clear that they do not want their currencies to be reserve currencies, and have therefore limited access to them. The fear is that as nations with reserve currencies, they would lose control over domestic monetary policy, one component of which is interest rate management. The policy link to capital costs is strong.

In finance, there is an equivalent to the nontariff barriers that stymie efforts to open trade. The variety of ways in which capital costs are manipulated suggests a large gap between formally stating that a financial system is open to the world and achieving that goal. Numerous institutions tie savers to their country. Relations among intermediaries or between intermediaries and those who use the financial services can persist when they are based on mutual benefit. A balance of power among groups of institutions will be hard to change if the balance is maintained by regulations that are designed to ensure the safety and soundness of a country's financial system. France's exchange controls are explicit. Japan's controls, which are much more complex, are likely to persist despite the appearance of change.

The second question one must answer in order to determine the future of Japan's complex financial system is whether the *internal* barriers are coming down permanently. Today, the structure in Japan still appears to be amenable to subtle guidance that helps firms competing in world industries. The laws and practices that undergird these relations are changing, however. Competitive pressures resulting from slower growth in demand force city and local banks to vie for the middle-market firms. Cost pressures force city banks, which are liability poor, to search for cheaper deposits. Big borrowers' access to foreign funds reduces the power of their domestic banks. The opportunity to invest abroad increases the options of some savers. The government's dependence on banks to finance the fiscal deficit, a change with roots in the mid-1970s,[78] means the banks can demand something in return. Free market interest rates have begun to appear, and changes in the banking laws have formalized new opportunities.

The important issue is not whether the Japanese financial system is open. It is not: for example, the free market interest rates affected

78. See M. Colyer Crum and David M. Meerschwam, "From Relationship to Price Banking: The Loss of Regulatory Control," in *America versus Japan*, ed. by Thomas K. McCraw (Boston: Harvard Business School Press, 1986).

barely 1.0 percent of total domestic credit as of December 1983. The important issue is whether the small changes that have occurred mark the end of the old strategy. Crum and Meerschwam argue that there was a sea change in Japan in the mid-1970s, from relationship banking to price banking, and this change, like the shift in the United States, is inexorable. Further, it is problematic whether the Finance Ministry's informal controls can survive in the future as some of the enabling conditions are eroded. The argument assumes that power has shifted from the Finance Ministry to the city banks. In a sense, the power relationship is bilateral. In my analysis, the government's power is multilateral and stems from the government's ability to play different groups in the financial system against one another. Thus one must look, for example, for erosion in the market segments that confine city banks and security companies. A few small signs of this have appeared. It is worth remembering that the controls survived earlier changes, such as the entry of the commercial banks into international markets in 1970–1971.

As financial markets evolved and banks diversified, the link between international trade and finance remained stronger than one might have expected precisely because of national strategies designed to promote exports. The evidence in this chapter suggests the tenacity of the trade-finance link for the banks. The large portion of banks' international lending allotted to trade is part of the story of the banks' growing exposure to developing countries, and its importance has been underestimated.

Government activities relevant to trade finance extend well beyond the microeconomic policies seen in the Sicartsa project. To promote their exports, some governments use the banking system at home in all stages of production, from ensuring access to raw materials to reducing costs of finance. In thinking about these national strategies, one can distinguish between government as regulator-manager of the aggregate economy, which is a familiar role to observers in the United States, and government as player, which is much less familiar. A government's power in the financial system can be derived from more than its position as sovereign. A government's ability to fuse both roles effectively, as in Japan, can make it a powerful force in financial markets. Indeed, in the preceding analysis, Japan stands out.

Into the 1980s, the G-5 governments used their banks to promote their own trade and, in the case of the United States, that of others. Given this dominant goal, one should not be surprised at the fate of conflicting policies. The main casualty was prudential regulation.

3

Official Oversight and International Bank Credit

Banks are among the most regulated institutions. Why, then, did regulation fail to control the rapid growth of loans to developing countries? Regulators cannot be expected to prevent every bad loan, but the debt crisis did not develop because a clever borrower hoodwinked the banks. People began to express their concern about loans to developing countries as early as 1974. Why did regulation fail?

A simple observation that might serve as an answer is that although banks are regulated at home, they are by tradition much less constrained in international operations. This is true of all G-5 countries, although the extent varies among them. But this truth begs the question. What explains this lesser regulation? If banking rules are designed to promote the safety and soundness of the financial system, and if the G-5 nations intend to continue to use them to this end, it is essential to know why international operations are less regulated and why those regulations did not work.

The easy answer to *my* question is that the national strategies of the G-5 countries and the existing regulatory processes deflected the necessary prudential rules. Principles of safety and soundness represent only one purpose of each home government's policy toward its banks. A notable goal, discussed earlier, is trade promotion. Other goals vary with the country, and home governments applied their regulations to promote their own goals. The regulatory process in each of the G-5 countries permitted this. Although individual regulators appear to have understood the dangers, they made and implemented policies that would insulate banks from efforts to allocate credit directly. At the same time, they did not vitiate broader policies such as export promotion that would guide banks' lending by using the system.

Prudential regulation is clearly linked to trade and other policies. One can better understand this by examining rules in the G-5 countries that govern portfolio diversification and country analysis. By discriminating among borrowers, these rules shape the allocation of credit worldwide. A clear case of the light hand of regulation abroad is the interpretation of the 10 percent rule in the United States during the 1970s. U.S. policies extended beyond concern about the balance of payments to include broader concerns about the world economy. Equally revealing is an analysis of the substance of the rules and the process by which the rules were framed and enforced.

The Enforcement Hiatus: A U.S. Case

During the 1970s, a U.S. law restricted bank lending to individual borrowers to 10 percent of the bank's capital. The goal was to ensure that banks diversified their portfolios, because a big loan to one customer was riskier than the equivalent amount loaned to many different ones.[1] During the late 1970s, it became apparent that some of the largest U.S. banks had loaned more than their limit to various agencies of the governments in developing countries like Mexico and Brazil. Their exposure appeared to violate the 10 percent rule.

In fact, the law that set the 10 percent rule did not explicitly include loans by banks to various government agencies. In his interpretation, the U.S. comptroller of the currency had to reconcile demands from various quarters, negotiating a solution to an issue that could have created diplomatic tempests while maintaining the integrity of his own regulatory agency.

The 10 Percent Rule During the 1970s

Mario Henrique Simonsen, Brazil's minister of finance in the late 1970s, helped orchestrate his country's external debt policy, which

1. See Note, "The Policies behind Lending Limits: An Argument for a Uniform Country Exposure Ceiling," *Harvard Law Review* 99 (1985): 430.

left Brazil owing foreign banks between $61 and $70 billion by 1982.[2] Of this, Brazil's public sector accounted for 70 percent. The nine biggest U.S. banks had loaned at least $12 billion, which equaled 46 percent of their capital.[3] One can estimate the banks' exposure to Brazil's public sector. Even if they had placed with the public sector a smaller share of their loans than the average—such as 50 percent— as a group they would have loaned 23 percent of their capital to government borrowers. This exposure raises two questions. Did the banks violate the U.S. law that set a ceiling on loans to any one borrower of 10 percent of capital and reserves? Particularly given the appearance of a violation, what was the role of U.S. regulators in this exposure? According to Simonsen, "before 1982, U.S. bank regulators never affected the Brazilian government's borrowing from U.S. banks."[4]

Title 12 of the United States Code provides the legislative framework for national banks.[5] Virtually the same since the first version was enacted in 1864, Section 84 set the lending limit during the 1970s:

> The total obligations to any national banking association of any person, copartnership, association, or corporation shall at no time exceed 10 per centum of the amount of the capital stock . . . and . . . surplus [of the bank].[6]

A perennial problem has been the scope of the word *person*. For example, are the subsidiaries of a diversified holding company part of the same corporate person? As early as 1972, national bank examiners had begun to combine loans to various unincorporated agencies in the same foreign government. Then in 1975, a money center bank itself

2. For the $70 billion figure, see Maxwell Watson, Peter Keller, and Donald Mathieson, *International Capital Markets: Development and Prospects, 1984*, Occasional Paper 31 (Washington, D.C.: IMF, 1984), Table 32, p. 91. For the $61 billion amount, see the commercial bank commitments to the Brazil Phase II new money facility of $6.5 billion.

3. Thomas H. Hanley et al., "Bank Stocks: The Brazil-Washington Connection," (Salomon Brothers, New York: June 10, 1983) p. 3. Total capital includes equity, subordinated debentures, and provisions for loan losses.

4. Interview, Boston, March 1985.

5. State banks are subject to other limits. See Note, "The Policies behind Lending Limits: An Argument for a Uniform Country Exposure Ceiling," *Harvard Law Review* 99 (1985) 430.

6. 12 U.S.C.A. S. 84. In 1982, after the bulk of the bank lending to Brazil and other developing countries, Congress amended the law.

raised the issue. If the bank made loans to various public-sector agencies in Italy, booking them through different units, did it have to consolidate them for purposes of Section 84? After deciding that consolidation was not required because of the multiple booking, the U.S. comptroller of the currency began to consider the second, knottier issue: when were public-sector corporations—owned in whole or even in part by the government—part of the central government for purposes of Section 84?

The problem had potentially serious consequences. If the comptroller decided that all such companies were part of one "person," then some of the biggest U.S. banks were at or near their legal lending limit in a few countries with large public sectors and large external debt. In Europe, this meant France and the United Kingdom in addition to Italy. In Latin America, it meant Argentina, Mexico, and Venezuela in addition to Brazil. Eventually, South Korea's debt became big enough to raise the issue. In the mid-1970s, when the problem first arose, trade deficits induced by the oil price rise still needed financing. The big U.S. banks played a major role. The comptroller first encountered the problem of interpretation in the context of current-account deficits in Europe rather than in developing countries.

To resolve the problem, John Heimann, the comptroller, chose a slow, adaptive approach under his own control. He waited until January 9, 1978, when he filed a proposed interpretive ruling in the *Federal Register*.[7] At the same time, in an unusual move, he sent copies to the press, congressmen, concerned agencies in the federal government, and international banks. During the sixty-day period allowed for replies, the comptroller received over fifty written comments, from "national banks, trade associations, law firms, and domestic and foreign government agencies,"[8] including the government of Mexico. Yet Heimann waited fifteen months before issuing the final ruling.[9] During that time, he adjusted the ruling (see Figure 3–1), and mobilized support for it inside and outside the government.

The substance of the interpretation did not change substantially from proposal to final ruling. The ruling stated that a public-sector borrower need not be treated as part of the government for Section

7. See Comptroller of the Currency, *News Release*, January 9, 1978.
8. *Federal Register*, April 17, 1979, p. 22712.
9. Ibid.

FIGURE 3–1. Department of the Treasury: Comptroller of the Currency

The following is the text of the interpretive ruling for Section 84. Language that was proposed but ultimately dropped is stricken out. Language added in the final ruling is underlined.

S. 7.1330 LOANS TO FOREIGN GOVERNMENTS, THEIR AGENCIES, AND INSTRUMENTALITIES

a. Loans to foreign governments, their agencies, and instrumentalities will be combined under 12 U.S.C. S.84 if they fail to meet either of the following tests:

1. The <u>borrower</u> ~~borrowing entity~~ must have resources or <u>revenue</u> ~~income~~ of its own sufficient over time to service its debt obligations ("means" test).

2. The loan ~~proceeds~~ must be <u>obtained for a</u> ~~used by the borrowing entity in the conduct of its business and for the~~ purpose <u>consistent with the borrower's general business</u> ~~represented in the loan agreement or otherwise acknowledged in writing by the borrowing entity~~ ("purpose" test). This does not preclude converting the loan proceeds into local currency prior to use by the borrowing entity. These tests will be applied at the time each loan is made.

b. In order to show that the "means" and "purpose" tests have been satisfied, a bank shall, at a minimum, assemble and retain in its files the following items:

1. A statement and supporting documentation describing the legal status <u>and the degree of financial and operational autonomy</u> of the borrowing entity ~~and showing its ownership and any form of control that may be exercised directly or indirectly by the central government~~.

2. Financial statements for the borrowing entity for a minimum of three years prior to making the loan or for each year minimum of three years prior to making the loan or for each year less than three that the borrowing entity has been in existence.

3. Financial statements for each year the loan is outstanding.

4. The bank's assessment of the borrower's means of servicing the loan including specific reasons justifying that assessment. Such assessments shall include an analysis of the financial history of the borrower, the present and projected economic and financial performance of the borrower, and the significance ~~or lack of significance~~ of any ~~guarantees or other~~ financial support <u>provided to the borrower</u> by third parties, including the central government. <u>A presumption of dependence arises unless the government support is less than the borrower's annual revenues from other sources. The presence or absence of a government guarantee raises no presumption concerning the ability of the borrower to satisfy the means test.</u>

5. A <u>loan agreement or other</u> written statement from the borrower <u>which clearly describes</u> ~~describing with particularity~~ the purpose of the loan. ~~Normally~~ <u>Such a</u> <u>written representation</u> ~~statement~~ will <u>ordinarily</u> be regarded as sufficient evidence to meet the "purpose" test requirements. ~~However~~, <u>But</u> when the bank <u>at the time the funds are to be disbursed</u> knows or has reason to know of other information suggesting a use of proceeds inconsistent with the written representation ~~in the statement~~ it may not, without further inquiry, accept that representation.

John G. Heimann

84 if it had the means to service its debt and if the purpose of the loan involved the borrower's business. The bank, rather than the comptroller, would carry the burden of deciding when the means and purpose tests were met. To show that it had applied the test, the bank was required to keep in its files evidence of the borrower's autonomy (subsection [a]) and a statement of the loan's purpose (subsection [b]). *Autonomy* was defined as "financial and operational," rather than as the absence of direct or indirect control by the central government. Thus the test delegated broad authority to the banks.

The comptroller took this tack after consulting with many different groups, who raised issues of practicality, foreign policy, and trade policy. The Bankers Association for Foreign Trade wanted Heimann to ask Congress to relax the law, arguing that the limit on loans to foreign governments should be raised to 25 percent of capital and surplus. The president of Chase Manhattan Bank noted numerous technical problems in applying the rule, saying it required judgments based on "tenuous distinctions" likely to be made "after the act." The director general of the Central Bank of Mexico wrote that sovereign states and corporations were fundamentally different and that mixed economies had special characteristics that required careful and flexible application of such a rule. Failure to do so, he said, could lead to "unequal treatment and . . . problems in the field of international politics." Even other parts of the U.S. government raised questions. The Commerce Department expressed concern, saying that "the possible restrictive effect this ruling may have on certain U.S. bank lending both current and future, could become a matter of concern to U.S. foreign trade, particularly since third-country banks will tend to favor exports from their own country."[10]

According to Simonsen, the government of Brazil had coordinated the external borrowing of its public-sector agencies for over a decade. Since the central bank held the foreign exchange, giving the borrower the cruzeiro equivalent of the loan, the government's action amounted to far more than ensuring an orderly approach to foreign credit markets. It is hard to see how this behavior could be exempt from the application of the 10 percent rule, but the comptroller exempted it by not seeking to regulate certain behavior. Recognizing that governments and private corporations are different creatures, he did not treat a foreign government like a "corporate parent subject to the parent-

10. All quotes are from *Econocast World Banker*, April 16, 1978, pp. 4–5.

subsidiary combining principles" already in force.[11] He did not stip-
ulate that the legal lending limit applied whenever a government
guaranteed its parastatal's debt or gave a temporary subsidy to help
the parastatal through a bad year. Above all, the comptroller did not
take into account transfer risk. In the case of Brazil, for example, most
loans from banks were to be repaid in U.S. dollars. Since a Brazilian
borrower's earnings were in cruzeiros, the loan was subject to the risk
that the borrower could not raise the dollars even though it had the
cruzeiros. All Brazilian borrowers were subject to this transfer risk.
Should that common risk mean that all Brazilian borrowers were one
person for the purposes of Section 84? The comptroller said no, in
subsection (a)(2). His rationale was that Section 84 was intended only
to diversify a bank's exposure among individual borrowers; the many
other lending risks—including transfer risk—were outside Section 84.

How would the means and purpose tests apply to the specific
borrowing policy described by Simonsen? His financially and operationally "autonomous" public-sector firms raised dollar loans as part
of the central government's budget for foreign currency and debt.
There was similar borrowing in Mexico, at least from 1981. The
Mexican government directed such parastatals as the oil company
Pemex and the power company Comision Federal Electridad (CFE)
to raise dollar loans abroad and pass the proceeds to the government.[12]
In these cases, the borrowers passed the means test. What of the
purpose test? The central bank automatically took the dollars, but
that merely created an excluded transfer risk. The question for the
bank and the comptroller was: What happened to the cruzeiro or peso
proceeds?

The problem with the purpose test is that money is fungible.
Consider the following. Suppose that the parastatal spends the req-
uisite funds for the designated purpose, but the dollar loan frees funds
that allow the parastatal to repay an outstanding government loan or
to buy government securities or make deposits in a local bank, which
in turn buys the securities. Such action would appear to violate the
intent of the ruling. On an analogous matter, the comptroller said he
would combine a loan to a private entity "with loans to the central
government when the entity is functioning merely as a conduit for
government borrowing and the lending institution is really looking to

11. *Federal Register*, April 17, 1979, p. 22714.
12. Interviews, Mexico, 1982 and 1983.

the government for repayment of the loan."[13] Yet as the hypothetical case shows, a conduit is hard to define. Under such circumstances, the question becomes, Whose job is it to decide whether the purpose test is met: comptroller, bank, or borrowing government?

In its allocation of responsibility, the 1979 interpretation may be seen as a friendly ruling that relieved the immediate players of a potentially onerous problem. As a result, the clarification did not have the effect of reducing loans by U.S. banks to heavily indebted governments in other countries.[14] Instead, it allowed U.S. banks to continue to lend by clearing up an uncertainty in the law. The relief came not in defining standards—the ruling went beyond technicalities to financial realities—but in setting the burden of proof for applying those standards. The comptroller would rely on the banks, who would in turn rely on the borrowing agency. U.S. banks could rely on the borrower's written representation about the loan's purpose unless they knew or had "reason to know of other information suggesting a use of proceeds inconsistent with the written representation."[15] Showing that the bank had reason to know requires a fairly high standard of proof.

The means and purpose tests thus fit the broader U.S. strategy described in chapter 2. They allowed indebted public-sector borrowers outside the United States to continue to borrow from U.S. banks. If a government had a parastatal that could pass the means test by showing that it was financially and operationally independent, that parastatal could effectively serve as a conduit for funds from U.S. banks to the central government. The Brazilian and Mexican governments understood this and their initial alarm at the interpretation evaporated. The interpretation put the burden of avoiding the limits on sovereign borrowers. The only threat to them was modest: U.S. banks might have to reduce their lending in the future.

The interpretation strengthened the pattern of bank-government relations: It reinforced the existing relationship between the regulator

13. Final interpretive ruling, *Federal Register*, April 17, 1979, p. 22713.

14. Although the total share of U.S. banks in bank lending to developing countries had been declining since 1975, it reached a plateau in mid-1979, about the time that the final ruling took effect. The plateau resulted from changes in the international banking industry when borrowers' conditions worsened after the second oil shock and as banks from other countries pulled back from the market.

15. Section 7.1330, subsection (b)(5).

and the banks, maintaining a formal distance between them. The comptroller rejected a proposal that he decide when the means and purpose tests required consolidation of borrowers. To have accepted the proposal would have placed him squarely in the middle of the banks' lending decisions. U.S. regulators have tried for years to avoid such a role on the grounds that in hard times they would then be responsible for what were bad portfolio choices.

The interpretation affected bank-government relations in a second way. It reasserted the comptroller's authority to regulate banks against an encroaching Congress. By acting, the comptroller muted potential critics in Congress. For John Heimann, the main problem was how to explain to Congress that he had acted responsibly in implementing a law—Section 84—that could be interpreted in several ways. He knew there had already been criticism in Congress. In the Senate Committee on Foreign Relations, Senator Frank Church's Subcommittee on Foreign Economic Policy had begun hearings in 1975 and issued a report in 1977 critical of the banks' foreign exposure. The report specifically questioned the effectiveness of the 10 percent rule.

> This 10 percent rule may not provide as much protection for the banks as one is led to believe. . . . Increasingly, the biggest borrowers on the Euromarket are public entities—municipalities, public utilities and state-owned enterprises. The ultimate obligor for all of these entities is one and the same, the foreign central government. Nevertheless, the banks and bank examiners are interpreting the 10 percent rule to mean that so long as any one of those entities is borrowing for its own use, is juridically an independent entity,[16] and has the apparent means to repay, it will be considered a separate borrower. Thus, a single U.S. bank may have loans outstanding to 20 different public entities in Brazil, none of which individually exceeds 10 percent of the bank's capital, but which taken together may far exceed the limit, and still not be in violation of the rule. The fact that the Indonesian Government recently had to assume a large foreign loan obligation incurred by Pertamina, the national oil company, illustrates that the central government is the ultimate obligor even in cases where the original borrower has a substantial independent source of revenue.[17]

16. The test is that the entity can be sued.
17. Staff "International Debt, the Banks, and U.S. Foreign Policy," U.S.

As it happened, the subcommittee report accurately described the consolidating role of central governments during the debt crises of the early 1980s. Yet its view did not influence the interpretation in the 1979 ruling.

The political context of this hearing suggests that although the comptroller had to act on Section 84, he did not need to accept the report's view that all parastatals were in reality "one and the same." Earlier, the banks and their regulators had successfully exercised their political muscles against the committee. Senator Church's subcommittee had recently completed hearings on the energy crisis, in which it had uncovered detailed, highly confidential information about that industry over the past fifty years. These hearings gave the subcommittee a prominence in public affairs that could not be ignored. In 1975, its inquiry into international banking had promised to be an important sequel. Yet the subcommittee ran into a stone wall in its search for data about each major U.S. bank's international lending. Powerful allies in the executive branch protected the banks from the congressional search.[18] Although the Church committee could not breach the confidentiality of the banking system, its inquiry kept attention focused on the issue of the banks' exposure abroad, as the comptroller knew it would.

Why would the U.S. regulator delegate so much to the banks and their borrowers? The comptroller's office offered two arguments for not being active, each based on the political process. One argument

Senate Committee on Foreign Relations, Subcommittee on Foreign Economic Policy, 95th Congress, 1st Sess., August 1977, pp. 55–56.

18. See Hearings, "Multinational Corporations and United States Foreign Policy," U.S. Senate Committee on Foreign Relations, Subcommittee on Multinational Corporations, 94th Congress, 1st Sess., July 16, September 11 and 18, October 9 and 29, 1975, Part 15. The ten largest U.S. banks declined to fill out a questionnaire from the subcommittee about their "deposits . . . in foreign branches and foreign subsidiary affiliates, on a country basis, and . . . the risk exposure for certain other countries on the loan side" (p. 1). These hearings report the ultimate success of the banks in this encounter with the subcommittee. They were supported by bank regulators and others in the executive branch, including Paul Volcker, then president of the New York Federal Reserve Bank, Philip Coldwell and Henry Wallich, governors of the Federal Reserve System, Edwin Yeo, under secretary of the treasury for monetary affairs (who went on to lead the First National Bank of Chicago), and Thomas Enders, assistant secretary of state for Economic affairs. The final compromise was to aggregate data supplied by the Federal Reserve Board.

concerned the domestic regulatory system, the other U.S. international interests. In the lore of U.S. financial regulation, "credit decisions are best left with the professional lenders who are responsible to management and shareholders."[19] For this very reason, the comptroller lacked the resources to decide about hundreds of parastatals in many other countries. It is true that resources were constrained. In practice, however, only half a dozen countries were involved; lending to no other borrowers approached the volume needed to equal 10 percent of the big banks' capital. Indeed, domestic precedent would have supported a more active role: as a matter of law, the comptroller already determined case by case whether municipal bonds are general obligations of the state and hence eligible for unlimited investment by national banks.[20] One must look further to explain the comptroller's delegation. The process for articulating U.S. international interests also played a role: according to a senior official in the comptroller's office, decision making about "foreign public sector entities" would place the comptroller "in a political posture . . . contrary to the role designated . . . by the Congress."[21] Resolving conflicts in domestic regulatory practice by appealing to the process for articulating international interests fits a U.S. strategy concerned with maintaining the international status quo (see chapter 2).

The domestic political weight behind this delegation was an alliance between bank regulators, other executive agencies, and the big international banks. All these groups, and those in Congress, saw that action was necessary to fill a lacuna in the law, yet they lacked a broad consensus about the nature of that action. The comptroller could not turn to Congress for a remedy without giving Congress a platform to examine the big banks' international and domestic lending more generally.[22] In exercising his only alternative, interpreting the law himself,

19. See Robert R. Bench, associate deputy comptroller of the currency, "Edited transcript of remarks," International Advisory Committee, Allied Bank International, St. Louis, Mo., May 4 and 5, 1978, p. 8.

20. Ibid. p. 9.

21. Ibid. There is no evidence that the comptroller issued his proposal to help Secretary of Energy James Schlesinger negotiate the Mexican gas pipeline, as a Mexican official charged. Interview, Lima, Peru, 1978.

22. The 1983 amendment to Section 84 that raised the limit above 10 percent resulted not from the needs of the big banks but from those of the small ones, which found themselves exceeding the 10 percent limit on loans to local firms. Interview, Washington, D.C., March 1985.

Heimann acted without the need for congressional support, and hence was less bound by the congressional view that international lending should be restrained. Thus the bargaining was solely among regulators, groups in the executive branch, and interested members of the financial community. The interested government agencies were those with an international bias, the Treasury and the State Department, which did not want the comptroller to allocate financial resources internationally.[23] His decision preserved their turf for them. The big banks wanted action to resolve ambiguities in the law; directors, for example, feared they might be liable for failure to comply. On the other hand, the banks did not want action that would curtail their discretion or their ability to compete with banks from other countries. That is essentially what they received.

This story illuminates the question I posed at the outset of this section: What was the role of the regulators while big U.S. banks accumulated loans to public-sector borrowers in Brazil far in excess of 10 percent of capital? Although there was some restraint, it was overshadowed by other effects of the Heimann ruling.

- First, by drawing attention to the legal lending limit as it applied to foreign governments, a limit that some banks had already exceeded by almost any definition,[24] the comptroller called for some adjustment, and in the long hiatus between proposal and final ruling, he gave banks the time to adjust.
- Second, the interpretation reduced uncertainty about the lending by resolving an ambiguity in U.S. law; in this sense, the regulators facilitated such lending.
- Third, the substance of the ruling left the banks with enough latitude to continue lending if public-sector borrowers could

23. Applied to U.S. borrowers, the 10 percent rule may simply spread loans among those banks, because as the biggest lenders reach their limit, the borrower will turn to other banks with less exposure. For non-U.S. borrowers, the 10 percent rule is likely to place a ceiling on the available credit. Because the borrower is more remote culturally as well as geographically, banks need a threshold infrastructure to evaluate the risk. This places barriers to entry that restrict lending by the smaller banks. Moreover, capital is concentrated in the big banks and the borrowers' needs are high.

24. For example, Bank of America was reported at the time to have exceeded the limit in lending to the Mexican government.

meet the means test and make a showing that they met the purpose test.

- Finally, to the extent that the ruling did restrain lending, it may have had a perverse effect. While directing bank lending away from direct loans to central governments, the ruling encouraged loans through channels outside the ambit of Section 84. Most notable was the exclusion from the lending limits, by interpretation of subsection (b)(9), of interbank deposits. A U.S. bank could deposit Eurodollars in the government-owned Banco do Brasil's London branch and that deposit would be outside the ambit of Section 84 even if the Brazilian bank loaned the funds to a government agency back home. In the 1982 debt crisis, interbank lending of this sort proved to be much larger than bankers had realized and was the least amenable to restructuring.

This is a story of the evolution of U.S. government policy toward its banks' international lending. At the time, the comptroller went far beyond the expectations of many observers. He raised for broader public debate the issue of massive lending to foreign governments. He narrowed the gap between the language of the law and its implementation. That law was not drafted originally to regulate lending to governments. Indeed, it was designed, not for the complexities of late-twentieth-century international banking, but for the domestic needs of the United States banking system in the mid-nineteenth century. The comptroller reconciled the need of the domestic banking system for clarity about the legal lending limit, a problem of immediate concern to him, with the need of the international economy for dollar financing, a problem of immediate concern to others in the executive branch. Congressional hostility to money center banks, well over a century old, and the complexities of the U.S. financial system dictated his incrementalist approach. He could not ask Congress to change the law.

This is not a story of adversarial relations between the executive branch and the big U.S. banks. Relations are symbiotic, based on common interests: the comptroller's decision fit the broader U.S. internationalist strategy that the banks wanted to maintain. In this regulatory action, there is no evidence of a regulator held captive by the interests he regulates, perhaps because outside the financial system there was sufficient interest in his actions.[25] The adversarial relations between business and government were greatest when Congress was involved.

The distrust of big banks and the internationalist concerns in the executive branch stymied action by either group during much of the 1970s. Congress could block attempts to loosen the 10 percent rule as it applied abroad, but could neither tighten the rule nor direct its enforcement. The executive branch, to avoid taking issues about international banking to Congress, acted as much as possible on its own authority. The balance of these forces shaped the regulating for the safety and soundness of cross-border lending. It gave the comptroller more latitude than he might otherwise have had if either had dominated, but no room for basic change. The resulting inertia suited the security and adjustment needs of the executive branch during the 1970s. The longstanding tradition that gave banks more leeway in their international operations than at home allowed U.S. banks to finance world current-account deficits smoothly.

Regulation and U.S. National Strategy

Embedded in U.S. law for at least sixty years has been the notion that U.S. banks are properly subject to less regulatory constraint in their operations outside the United States than at home. The areas of freedom are major: exemptions from the interest rate ceilings of Regulation Q, from the interstate branching prohibitions of the McFadden Act, from the reserve requirements of Regulation D, and from the underwriting prohibitions of the Glass-Steagall Act. The law did not distinguish between domestic and international operations on matters of safety and soundness, however: with minor exceptions, the exemption did not apply to the 10 percent rule.[26]

25. See Douglas D. Anderson, *Regulatory Politics and Electric Utilities* (Boston: Auburn House, 1981). According to Anderson, a regulator who must make a specific decision (not plan) in an environment that has no tight external constraint will not be subject to "capture" but will have considerable leeway in which to act (see p. 22).

26. The Federal Reserve's Regulation K, Section 211 governs the international operations of national and state member banks. It extends the powers of foreign branches to make guarantees and underwrite government obligations subject to the 10 percent limit per person (Section 211.3). It limits the exposure of Edge Act Corporations to 10 percent (Section 211.6 [b]), with one exception:

Several motives could explain the U.S. regulatory exceptions for banks' international operations; the dominant motive appears to be a concern for U.S. international competitiveness and for the stability of the international system. Other explanations, such as practical and operational matters or ideology, seem less important. One might imagine that several practical matters meant U.S. banking law would restrict banks abroad less. To the argument that regulators need be less concerned about international operations, which are largely carried out by banks with long experience, one need only observe that the experienced banks are closely monitored at home. Again, perhaps the banks' foreign operations, relatively small, posed no real threat to domestic banking. Although that was certainly true in the past, the largest banks' foreign operations have been significant for the last decade, yet the gap between foreign and domestic regulation persists. Or, limited staff in the agency might have been a motive: perhaps the far-flung operations of the banks were hard to reach, especially by regulators unskilled in international banking. Although staff shortages might explain the slow implementation of safety and soundness standards during the 1970s, the shortages are more an outcome of policy than a cause. The U.S. regulators, who unlike those in several other G-5 countries have traveled abroad to inspect their banks for decades, could have developed even greater skills had they chosen to do so. At issue here is the reason for choosing not to develop these capabilities sooner.

A second possible motive—ideology—also does not help explain the difference between domestic and foreign regulation. One might decide, as some European governments did, that for the most part the jurisdiction of home regulators should not extend beyond the borders of the country. But the U.S. government has not accepted this view of its authority: the extraterritorial reach of U.S. law stirs controversy in many other areas (tax and antitrust laws are examples). Something else must explain the limited extraterritorial scope of the U.S. banking laws.

The more compelling motives for the different regulatory standards are the competitive and systemic concerns of the U.S. government. Conceptually distinct, the two are hard to disentangle in practice.

---

the limit is 100 percent when 25 percent or more of the transaction is "supported" by multilateral agencies like the Inter-American Development Bank (Section 211.6[b][3][v][A]).

Some of the exceptions for international banking result from the U.S. government's concern for the relative competitiveness of U.S. banks and exporters. The government has sometimes justified exceptions in terms of the stability of its allies or of the international system. The history of the Edge Act Corporations (EACs) illustrates these motives.

For over sixty years, the U.S. government has exempted from certain domestic laws the operations of U.S. banks' EAC subsidiaries. The law constrains U.S. commercial banks at home in many ways, forbidding them from acting as investment companies and from much interstate branching, for example. The law permits banks to set up these wholly owned subsidiaries to finance international commercial and financial transactions. In a sense, these banks are treated more as other businesses when they operate abroad. First, since a bank can set up an EAC in a state other than its headquarters, the EAC is not bound by the laws against interstate banking. Second, the EACs partially span the chasm dug by the Glass-Steagall Act between commercial banking and underwriting. They can make direct equity investments in foreign financial trusts and in nonfinancial companies, and can underwrite security issues abroad. They can also hold shares in other corporations that can, depending on the degree of ownership, engage in nonbanking and nonfinancial activities barred to the parent national bank. As a subsidiary, and thus distinct from the parent bank, the EAC can be allowed to take on business unrelated to the parent's without jeopardizing the parent. Foreign branches, as an integral part of the bank, are more circumscribed.

The motives prompting these exemptions are found in the legislative history of the Edge Act of 1919, amending Section 25 of the Federal Reserve Act of 1913.[27] Although the exemptions evolved as the decades rolled by, Congress originally had two purposes in accepting the bill proposed by Senator Walter Edge of New Jersey. One was to improve the competitive position of national banks and the exporters they financed, the other to help Europe recover from the devastation of the First World War.[28] The importance of the second goal is apparent in the testimony of Robert Latham Owen, a Democrat who

27. Public Law 270 of September 7, 1916, 39 Stat. 755 (1916) and see *U.S. Congressional Record*, Vol. 53, Parts 8 and 13, 1916, cited in James C. Baker and M. Gerald Bradford, *American Banks Abroad* (New York: Praeger, 1974), p. 26 (hereafter cited as Baker and Bradford).
28. Baker and Bradford, p. 50.

was Oklahoma's first senator, before the Senate Banking and Currency Committee in 1919. Senator Owen said that the bill provided the

> means by which quick and large capital can be made available for the purpose of extending credit to Europe through the process of buying European bills; of making agreements by which European bills may be renewed three or four times per annum; and carried along until the people in Europe shall be able to repay the loans which are extended. The purpose of this Edge bill is to organize a means by which European credits can be marketed with the American investing public.[29]

Before isolationists captured United States foreign policy, the U.S. government was prepared to use its banks to achieve national purposes abroad. This is not far removed from the use made of the banking system in the 1970s after the oil shock.[30]

The Edge Act Corporations illustrate how a nation—the United States—uses international banking to accomplish national purposes in an active rather than a passive manner. The EACs demonstrate as well that the active approach is not new: EACs have existed almost as long as the Federal Reserve System itself. Indeed, the EACs evolved into a major vehicle by which big banks cross state lines,[31] since to succeed the EAC must add value for the bank as well as for the government. This active posture by government suggests another way to look at its regulation.

Many see national regulation of international banking as so many dikes erected against the relentless force of world markets. In this view, regulation is futile: banks in international markets have too many avenues for escaping the controls of the home or, for that matter, any other country. The common example is the financial haven, a country like Singapore or Panama, in which the banks are free of myriad controls over their offshore operations. The history of EACs and the

29. U.S. Congress, *Amendment to the Federal Reserve Act,* Hearings before the Senate Committee on Banking and Currency, 66th Congress, 1st Sess., S.2472 (Washington, D.C.: U.S. Government Printing Office, 1919), p. 8, quoted in Baker and Bradford, p. 50.

30. That the banks did not respond immediately is not germane to the argument.

31. See Seung H. Kim and Stephen W. Miller, *Competitive Structure of the International Banking Industry* (Lexington, Mass.: Lexington Books, 1983), p. 23.

10 percent rule suggests that the U.S. banks' freedom from regulation, relative to the controls at home, is a deliberate choice by the U.S. government. The home government chose not to regulate, for a reason.

Comparing G-5 Countries: Two Key Issues

Regulation of banks' international lending usually refers to the prudential matters discussed above, notably the safety and soundness of the banks, which in turn are of interest because of their impact on the broader economy.[32] Governments also use the banks to achieve other goals, such as supporting a particular structure of finance and industry at home, demand management, a stable balance of payments, and even national security. These interests extend far beyond the needs of the banks themselves, which indeed are often secondary to the broader goals. As a result, banks that move abroad do not escape home control, and the ties to the home country generally remain strong.

The extent to which banks' international lending is subject to regulation at home differs considerably among G-5 countries, and these differences have several consequences. First, the extent of the regulation will affect bank decisions to operate abroad rather than at home. For example, German banks must escape leveraging rules by setting up subsidiaries in Luxembourg; elsewhere, leveraging rules that consolidate foreign operations do not prompt banks to try to escape. The literature admirably charts this first effect, and I do not pursue it here. Second, the different leveraging rules create diverse cost structures for banks from various homes, giving banks from a low-leverage country like Japan a cost advantage over the others (see chapter 4). Third, the different rules lead banks from different home countries to allocate international credit in different ways. Banks from low-leverage countries, because they have institutional support at home, can accept greater risk in their portfolio than can other banks. They could thus accept a portfolio with a larger portion of risky developing country debt than could others. This effect is especially relevant here. The list below summarizes the range of regulatory differences.

32. See, for example, James W. Dean and Ian H. Giddy, *Averting International Banking Crises*, Monograph Series in Finance and Economics, 1981–1, Graduate School of Business Administration, New York University.

1. *Prudential rules.* U.S. and Japanese banks are most carefully regulated for risk analysis, matching, reporting, on-site inspection, reserves, and capital adequacy of international operations. The British banks comply with informal review by the Bank of England; the subsidiaries of German banks are beyond the legal powers of their home regulators; and the big French banks are effectively beyond the reach of the controller of banks.

2. *Administrative forms.* U.S. and Japanese banks are subject to closer controls by their central banks when establishing foreign offices than are the others.

3. *Taxation.* British, German, and U.S. banks are subject to tax at home on their foreign earnings; French banks are not.

4. *Credit allocation.* Japanese banks are subject to administrative guidance in their foreign lending, which sometimes extends to credit decisions about particular country or corporate borrowers. German banks are protected by law from such guidance.

5. *Home currency lending.* Japanese and French banks have been limited in lending their home currencies internationally, in contrast to U.S. banks.

6. *Product restrictions.* U.S. and Japanese banks are constrained in the financial services they can offer abroad, although less so than at home. German banks can offer universal financial services in both places.

Two major types of regulation affect banks' allocation of international credit: portfolio diversification and credit quality. These are major issues for regulators of domestic banking, and international lending introduces new twists in both. *Diversification* among unrelated borrowers is a cardinal principle of lending, designed to reduce risk. The U.S. Congress that enacted the 10 percent rule focused on domestic lending, where one method of accounting and one legal system set standards for what is "unrelated." John Heimann had to define diversification in foreign corporate and governmental contexts alien to the original framework of the law. *Credit quality* also concerns regulators charged with the safety and soundness of the financial system. Domestic quality standards assume a common national economy, but a bank that lends to borrowers abroad confronts risks associated with the second country. To address the problem, banks and their regulators analyze country risk.

The following subsection explores the counterparts of the 10 percent rule in other countries. The next subsection explores the regulators' power to judge the quality of their banks' overseas portfolios.[33]

Standards for International Portfolio Diversification

Among the G-5 banks, the European banks have been more indepen-dent of home rules about portfolio diversification abroad than have banks from either Japan or the United States. Since regulatory systems vary, the 10 percent rule is not duplicated precisely elsewhere. Ana-logues are apparent in the ceilings regulators set on foreign loans in the aggregate as well as in the ceilings on loans set by individual banks to individual foreign borrowers. Two countries do not set formal rules and I do not examine them: France and England. French regulators left the question to their big banks. The Bank of England applies its standards during individual consultation with each bank, rather than through uniform rules. I am concerned here with the other three G-5 countries.

Over the past decade, the German banks avoided the imposition of ceilings, whereas the U.S. banks were at least nominally subject to ceilings, and the Japanese banks were regulated in form and practice. In Germany, the banks fought the regulators, going outside the finan-cial system for allies. As in the case of Sicartsa, a bank-government alliance was moot. In the United States the banks and regulators joined forces against Congress, and in Japan the banks ended up cooperating with their regulators in return for trade-offs elsewhere. Here the bank-government alliance is effective.

In Germany, clear regulatory principles applied to banks and their foreign branches but not to their foreign subsidiaries, which consis-tently loaned big sums.[34] Since the mid-1970s, technocrats in the

33. Both sections are deliberately brief. For detail, the reader may consult a broad literature describing the regulation of international banks. See, for ex-ample, Richard Dale, *The Regulation of International Banking* (Cambridge, England: Woodhead-Faulkner, 1984); R. M. Pecchioli, *The Internationalization of Banking* (Paris: OECD, 1983); and Robert S. Rendell, ed., *International Financial Law* (London: Euromoney Publications, 1980). There are many other good descrip-tions of the laws.

34. Principle I limits a bank's total credit to eighteen times equity. Section 19 of the banking law limits credits to a single borrower or related group to 75 percent of equity. H. Schneider, H.-J. Hellwig, and D. Kingsman, *The German*

German Finance Ministry and regulators in other industrial countries have urged consolidation of the foreign subsidiaries' operations, even though such a move would force the banks to increase their equity or greatly reduce their foreign lending. Until 1985, however, the big private German banks managed to elude consolidation. In this they were supported by big German firms, which could borrow deutsche-marks from the unregulated Luxembourg subsidiaries of German banks at lower cost. The banks' political strategy was to delay legislative action and to prove that they could manage problems that might arise as a result of the nonconsolidation.

- The banks informally reported figures that consolidated wholly or almost wholly owned subsidiaries in order to avoid formal change.
- They gained time because of the disintegration of the Schmidt government after 1979 and the slow start of the Christian Democrat government.
- They had the support of the economics minister, a leader of the Free Democratic party and a proponent of free markets.
- To make government assistance unnecessary, they aided small banks that went bankrupt partly because the absence of rules allowed them to behave imprudently.
- They did not adjust their own balance sheets to comply with the intent of the law setting credit-equity ratios.

As late as February 1984, when the finance minister submitted a draft of a law to consolidate, the economics minister still opposed him.[35] When the act took effect in March 1985, it included a five-year transition period. The Big Three banks had delayed consolidation for over ten years.

In Japan, under the authority of the Banking Law of 1981, the government limited to 20 percent of capital and reserves the loans a city bank could make to any one customer, including medium and

---

Banking System (Frankfurt am Main: Fritz Knapp, 1978), pp. 41–43. That this is much higher than one sees in the United States reflects the importance of the ties between the big German banks and their major corporate customers, both to the banks and to the state.

35. See John Davies, "Bonn Wrangles over Bank Laws," *Financial Times*, December 23, 1983, p. 2, and Peter Norman, "Germany Drafts Tougher Rules for Its Bankers," *The Wall Street Journal*, February 3, 1984, p. 27.

long term loans to any one country. The city banks had opposed rigorous application of the 20 percent limit to overseas lending. In an interview published one month before the Finance Ministry's action, the president of Fuji Bank said,

> Suggestions are being made by the Ministry of Finance for guidance but I believe decisions should be left to the individual banks' management. Of course, whether 20 percent of capital or 25 percent is a good limit is open to discussion, but the decision should be made by the individual bank. There are some banks that are going into international lending, and others that are not. So a universal application of the 20 percent limit is unrealistic.[36]

The move was preceded by years of informal discussions, during which many banks moved toward the new government standard. By the time the limit was imposed, only Mitsui Bank lacked adequate capital for its outstanding loans to important corporate customers.

The long period of discussion, compromise, and adjustment was characteristic of the regulatory system in Japan. So was the government's extensive reach. Since the mid-1970s, the Finance Ministry has

1. twice pulled Japanese banks out of syndicated loan markets, once between 1974 and 1976, the second time in 1979 and 1980;
2. limited the share Japanese banks as a group could take in any dollar syndicated loan (it stood at 20 percent in late 1983);
3. fixed six-month ceilings on offshore loans to be allocated among the banks;[37]
4. set rules for matching the maturities of foreign liabilities to foreign assets;

36. "Bank's Leader Pushes for Reform," *Euromoney*, March 1983, pp. 125, 128.

37. For the six months starting in April 1983, for example, the banks received Y 700 billion ($2.9 billion) for yen loans and $8 billion for dollar loans. Yoko Shibata, "Limits Raised on Offshore Loans by Japanese Banks," *Financial Times*, April 19, 1983, p. 18.

5. required the banks to report all offshore lending, though foreign subsidiaries could report loans after they were made;

6. reviewed in advance the lending program of each bank, through the Finance Ministry every six months and through the central bank monthly.

Once agreement was reached on the lending ratios, the Japanese banks were expected to comply with both the spirit and the letter of the law.[38]

Standards for Credit Quality in International Portfolios: Country Risk

In the rules that set standards for credit analysis, regulators have not developed equal authority in country analysis. Given the high volume and growth of country lending, this might be surprising. Regulators in Germany and France deliberately did not cultivate this capability, leaving to their own big banks the decisions about country risk. Regulators in the other three G-5 countries developed a capability in country analysis.

In Japan's Ministry of Finance, the research unit of the International Finance Bureau analyzes countries. Although the Finance Ministry says it does not place countries in risk categories, it has designated high-risk countries on the verge of, or enmeshed in, debt problems.[39]

In the United Kingdom, the Bank of England employs about twenty economists and sixty other specialists, mainly territorial, to analyze country markets. Rather than group the countries according to risk, the bank uses its research in individual discussions with the banks it supervises. In addition, the Bank of England and the clearing banks' Sovereign Risk Committee have met monthly since 1981. Limited to the clearers, and therefore excluding even the largely international Standard Chartered Bank before it became a clearer in 1985, the

38. It might be argued that the Japanese banks violated the spirit of the limits on medium- and long-term lending when they dramatically increased their short-term loans in 1981 and 1982. I believe they acted within the spirit of the rule, which was intended to leave them free on the assumption that short-term lending finances trade.

39. Tom Bodgett, "Japan Reacts to the Rescheduling Procession," *International Financial Law Review*, April 1983, p. 19.

Sovereign Risk Committee members share data about borrowing countries. This approach fits Britain's informal system of bank regulation.

The U.S. regulators place countries in one of three risk categories and examiners inform a bank's directors when that bank's exposure in any one group exceeds set fractions of capital. In the spring of 1979, the federal bank regulators began to categorize countries as strong, moderate, or weak according to past and prospective performance. Banks would be expected to limit their exposure in each group of countries. No more than 5 to 10 percent of capital could be loaned to a weak country, no more than 25 percent to a strong one. Loans to a country in the weak category could be classified as substandard, doubtful, or a loss, and the bank would have to make an appropriate charge against its capital. The method of classifying countries was at the heart of the new system. The comptroller, the Federal Reserve Board, and the Federal Deposit Insurance Corporation worked together, drawing on information from government agencies—including the State Department and the Central Intelligence Agency—and from the big banks themselves. If the comptroller believed a bank was concentrating too heavily in one group of countries, particularly the weak, he would inform the bank's board of directors. But he had no authority to impose sanctions, and he would not ask the bank to reduce its lending to a particular country, only to the group. His goal was portfolio diversification.

Style of Governance and National Strategy

Rules governing the safety and soundness of banks' international lending reflect the broader policy objectives, or strategy, of the banks' home government. The rules do not simply ensure prudential behavior by the banks, which one assumes would be their primary object. Nor do they simply reflect the usual process of rule making at home, the style of governance. One must understand a nation's strategy in order to understand the prudential rules for its banks. This is apparent in the degree to which various governments gave their banks independence in international lending.

Style of Governance

Style of governance, a phrase taken from Raymond Vernon's work on multinational corporations and national governments, refers to the process by which official policy is made and implemented. Vernon rightly observes that it is necessary to know this process to gauge the effect of policy on multinationals.

> The capacity of any government to command a particular firm to undertake a specified task in support of a public policy . . . has been reduced. . . . At the same time . . . more enterprises exist to which a government can turn for the discharge of some national task. In some situations, the proliferation in the number of enterprises can prove to be the controlling factor and can increase the powers of government; in other situations, the increased mobility of enterprises can be the controlling factor and can weaken the powers of government. We cannot be sure of the net effect without specifying the nature of the problem and the style of governance of the country concerned.[40]

In the regulation of banks' international lending, it would at first appear that the "increased mobility of enterprises" did "weaken the powers of government," since in all five countries the banks enjoyed greater independence abroad than at home. Two points now qualify this view, however. First, there are important differences among the countries' regulations that result from more than the style of governance at home and the number of players. In some cases where the outcomes differed, the political processes surrounding the regulations were alike and the players of about equal number. The different outcomes are explained by what the governments want to accomplish. Second, the big banks and their home governments are not always adversaries for whom one's gain is the other's loss.

Style of governance is helpful in explaining the degree to which German banks' international lending is regulated. Germany refrained from regulating for reasons of law and politics. Germany's Finance Ministry honored the rule of official neutrality toward individual credit decisions, a reaction against the close ties between government and banks in the Third Reich. Embedded in the German Banking Law, these rules prevented the ministry from readily consolidating the banks' overseas accounts. To ensure this policy continued, the

40. Raymond Vernon, *Storm over the Multinationals* (Cambridge, Mass.: Harvard University Press, 1977), pp. 136–137.

minority party used its pivotal role in framing the strategy of the coalition government.

A comparison of all five countries leads to a surprising observation, however. In regulating the diversity and risk of banks' international loans, the least restrictive government was France, whose banks are most subject to controls at home.[41] Germany followed France closely. The United Kingdom was less liberal, the United States even less so, and Japan was most restrictive. Single factors, such as the banks' length of foreign experience[42] and the number of banks being regulated,[43] do not account for these regulatory differences. A major surprise is that France and Japan are at opposite ends of the spectrum. By some measures, they regulate similar aspects of their banks' activities and in fact share similar financial systems.

The type of domestic regulation fails to account for the different degrees of freedom in international lending. All G-5 countries regulate bank assets and liabilities, though in the period I emphasize, the British, Germans, and Americans focus more on the liability side, the French and Japanese more on assets. The governments that rely on the liability side keep their relations with their banks more at arm's length, working through market mechanisms. (Indeed, the arm's–length relations carry over into the regulation of bank assets, since the governments examine portfolio diversification rather than allocate credit.)[44] The governments that also use the asset side are less apt to

---

41. The government enforced the *encadrement de crédit*, a strict corset on the growth of the banks' domestic lending with exceptions for preferred uses such as housing.

42. Although even big Japanese banks have barely ten years of international experience in contrast to the century of experience of big U.S. banks, Japanese and U.S. banks are most constrained abroad.

43. Over one hundred U.S. commercial banks were somewhat less regulated than barely thirteen from Japan, which in turn were much more regulated than the small number of banks from France and Germany. Small numbers may affect regulation indirectly, however. If the big banks' small numbers helped them win or hold an important place in the home political process or in their relations with home firms, the banks had power. For example, the Big Three German banks occupied a pivotal position in their home financial system, responsible for many functions ranging from shareholding to trade finance to industrial planning. They had the greatest success in avoiding control by regulators who wanted more stringent rules.

44. Relations at arm's length do not mean that regulators and the banks necessarily act as adversaries. It is true that in the United States pressure to limit

be at arm's length. An important characteristic of the French and Japanese financial systems is that the banks are constrained by state ownership or authority and the regulators are constrained by their involvement in the credit side of the banks' operations.

Others who have studied the financial systems of the G-5 nations have noted basic policy differences between the two groups of countries. Franco Modigliani and Lucas Papademos have described two paradigms for national monetary policy.[45] In their view, the liability management of the Federal Reserve System and Bank of England is based on a money paradigm, whereas the asset management of central banks in Japan and France is based on a credit paradigm. The two paradigms reflect different domestic relations between regulators and the banks. The credit paradigm involves the central bank in decisions about those to whom the banks lend and is a form of credit allocation. Others find that these differences affect the banks' domestic lending[46] and the industrial performance of the country.[47]

The structure of the home financial system does not fully explain the various degrees of freedom from regulation abroad. To see this, one can use John Zysman's classification of the financial systems of the G-5 countries into three groups: (a) credit-based and price-administered countries (France and Japan); (b) credit-based and institution-dominated (Germany); and (c) capital-market-based (the U.K. and the

---

the power of the big banks at home makes government willing to restrain their international activities. An example from the past is in the legislative history of the Edge Act. Congress reduced the capital requirements to become an agreement corporation (a predecessor of the Edge Act Corporation) when the original threshold was open only to the biggest banks. A recent example is the House of Representatives debate about the supplementary quota for the IMF in 1983. Recall, however, that in interpreting the 10 percent rule John Heimann cannot be said to have adopted an adversarial stance.

45. Franco Modigliani and Lucas D. Papademos, "The Structure of Financial Markets and the Monetary Mechanisms," in *Controlling Monetary Aggregates III* (Boston: Federal Reserve Bank of Boston, 1980).

46. See, for example, Melitz's comment that the hypothesis that capitalist financial systems are inherently unstable may not apply in countries "where every financial intermediary automatically has heavy access to the lender of last resort, such as Japan, France, and some of the Scandinavian ones." C.P. Kindleberger and J.-P. Laffargue, *Financial Crises: Theory, History, and Policy* (Cambridge, England: Cambridge University Press, 1982), p. 47.

47. John Zysman, *Governments, Markets, and Growth: Financial Systems and the Politics of Industrial Change* (Ithaca, N.Y.: Cornell University Press, 1983).

U.S.).[48] These groups do not reflect the extent to which international operations are regulated.

- The most regulated banks (from Japan and the U.S.) are not in the same group, nor are the least regulated (French and German).
- Banks within a given group have different degrees of freedom abroad: Japanese banks are highly regulated, French banks almost unregulated; U.S. banks are much more controlled than U.K. banks.
- Although all countries allow their banks greater freedom abroad than at home, the difference between domestic and international regulation is much greater for French and German banks than for others.

To explain the regulatory differences, one must go beyond the process by which policy is made at home and look at both the process used to formulate and implement policy and the substance of that policy.

The Role of National Strategy

During the mid-1970s regulation was a supporter of a nation's broader strategic interests, not the driving force. In France and Japan, national interests account for the striking regulatory differences. French and Japanese macroeconomic, trade, and investment policies appear to have encouraged banks to import foreign capital and discouraged them from lending abroad except to finance exports. These policies were designed to help the country adjust to the oil shock. Prudential rules took second place to these goals.

After the first oil shock, the French government used bank regulation to promote exports. It excluded export credits from the *encadrement*, which fixed ceilings on domestic credit, with the result that the share of all credit devoted to exports grew from 4.9 percent in 1973 to 12.6 percent in 1979. The government prohibited banks from making franc loans to nonresidents for anything but exports. Although

48. Ibid. Zysman's groups were designed to explain domestic economic policy.

the French government owned the Big Three French banks, it chose to use regulatory devices rather than direct commands to achieve these export goals. The strategy promoted domestic distribution rather than production, then vainly sought an external balance with a cruder set of policies, the capital controls and export subsidies. The resulting current-account deficits needed financing. The big French banks helped arrange it for public and private borrowers. Their success required the government's implicit guarantee of their liabilities and its noninterference in their international activities. In effect, the French government needed its banks' independent stature in the world financial community because government economic strategy forced France into international capital markets.[49]

The Japanese banks operated on a tight rein. After both oil shocks, the government restricted the banks' external loans, during 1974–1976 and 1979–1980. It encouraged export credits in many ways, outlined above. Through administrative guidance, government lending, and other informal mechanisms, the Bank of Japan had already set the parameters and influenced the direction of lending in the domestic activities of Japanese banks when the oil shock hit, an influence that carried over to foreign lending. Japan needed to control its borders if it was to use its own financial system for development purposes. In contrast to the French banks, the Japanese banks could not be allowed to gain independence abroad lest that freedom threaten the government's strategy at home.

49. Note that French strategy reflects some realities in international markets. The government could have simply issued direct commands to its own banks. By relying on regulation, the government may be responding to its position in a world economy more open than before. As early as 1967, an official commission had observed the need to "more and more employ [policy] forms which preserve the market mechanism" because the country's borders offered less protection than in the past. (Stuart Holland, "Europe's New Public Enterprises," in Raymond Vernon, ed., *Big Business* [Cambridge, Mass.: Harvard University Press, 1974], p. 36). This stance is apparent in its use of its own banks despite reports of the continuing power of "concertedness," the close relation between the government and large companies (Charles-Albert Michalet, "France," in Vernon, *Big Business*, p. 124), and reports of the integration of state officials with the business community, which suggested a "formidable set of policy instruments which impinge on particular sectors of the economy and individual firms" (Peter J. Katzenstein, ed., *Between Power and Plenty* [Madison: University of Wisconsin Press, 1978], pp. 20–21).

Prudential Regulation and Other Goals

Tension between prudential rules and other, possibly competing, goals hampers the G-5 governments' regulation of international lending. On one side are the interests in a stable financial system, a matter of particular concern to the bank regulators and the banks. On the other side are interests, such as trade performance, embodied in other government agencies, many firms, and again, the banks. Banks are on both sides. The tension was resolved during the 1970s in ways that protected the interest of the financial system in its own self-governance while at the same time helping to achieve the broader goals of the government's strategy.

The Bureaucratic Independence of the Financial System

The interests of the financial system were indeed protected in the process by which regulators and banks arrived at acceptable rules. This raises the question of whether bank regulators really supervised or were captured by the big banks.

There is a hint of capture from a striking similarity in the political processes in the five countries: the formal distance that regulators and banks, both part of the financial system, tried to maintain between themselves and others inside and outside the government. Across this divide, both sides maintained informal contact, though the extent varied among countries. The appearance of distance affected the procedure by which decisions were made and thus the distribution of power.

The formal wall separating those inside the financial system from outsiders is apparent in the government's capacity to analyze the countries to which their banks made loans. Despite the interest a foreign affairs ministry might have in the impact of a bank's country lending, only regulators analyzed country risk, in vivid contrast to the German practice described by the Dresdner Bank official who said in 1906 that his bank consulted with the Foreign Ministry in advance of each major loan. In the United States, a recent comptroller of the currency gave voice to the formal distance when he said, "We have had no pressure from [the State Department] or Congress; if we did we'd tell them to go fly a kite. Of course, if a country were strategically important, we would certainly contact State or other agencies if we were about to do anything."[50] In practice, informal contacts by senior officials of the Treasury and the State Department would communicate broader concerns to the comptroller. Both departments had at least one staff officer who followed the banks' activities.

In Britain, the distancing was still stronger than in the United States. Jealous of its prerogatives, the Bank of England was the conduit for Treasury and Foreign Office communications with the banks. Neither ministry could muster a staff of country analysts to approach the Bank of England's. Like U.S. government departments, each did have a staff officer who followed the banks' activities and whose pressure on the banks' lending was informal.

In country risk analysis, at least, the extent to which regulators formally consider the home government's broader, nonprudential interests may depend on the portfolio of the regulator. That the official analyst for country risk in Japan was the Finance Ministry set the country apart from the United States and the United Kingdom. The Finance Ministry, in the words of one official, "functions like the U.S. Treasury, the Office of Management and Budget, the Securities and Exchange Commission, and the Internal Revenue Service" in addition to setting and implementing policy for the entire financial system.[51] Compared with multiple bank regulators in the United States, whose activities were characterized as a competition in laxity, this single regulator in Japan wielded incomparably more authority. Japan's Foreign Ministry could not have even a banking officer, let alone the capacity to analyze countries for bank exposure. Given the small number of big banks, the Ministry of Finance (MOF) could talk with each and reach not only most of the international lending but most of the domestic lending as well. It is difficult to imagine any of the Japanese city banks saying, as did a senior vice-president of the American Citibank, "If the [National Bank Examiners'] ranking of a particular country isn't justified by our own research, we follow our own analysis." In the U.S. policy-making process, only the regulators dealt with the banks directly. Their province was safety and soundness. To ensure their continued sway, however, they did not counter other government policies that influenced the banks indirectly.[52]

50. Quoted in Philip A. Wellons, *World Money and Credit* (Boston: Harvard Business School, 1983), p. 124.

51. Interview, New York, October 1982.

52. Quoted in Wellons, *World Money*, p. 121.

Safety and soundness rules

The prudential regulation of international credit reflects a trade-off that will vary by country and go far beyond issues of safety and soundness. Japan controlled its banks' external lending according to its balance of payments. It did not need to give them independence abroad because, unlike the French, it did not need to attract dollar depositors, but it did need to keep control at home. The other countries focused less on their trade or capital-account balances. The U.K. government, working through the Bank of England and the clearing banks, sought instead to preserve London as the preeminent financial center in the world. The U.S. government was more concerned with the stability of the international system. Both governments regulated their banks, in other words, to achieve goals associated with their broader strategies.

The overall result was that during the 1970s banks in most countries were able to lend substantial amounts to borrowers in developing countries, yet still have their regulators as allies within the government. The banks and regulators formed coalitions to counter direct credit controls by others in the government while at the same time submitting to broader policies that encouraged lending. Even in Germany, where regulators and banks struggled over control, the result was to ensure the banks' independence. Was this good policy?

Conclusions

The combination of national strategies and process in the G-5 countries led to a peculiar mixture of conservative and short-term policy. The process that insulated the financial system was conservative, for the distance between the financial system and those outside it reinforced the status quo by impeding efforts to build constituencies that would change the regulations. In Germany and the United States, no constituencies outside the financial systems developed in support of limiting the banks' international lending. The German regulators were unable to change the status quo alone and the U.S. regulators did not feel compelled to do so, despite some congressional interest. In Japan, the Finance Ministry did not need to look outside the financial system for support to regulate the banks' international lending; MOF control was the status quo.

The U.S., U.K., and Japanese banks benefited when their regulators developed the capability to analyze countries. Having built their own cadres of analysts, the Bank of England, the U.S. bank examiners, and the Japanese Finance Ministry could speak authoritatively not only to the banks but also to other government agencies. Officials from the U.S. comptroller's office, for example, regularly appeared before congressional committees inquiring into the big banks' exposure in developing countries. Further, officials could guard the banks from other agencies that represented different state interests in the foreign country or in the outcome of a debt crisis. They could also speak to each other in such a crisis.

More than just another example of regulatory capture, these impediments to change built stability and continuity into the financial system. Although they may have retarded adjustment during rapid economic or technological change, they also served as a buffer in times of crisis. But no one managed the system before the crisis. The G-5 governments mixed permissive prudential regulations with policies actively promoting loans to developing countries that were markets. This fit their short-term needs. It also reflected the end of U.S. hegemony. U.S. policy, oriented more than any other nation's toward maintaining an open system, did not guide others to a healthy competition in that system. No major industrial nation took the lead. None could step in to weigh the contending policies and shift them toward the world economy's long-term need for balance. No regulators could take the lead within their governments, because a broader political consensus limited their power.

This means that if one wants more effective prudential regulations, one must negotiate a home strategy that does not rely on the banks to finance home exports to achieve competitive advantage. One must also ensure that regulators are not satisfied with rules reinforcing their authority in the financial system. Steps such as simply tightening the lending limits, for example, do not address the underlying problem.[53]

The active role of the banks' home governments and the purpose of that active role may have varied by country but overall government policies tended to promote trade. Trade-related finance, however, is only part, though a large one, of the developing countries' debt. National strategies do not explain all lending by the banks to devel-

---

53. See "The Policies behind Lending Limits: An Argument for a Uniform Country Exposure Ceiling," *Harvard Law Review* 99 (1985): 430n.

oping countries, and I now turn to other factors influencing international lending. Banks have their own interests; just as the regulators were not the banks' captives, so banks were not captured by their home governments. The banks' own ties to their home encouraged them to play an active role in trade-related finance and also influenced their lending for purposes other than trade.

4

Banks' International Lending: The Home Is the Key

I have explored three areas that show the pervasive impact of the home strategy on the banks' international lending. First, when it promotes exports, the home stimulates demand for the banks' credit, as in the case of Sicartsa. Second, the home shapes the supply of funds at home. In both ways, financing home-country trade links the banks to their government's broader policies. Third, the home uses regulation to support national goals that extend beyond the banks' immediate interests and beyond concerns about financial stability. In each chapter, the analysis focused elsewhere than on the banks themselves.

Here I shift to the perspective of the banks, drawing on and supplementing the conclusions from earlier chapters. The object of this chapter is to show how the banks' international business strategies can draw on policies and institutional ties in their home countries. Existing views of bank-government relations in international lending paint two very different views. I start with the two views to set the stage, making this chapter more abstract than its predecessors. Chapter 5 tests the two views against the actual behavior of twenty-eight lead banks in the massive, global market of loan syndications.

By its nature, banking lends itself to home influence. Banks, after all, are in a commodity business: money is a commodity. One of the hardest tasks for a firm selling a commodity is to differentiate itself from competitors. Banks are no exception. In a study of the strategies of the one hundred largest banks based outside the United States, for example, the big banks examined here appear in only two of the six groups of banks defined by business strategy, and hence have little to distinguish themselves from one another.[1] In international credit markets a bank's home affiliation permits it to differentiate itself effectively from the banks in other countries. The home also provides its banks with a distinctive cost structure and the opportunity to protect key markets. Although many of the home's influences are indirect, the home government acts directly often enough for banks to build the alliances at home that will help them compete abroad. For the bank, the home thus becomes a key part of its international lending strategy.

Since homes differ in important ways, and since the home is important to a big bank's strategy, the world has few, if any, banks that are politically independent of all nations. We can best understand the expansion of international debt and the ensuing debt crisis, therefore, by examining the interests and policies of the major home countries and the process by which those policies are shaped.

Relations Between International Banks and Their Home Governments

Of various models for governments and multinational corporations (MNCs), two help one think about banks and their home governments. In the liberal model, described by Gilpin, the MNC is a beneficent challenger to national governments, acting in the interests of global economic efficiency. In the mercantilist model, also described by Gilpin, the MNC is the instrument of the nation-state.[2] The liberal model approximates the image of international banks held by many American bankers and government officials; it lies behind the notion of a "Eurobank" found in international finance. The mercantilist

1. Martin Ramsler, "Strategic Groups and Foreign Market Entry in Global Banking Competition," Ph.D. diss., Harvard University, 1982.
2. Robert Gilpin, *U.S. Power and the Multinational Corporation* (New York: Basic Books, 1975). A third, the dependency model, is not suitable here, since it applies more to MNC relations with governments of host rather than home countries. It assumes that the home government simply does the bidding of its MNCs. The relation between the banks and their home governments is much more complex than that. There is critical analysis of this model in Gilpin, in C. Fred Bergsten, Thomas Horst, and Theodore H. Moran, *American Multinationals and American Interests* (Washington, D.C.: The Brookings Institution, 1978), and in Raymond Vernon, *Storm over the Multinationals* (Cambridge, Mass.: Harvard University Press, 1977), chap. 8.

model is an alternative view: the home government's political and economic interests remain dominant despite increasing integration of financial markets. According to the evidence, American banks have been closer to the liberal model, European and Japanese banks closer to the mercantilist, though for reasons that extend beyond the mercantilist explanation of home government policy. In the following discussion I treat these two approaches as opposing views of international banking. Few writers actually argue either in its pure form, but many tend toward one rather than the other.

The Liberal Model

In the liberal model,[3] the MNC is "an anational force."[4] It is "increasingly indifferent to national boundaries in making decisions" about "markets, production, and sources of supply." This view, though recognizing a political dimension to the international system, emphasizes the primacy of economic forces,[5] particularly in the literature about international banking. Because of "economic interdependence and technological advances in communications and transportation," the MNCs "are escaping the control of nation-states, including that of their home governments."[6] One may extrapolate from this the idea that national differences among the MNCs have little significant impact on bank behavior. The big banks qualify as MNCs by many measures.

The Eurobanks

The idea that financial markets are integrated and market forces dominant in banks' behavior is consistent with the liberal model. The idea leads to the notion that the behavior of banks from different countries is becoming similar as they sail onto the high seas of world finance.

3. This model is also called the Sovereignty at Bay model, based on the book of that title by Raymond Vernon. Raymond Vernon, *Sovereignty at Bay* (New York: Basic Books, 1971). In fact, the liberal model is an amalgam of many writers' views. A careful reading of Vernon's works reveals that his views are not entirely congruent with Gilpin's description of the liberal model.

4. Bergsten, Horst, and Moran, *American Multinationals*, p. 329.

5. Robert O. Keohane and Joseph S. Nye, *Power and Interdependence* (Boston: Little, Brown, 1977).

6. Gilpin, *U.S. Power*, pp. 220–225.

Many analysts suggest that the banks jettison the peculiar features of their nationality and become functionally equivalent: in a word, Eurobanks.

The Eurobank is "a financial intermediary that simultaneously bids for time deposits and makes loans in a currency, or currencies, other than that of the country in which it is located."[7] The term became popular in the 1970s. For example, in one text we find this: the "essence of the transactions in the [Euro-] market is to sever the nationality of the bank from the nationality of the currency in which it deals."[8] At one level, the term and related forms are just an analytical device. They serve merely as a shorthand for banks operating in Eurocurrency markets,[9] or they enable writers to explore Eurocurrency operations in the abstract, independent of the participants' "legal form and organizational structure" or home country.[10] In practice, however, there is a metamorphosis. The analytical device takes on its own reality. The tendency to strip banks of their nationality is found in texts about international banking and finance,[11] and in studies about competition and pricing.[12]

The idea of the Eurobank gained favor for several reasons. It fits the free market goals of those officials who shape policy toward international trade and politics, as well as of regulators and monetary policymakers who are concerned with banks. The concept of the Eurobank also coincides with a popular ideology: Government should

7. Gunter Dufey and Ian H. Giddy, *The International Money Market* (Englewood Cliffs, N.J.: Prentice-Hall, 1978), p. 10.

8. Richard E. Caves and Ronald W. Jones, *World Trade and Payments*, 2d ed. (Boston: Little, Brown, 1977), p. 354.

9. See M. S. Mendelsohn, *Money on the Move* (New York: McGraw-Hill, 1980), pp. 46–47.

10. Dufey and Giddy, *International Money*, p. 12.

11. A recent text on international lending devoted an average of three paragraphs to each banking system of ten industrial countries and then proceeded to analyze types of lending by banks with little or no reference to these differences. T. H. Donaldson, *International Lending by Commercial Banks* (New York: John Wiley, 1979). Another text recognized that "the 20 or so of the world's biggest banks . . . play a dominant role in the Eurodollar market" without then exploring the consequences of this dominance. Dufey and Giddy, *International Money*, p. 213.

12. K. Inouye, "Determinants of Market Conditions in the Eurocurrency Market—Why a Borrowers' Market?" Bank for International Settlements Working Paper No. 1, Basel, Switzerland, April 1980.

not play a role in bank decisions.[13] The sociology of international banking also probably fosters the idea of the Eurobank.[14] Certainly, the Eurobank fits the metaphor of international banking today, which is aquatic.[15] Forces of supply and demand for funds are like tides on which a bank rides. Perhaps the bank navigates the seas but if it does so, the craft's activities affect only its own destination, not the direction or force of the current. By implication, only the captain is concerned about the direction of the ship; policymakers should study the tides, treating the ships as essentially the same. The banks, as Eurobanks, fit the liberal model of MNC-government relations.

Lending by the Eurobanks

Much of the extensive literature prompted by recent lending is implicitly built around the concept of global economic efficiency. A central question in this literature is why the banks loaned as much as they did to the many countries that eventually defaulted. Most people who have written on this have taken a liberal position. For most observers, the 1973 oil shock was the key, but was taken as a starting point rather than a full explanation.[16] Analysts usually consider five

13. See, for example, Robert W. Russell, "Three Windows on LDC Debt: LDCs, the Banks, and the United States National Interest," in Lawrence G. Franko and Marilyn J. Seiber, eds., *Developing Country Debt* (New York: Pergamon Press, 1979). Russell argues against any effort to guide private credit, saying the "highest priorities for United States policy, which happily serve both domestic and international interests, should be a steady economy and a liberal trading policy" (p. 265).

14. In this market, bankers share a common society. Banks of all kinds provide similar services according to similar conventions. The U.S. dollar is the dominant currency, English is the dominant language for transactions and contracts, and in most cases the law of New York State or the United Kingdom governs.

15. There are many examples of the aquatic or nautical metaphor. A bank that goes international is swept along with the current. A short-term trend is merely a ripple. The main commercial bank of a financial conglomerate is called its flagship.

16. See Benjamin J. Cohen, *Banks and the Balance of Payments* (Montclair, N.J.: Allanheld, Osmun, 1981), p. 22; Richard S. Dale and Richard P. Mattione, *Managing Global Debt* (Washington, D.C.: The Brookings Institution, 1983); William R. Cline, *International Debt* (Cambridge, Mass.: MIT Press, 1984), p. 8; Darrell Delamaide, *Debt Shock* (Garden City, N.Y.: Doubleday, 1984), p. 27; Irving S. Friedman, *The World Debt Dilemma: Managing Country Risk* (Philadelphia:

economic variables in explaining the banks' lending and often emphasize one: macroeconomic forces, market disequilibria, structural
changes in the international economy, the dynamics of intermediation,
and structural disequilibria.

In the argument focusing on macroeconomic forces, the banks
loaned to developing countries because of the response by the industrial countries to the first oil shock. Expansionary policies by the
OECD governments permitted world inflation and led to the "break-
down in the world adjustment process."[17] The results included low
real interest rates and high commodity prices. Banks, assuming this
environment would continue indefinitely, loaned to developing countries.[18] Bankers tend to see this decision as an honest mistake, but
others see it as "administrative miscalculation and outright bungling
and . . . the misjudgment of Western lending institutions."[19] Both
views capture a permissive environment but fail to explain why the
banks acted as they did.

A related explanation focuses on disequilibria in the banks' major
markets, looking particularly at demand, performance, and returns.
In major developing countries, compared with industrial markets, the
banks found higher returns and a history of strong growth based on
exports of manufactured goods.[20] Opportunities for higher profitabil-

---

Robert Morris Associates, 1983), p. 53; and Staff, "International Debt, the Banks,
and U.S. Foreign Policy," U.S. Senate, Committee on Foreign Relations, Subcommittee on Foreign Economic Policy, 95th Cong., 1st Sess., 1977, p. 31
(hereafter cited as the Church Committee Report). Since "deficits in developing
countries require loans," whether deficits or loans come first "can be a chicken
and egg question." David Gisselquist, *The Political Economy of International Bank
Lending* (New York: Praeger, 1981), p. 155.

17. On inflation see Alexander Fleming, *Private Capital Flows to Developing
Countries and Their Determination: Historical Perspectives, Recent Experience, and Future
Prospects* (World Bank Staff Working Paper No. 484, Washington, D.C., 1981),
p. 13. The quotation is from William A. Noellert, "The International Debt of
Developing Countries and Global Economic Adjustment," in Lawrence G.
Franko and Marilyn J. Seiber, eds., *Developing Country Debt* (New York: Pergamon
Press, 1979), p. 270.

18. Robert Z. Aliber, "International Banking: A Survey," *Journal of Money,
Credit, and Banking* (November 1984, Part 2), p. 661. See also Carlos F. Diaz-
Alejandro, "Latin American Debt: I Don't Think We are in Kansas Anymore,"
Brookings Papers on Economic Activity, 2: 1984, p. 337.

19. Dan Dimancescu, *Deferred Future* (Cambridge, Mass.: Ballinger, 1983),
pp. 58–59.

20. On returns see George E. Phelan, "Discussion," in *Key Issues in Inter-*

ity extended beyond lending to encompass many related services: deposits, correspondent banking, local branch operations, and corporate finance.[21] In a growth environment such conditions gave the banks strong incentives to lend. These multiple ties to developing countries did not exist for many banks as recently as 1970, however, and as a result this interpretation misses certain changes in the structure of world finance.

A third argument holds that structural changes in the international economy under way for over a decade by 1973 prompted the banks to act. One group of writers finds important changes in the environment. "Multinationalization" prompted some banks to follow multinational corporations abroad and then prompted others to follow the first wave of banks.[22] These new entrants pushed the search for new customers, which led banks to developing countries that were newly industrializing as part of a long-term transformation of the world economy.[23] World financial markets opened as many countries relaxed regulations such as exchange controls and barriers to access by foreign banks.[24] The greater role of the International Monetary Fund (IMF) reduced the risk associated with lending to developing countries.[25] These four changes are all outside banking itself. A second group of

national Banking (Boston: Federal Reserve Bank of Boston, 1977), p. 42. A survey by the Group of Thirty later confirmed that bankers found stronger growth and better returns in developing countries: Group of Thirty, *How Bankers See the World Financial Market* (New York: Group of Thirty, 1982), p. 8. On growth see Jeff Frieden, "Third World Indebted Industrialization: International Finance and State Capitalism in Mexico, Brazil, Algeria, and South Korea," *International Organization* 35 (Summer 1981): 407, 409. On exports, Noellert, "International Debt," p. 273.

21. Richard O'Brien, *Private Bank Lending to Developing Countries* (World Bank Staff Working Paper No. 482, Washington, D.C., 1981), p. 15.

22. R. M. Pecchioli, *The Internationalization of Banking* (Paris: OECD, 1983), p. 52; see Herbert Grubel, "A Theory of Multinational Banking," *Banca Nazionale del Lavoro Quarterly Review*, December 1977, p. 349. Norman S. Fieleke, "The Growth of U.S. Banking Abroad," in *Key Issues in International Banking* (Boston: Federal Reserve Bank of Boston, 1977), pp. 9, 30, found, for example, that U.S. foreign direct investment was associated with the level of U.S. branch assets in various countries.

23. Michael Moffitt, *The World's Money* (New York: Simon and Schuster, 1983), p. 93; Frieden, "Third World Indebted Industrialization," pp. 407, 430.

24. Pecchioli, *Internationalization*, p. 53.

25. Charles Lipson, "The International Organization of Third World Debt," *International Organization* 35 (Autumn 1981).

writers focuses on changes in lending procedures that permitted banks to make the kind of loans that fit developing countries' needs. New techniques included syndication and cross-default clauses; new technologies included the computer and improved telecommunications.[26] New conventions permitted banks to go directly to the prospective customer rather than through correspondent banks, creating "a less tidy market" and changing the nature of competition among the banks in ways that undermined the market's structure.[27]

According to the views just discussed, changes in the international economy prompted banks "to bravely go where few banks had gone before." According to another view, also based on the idea of global economic efficiency, the dynamics of international lending—seen in banks' strategies, long since at work—explain the response of the banks. Writers assert that the global money markets were "in place" by the time of the oil shock.[28] They then trace different causal lines. One approach assumes competitive strategies: lead banks made their money from fees and therefore had to find and arrange ever more loans; as lending grew, banks continued to lend even more in order to retain market share.[29] Another approach notes the cooperative strategies of the players, especially compared with prewar antagonisms: by working together, banks and borrowers reduce the risk of default.[30] A third view, that the banks were simply diversifying their assets, is difficult to demonstrate, either by showing that the banks' rate of return was higher abroad than at home or by showing that the variance of returns declined as banks loaned to more countries.[31] The fourth and best-known explanation is Charles Kindleberger's. He argues that euphoric lending, like that in the mid-1970s, is inherent in international banking. The many players match one another's lending, overestimating the upswing in the economic cycle. In the absence of an international lender of last resort, a crash follows the euphoria. The

26. Dale and Mattione, *Managing Global Debt*.

27. Mendelsohn, *Money on the Move*, p. 88.

28. Moffitt, *The World's Money*, p. 94.

29. Mendelsohn, *Money on the Move*, p. 83; Aliber, "International Banking," p. 678.

30. Jeffery Sachs, "LDC Debt in the 1980s: Risk and Reform," in Paul Wechtel, ed., *Crisis in the Economic and Financial Structure* (Lexington, Mass.: Lexington Books, 1982), p. 200.

31. Pecchioli, *Internationalization*; Fieleke, "Growth of U.S. Banking Abroad."

boom-bust pattern has been repeated for centuries in international banking; in Kindleberger's view, the episode in the mid-1970s was merely one of many.[32] This interpretation comes close to a structural argument.

Finally, advocates of global efficiency explain the lending of international banks by looking for the competitive advantage that some banks have over others. At least two approaches—one based on theories of industrial organization and the other on theories of international trade[33]—find that this advantage is derived from structural imbalances. In the first, banks from countries in which margins are narrow are presumed to be more efficient than others and hence have opportunities to grow abroad at the expense of the less efficient. In the second, countries whose banks have greater scale, technology, or access to information, or a lower cost of capital, have an advantage in foreign competition.[34] Unfortunately, these approaches are too general to explain why banks loaned so much to developing countries in the 1970s.

These five approaches share the view that global market forces, independent of the politics of nations except to the extent that states create market imperfections, explain the behavior of banks. Even Robert Aliber, after admitting that "there are few uniquely international" banks, proceeds to concentrate on market phenomena.[35]

The Mercantilist Model

A different approach focuses on economic and political objectives at the national level. In the mercantilist model, MNC-government relations are hierarchical, with the government dominant. Despite the

32. Charles P. Kindleberger, *Manias, Panics, and Crises* (New York: Basic Books, 1978).

33. Aliber, "International Banking," and Yoon S. Park and Jack Zwick, *International Banking in Theory and Practice* (Reading, Mass.: Addison-Wesley, 1985).

34. See Ian H. Giddy, "The Theory and Industrial Organization of International Banking," in Robert G. Hawkins et al., eds., *The Internationalization of Financial Markets and National Economic Policy*, Research in International Business and Finance, Vol. 3 (Greenwich, Conn.: JAI Press, 1983), p. 195, cited in Park and Zwick, *International Banking*, p. 25. See Grubel, "A Theory," on multinational wholesale banking.

35. Aliber, "International Banking," p. 661.

trend toward integration of industrial economies, the nation-state remains the organizing force for economic activity.[36] According to Gilpin, "the essence of contemporary mercantilism is the priority of
national economic and political objectives over considerations of global
economic efficiency."[37] Again, "the mercantilist model . . . views the
nation-state and the interplay of national interests (as distinct from
corporate interests) as the primary determinants of the future world
economy."[38] It follows that "the management and the analysis of
interdependence must start at home."[39] Implicit here is the assumption
that global economic efficiency would be in the interests of the MNCs;
when their interest in global efficiency conflicts with their government's national objectives, the MNCs lose. Some analysts go even
further, arguing that "the government uses the activities of businesses
abroad to advance the interest of the state."[40]

Two conditions must be met before the mercantilist model can
apply to banks' worldwide lending operations: the home government
must be able to control its banks and it must act with the intention
of doing so. In the mercantilist view, international financial markets
are not so integrated that the home governments have lost control
over their banks. Periodically during the postwar era, for example,
each of the major home governments has placed barriers around its
domestic capital market. The U.S. government did so in the 1960s,
governments in Europe and Japan continued to do so sporadically to
1981. Yet a mercantilist interpretation of international banking would
have to assert that home governments' power extends to bank activities
beyond domestic capital markets, to the Eurocurrency markets and
financial markets in other countries. The basis for such an assertion
is not readily apparent, however; the absence of governments' regulation is the hallmark of the Euromarkets.

Little in the literature about banks' international lending examines
this perspective. One common view does hold that banks go abroad

36. In a study of Western European MNCs and governments, for example,
Vernon concluded that the abiding strength of nationalism prevented cooperation
among the MNCs in joint ventures or technological development. Raymond
Vernon, *Big Business and the State* (Cambridge, Mass.: Harvard University Press,
1974).
37. Gilpin, *U.S. Power*, p. 232.
38. Ibid.
39. Peter J. Katzenstein, ed., *Between Power and Plenty* (Madison: University
of Wisconsin Press, 1978), p. 22.
40. Bergsten, Horst, and Moran, *American Multinationals*, p. 324.

in response to low demand at home, but this is outside a mercantilist interpretation, which presupposes an active state.[41] The literature about international banking comes closest to the mercantilist paradigm in the work of two writers who draw upon the notion of competition among nations. To explain the banks' lending, David Gisselquist notes that the "major nations compete for current-account surpluses."[42] He does not, however, explicitly connect government action to win these surpluses and the lending of banks. In a study of foreign policy and international banking, Andrew Spindler finds that Japanese banks act abroad to "support . . . broader Japanese strategic objectives."[43] Other writers recognize the role of apparently disparate home government policies but fail to connect them. Many have noted that banks establish foreign offices because of legal restrictions in home markets, tax laws and foreign-exchange controls among them.[44] In 1977, by contrast, a study by the Church committee of the U.S. Senate suggested that banks had an incentive to lend if they expected their home government to bail them out should their developing country borrowers default.[45]

These two approaches—global efficiency and mercantilism—describe different relations between governments and international banks. In the model of global economic efficiency, the big banks are transnational agents, independent of any nation, including their own home. In the mercantilist model, they depend on their home. The two models are, of course, extremes. Few in either camp would deny that financial markets are more integrated than in the 1950s or assert that home governments exercise no regulatory authority over their banks' foreign lending. The question is therefore a relative one: Is the home government more impotent or more in command?

Banks and Government in Alliance

A close inspection of the G-5 countries suggests that the observed differences among banks from these countries do not result simply

---

41. On low demand, see the annual reports of the Bank for International Settlements in the early 1970s; Richard Russell, "Three Windows on LDC Debt," in Franko and Seiber, *Developing Country Debt*.

42. Gisselquist, *Political Economy of Lending*, p. 156.

43. J. Andrew Spindler, *The Politics of International Credit* (Washington, D.C.: The Brookings Institution, 1984), p. 175.

44. Pecchioli, *Internationalization*, pp. 53, 56.

45. Church Committee Report, pp. 67–68.

from differences in home culture, economic structure, or management style. The evidence below does not confirm the argument that powerful transnational banks force weak home governments to create a favorable banking climate. Instead, that climate reflects complicated bargaining among many players at the national level who ally to further their own interests. Not surprisingly, the five nations differ, and these differences affect the international system, defining the economic behavior by the banks—entry, exit, allocation, pricing, rescheduling—that in turn affects the stability of the system.

In the abstract, many factors indicate that the home country is not an anachronism in world banking. Common home market structure, market growth, regulation, trade, and stock markets suggest that banks from the same home country should behave similarly. Moreover, because these factors vary by country, one would expect banks from different home countries to behave differently: there are no Euro-banks. There are many reasons not distinctively mercantilist that support this view. First, oligopoly theory suggests common moves by banks where, as in France, Germany, and Japan, the industry is concentrated.[46] Second, to the extent that banks follow trade and direct investment,[47] one would expect banks from the same home country to concentrate in the same regions, with regions differing by home country as the directions of trade differ. Third, since home regulators apply common rules to banks from their country, they would impel or constrain the banks in the same way.[48] Fourth, the structure of the home monetary system appears to affect banks' domestic lending,[49] and this may affect their external lending as well. Fifth, the structure of the home capital market may affect banks' decisions to lend abroad; compared with that in the United States, the relatively small securities markets in France, Germany, and Japan pose less of a domestic challenge, as competitors, to banks from those

46. Frederick T. Knickerbocker, "Oligopolistic Reaction and Multinational Enterprise," D.B.A. diss., Harvard Business School, 1972; see also Janet Kelly, *Bankers and Borders* (Cambridge, Mass.: Ballinger, 1977).

47. See Fieleke, "The Growth of U.S. Banking Abroad," pp. 9–40.

48. See C. Stewart Goddin and Steven J. Weiss, *U.S. Banks' Loss of Global Standing*, U.S. Comptroller of the Currency Staff Papers (Washington, D.C., 1980).

49. Franco Modigliani and Lucas D. Papademos, "The Structure of Financial Markets and the Monetary Mechanisms," in *Controlling Monetary Aggregates III* (Boston: Federal Reserve Bank of Boston, 1980).

countries and therefore tend to be less of a goad for banks to expand abroad. Sixth, when the economies of the major OECD countries perform out of phase, one would expect that at any one time the demand for domestic credit would vary by home country, thus affecting banks' foreign lending. Finally, judgments about the banks made by their home stock markets may provide incentives and disincentives for management; shareholders' concern about a bank's exposure in developing countries affects all but the most valiant directors and executives.

The dynamics of the industry encourage banks to forge their alliances at home. Competition in the industry is based on price. The supply of and demand for funds at home reflect macroeconomic policies. The cost equation can be changed. Banks sell safety to their depositors, drawing on their special relations with their home government and its capacity to help them to reinforce their depositors' perceptions of safety, which in turn affect the banks' ability to attract low-cost funds and to maintain low yet acceptable ratios of capital to assets. Banks, acting with the help of their branch networks, also sell credit to borrowers lacking access to public markets, so the home government's capacity to control the banks' foreign branch networks is another source of government leverage. Each of the governments considered here has these capabilities; the difference lies in the way they use them.

Against this background, the models discussed above have a distinctly national cast. In the abstract, they present ways to organize corporate-government relations worldwide. In the case of international banking, the two models resemble existing relations in specific countries. Banks from France and Japan fit more closely the mercantilist model, though the home government does not make all the major decisions. U.S. banks are closer to the liberal model. The British and German banks have elements of both models.

The current definition of mercantilism in the international political economy is flawed, it seems, when used to explain international bank lending. It rings true that "the essence of contemporary mercantilism is the priority of *national* economic and political objectives over considerations of global economic efficiency."[50] The suppressed minor premise, that these banks' corporate interests lie in global economic efficiency, as implied by the mercantilist model's hierarchy of domi-

50. Gilpin, *U.S. Power*, p. 232.

nant governments and subordinate banks, is not quite right, however. The impact of the home government goes beyond government regulation in the narrow sense and the process is much more complex than one in which the government simply calls the tune. The home government's greatest impact often comes, not through command or direct regulation, but through manipulation of the domestic environment of the banks, for example, by affecting the banks' costs, access to borrowers, or supply and demand for funds. The government-business relation is not a simple hierarchy with the government on top. The banks themselves may, as we have seen, play a significant role in the policy process.

Each bank may gain more by maintaining its home country links than by achieving global scale. As I explore below, the international banks' corporate interests may profitably lie in their role in the home country's national strategy. Moreover, the banks' activities are not bound up only in their home government's strategy, but are intimately linked to the interests of their home corporations and markets as well.

The Home Country and Bank Strategy

A big bank confronts important issues in international lending when it builds alliances with other players at home. One or more of four basic issues arise when the big banks look to their home country to fix the parameters of international lending: the cost structure, barriers to entry or mobility, regulation, and recourse in the event of imminent loss. In reviewing these I refer only briefly to policies described in earlier chapters and elaborate on those not introduced earlier.

The underlying question is the extent to which important differences in banks' international portfolios are a function of nationality. Even integrated markets do not imply homogenous portfolios among all big banks. Major differences should result from the banks' business strategies. The more integrated the markets, however, the less significant should be a bank's nationality. In fact, the home itself is integral to the big banks' international lending. I begin with cost, obviously an important factor for the banks.

Cost Structure of the Home Country

Banks manage the components of profitability, often expressed in a standard formula: (unit revenue less unit cost) times (volume). A

146

common measure of banks' performance in the United States is return on assets: bankers relate their net income after tax to their asset volume. The banks' volume at home is so large that they are much more sensitive to their home's influence than to the influence of other countries. At home, moreover, the banks have substantially greater opportunities to reduce costs.

For all the big banks, the home market is by several orders of magnitude the dominant geographic market. The big banks do not simply divide their markets between domestic and international. Most break their international operations geographically into national markets. Thus the important comparison is among countries. For most, the home country accounts for the majority of assets, liabilities, and profits; for big U.S. banks, the United States is by far the largest market. From 1979 to 1983, for example, the domestic earnings of the ten largest U.S. banks ranged from 44 to 56 percent of all earnings. Domestic deposits ranged from 44 to 49 percent of all deposits, and loans by domestic branches averaged 53 to 54 percent of all loans.[51] Thus costs in the home country are crucial for the banks.

Even an extreme case—one of the world's most international banks, Citicorp—shows the importance of the home market as a volume base. According to Citicorp's income statement for 1983 (Table 4–1), Citicorp has at least 40 percent of its costs in its home country, and no other political jurisdiction comes remotely close to a 40 percent share.[52] Almost every other big U.S. bank would report a much higher share of costs as domestic in origin.

All costs are important because margins are narrow. At first it might seem that the cost of money swamps other banking costs, and any policy that reduced the cost even a little would have a big impact on expenses. For Citicorp in 1983, borrowed money (largely deposits) is 71 percent of gross expenses, overhead is 25 percent, and loan loss provisions—as close as the bank comes to allocating for possible as well as actual losses—are only 3 percent. But all banks have similar costs for funds in international lending because they fund much of their cross-border lending in Euromarkets. This common source puts

---

51. Salomon Brothers, *A Review of Bank Performance* (New York, 1984). Given the vagaries of booking, the quoted ranges are rough approximations.

52. This allocation by Citicorp shows at best orders of magnitude. It is extremely difficult to allocate income and cost geographically. Since Citicorp reports bookings in U.S. and other offices, it probably underestimates the U.S. component. It discloses, however, more than do non-U.S. banks.

TABLE 4–1. Citicorp's Expenses and Revenue (in billions), 1983

	U.S.		90 Other Countries		Total	
a. *Gross expenses*	$6.2	(40%)	$9.1	(59%)	$15.5	(100%)
Borrowed money		(26%)		(45%)		(71%)
Provisions*		(1%)		(2%)		(3%)
Overhead**		(13%)		(12%)		(25%)
b. *Net revenue*	$2.9	(49%)	$3.0	(51%)	$ 5.9	(100%)
c. *Net expenses and profit*						(100%)
Overhead						(64%)
Loan losses and provisions						(8%)
Taxes						(14%)
Dividends						(3%)
Retained earnings						(10%)

Citicorp's Expenses and Revenue (in billions), 1979

	U.S.		90 Other Countries		Total	
a. *Gross expenses*	$3.5	(35%)	$6.5	(65%)	$10.0	(100%)
Borrowed money		(23%)		(53%)		(76%)
Provisions*		(1%)		(1%)		(2%)
Overhead**		(11%)		(11%)		(22%)
b. *Net revenue*	$1.6	(48%)	$1.7	(52%)	$ 3.3	(100%)
c. *Net expenses and profit*						(100%)
Overhead						(67%)
Loan losses and provisions						(6%)
Taxes						(9%)
Dividends						(6%)
Retained earnings						(12%)

* Includes losses. Author's allocation based on distribution of actual loan losses.
** Author's allocation based on distribution of employees in 1983.
Note: Percentages may not sum to 100 because of rounding.
SOURCE: Citicorp, *Annual Reports*, 1983 and 1981.

them on an almost level playing field—one that they try to leave. Squeezed between the common cost of funds and price-sensitive customers, banks compete in wholesale lending on fine price differentials, and thus a large part of the game is to keep one's own costs lower than those of competitors. If Citicorp were to subtract out the cost of funds and account simply for net income, its distribution of costs (broadly defined) would be different (see "Net expenses and profit" in Table 4–1). Few if any costs are insignificant. Consider the following illustration.

Costs Affected by Home Country

A bank's major costs (and revenues), measured against assets and then earnings, are as follows:

Net interest spread/Assets
+ Fee/Assets
− Operating expenses/Assets
− Loan loss/Assets

= Profit before tax/Assets
× (1–tax rate)/Assets

= Profit after tax/Assets
× Assets/Equity

= Return on equity

The home shapes each of these costs. Any change from what might be called the free market level has a much more powerful effect on the banks' profitability than a similar cost change elsewhere because of the volume at home. In this formulation costs at home need not fall below those abroad (although in some cases they may) for the home to be important. The following sections explore where the opportunities for changing costs at home exceed those abroad. Many involve government action, raising overtly political issues.

NET INTEREST SPREAD/ASSETS   Embedded in the net interest spread is the cost of funds to the bank. For the big banks that manage all liabilities together, the cost of funds includes domestic as well as foreign funds even for international loans. As chapter 2 shows, the financial system at home may change the cost of domestic funds. In France, government ownership reduces risk for depositors and private shareholders in the banks, and therefore cost to the bank. In Japan, systemic effects accrue through government policy and by institutional practices that encourage savings and reduce risk. An official guarantee to a bank reduces its cost of funds, in the abstract, to the risk-free level paid by government itself. Compared with what costs would otherwise be, the overall cost of funds is lower.[53]

OPERATING COSTS   The home's major beneficial effect on operating costs comes in administrative and transactions costs rather than in the cost of labor (since the G-5 countries are high-wage economies) or of property (since each country's financial city is high-cost). Fewer reporting requirements, because of prudential regulation, mean lower administrative costs. Implicit guarantees by the home government reduce overhead costs such as country and credit analysis. Access to privileged information about borrowers reduces transactions costs. Banks rarely have an insider relationship with borrowers from other countries, especially governments. Some banks own equity in corporations or have exclusive relationships with corporate customers in their home country. As a *haus bank* or as part of a *keiretsu*, for example, a bank has access to information not available to ordinary lenders. In this sense the bank-as-owner shares costs with the bank-as-lender. As home firms go overseas and the banks follow their customers, they take these competitive advantages with them. Such privilege is limited to banks from the firm's home country.[54]

LOAN LOSSES AND PROVISIONS   Regulations and accounting practices in the banks' home country set the standard for

53. The home may also affect revenue: the export promotion agencies discussed in chapters 1 and 2 change the cost structure of transactions by taking the long-term end of the financing. Such a subsidy may make a project viable, allowing the borrower to pay market rates (at least) to private banks.

54. Privileged relations with home customers also benefit the banks on the pricing side. If they choose, they can accept lower prices than in an arm's-length loan to foreign borrowers yet keep the same margins. A bank that holds equity in the borrowing firm may take a longer view, accepting lower interest rates in return for eventual appreciation in the value of the firm's stock. The alternative is for the banks to use their power as equity holders to force higher margins on these customers. In either case, the base allows more competitive pricing elsewhere.

recognizing loan losses, as well as making provisions for them. Loan losses are, moreover, the outcome of risks taken earlier. Systemic effects, described in chapter 2, reduce risk, permitting lower reserves to provide against loss. Government subsidies and implicit guarantees reduce risk. An obvious example is export credits: the export promotion agencies discussed in chapter 1 take the long-term end of the financing and reduce the risk a bank might otherwise have borne.

A second example is the guarantee implicit in international lending. All G-5 governments support the overall international exposure of their biggest banks. The financial system defines the biggest banks; each bank's job is to make sure it is in the inner circle that can hold a riskier portfolio without a commensurate increase in costs. Both banks and governments recognize that the home financial system is hostage to the performance of its biggest banks. The more explicit the guarantee, in theory, the more the bank will benefit in reduced costs. Yet big banks have generally not been able to wrest explicit guarantees from their governments.

TAX RATES   Obviously, the home government writes the tax laws and negotiates the double taxation treaties.

EQUITY   At home, regulations, accounting practices, and capital markets set the standard for capital to asset ratios and return on equity. Higher leverage means lower capital costs and is particularly important, since it allows the bank to lend at lower prices, both at home and abroad.

In sum, each cost effect at home is, by virtue of the home's size as a market, qualitatively larger than what other countries can provide. Combined, the home's cost effects would be substantial. They come at several levels: in the financial system as a whole, in individual transactions, and for individual big banks. Privileged relations between banks and customers also reduce costs at home. On the basis of costs, one can see that even the biggest banks are creatures of their home country.

Home Costs and International Lending

The many ways the home can change its biggest banks' costs do not always aim specifically at international lending. Nor need they do so. Of ultimate concern to the bank is overall profitability, not just domestic or foreign profitability. This truism is grounded in the business itself, for it is difficult to compartmentalize banking operations in geographic terms.[55] Therefore, I consider here the effect of the home on overall revenues and costs. The alternative, allocating costs and revenues between home and abroad to estimate domestic and foreign net income, yields few useful insights.

Many of these costs directly affect international lending.[56] For example, big banks from Japan and France have pursued low-price strategies in international markets with the aid of systemic cost advantages.[57] The export subsidy programs draw more on home than on foreign banks. Programs in the G-5 countries are now open, at least in part, to banks headquartered in other countries. In practice, however, home banks take the lion's share of such programs, if only because of their close ties with home customers that export.[58]

Even such a world-class activity as syndicating a Eurocurrency loan can benefit from some of these cost effects. On a Eurocurrency loan the bank typically earns the London interbank offered rate (LIBOR) plus a small net interest margin and often some modest fees. The bank typically has several costs—the cost of funds (LIBOR), overhead, risk, and capital (dividends and, to increase the capital base as assets rise, retained earnings).[59] In this simple equation LIBOR cancels out

55. Banks have a hard time in their own analyses allocating revenue, costs, and volume among countries or between domestic and international operations. How, for example, should a bank allocate revenue from serving multinational clients worldwide or from such fee-earning services as syndication? How should it allocate costs of capital or headquarter costs that benefit the entire organization? Should it account for money deposited in its London branch by the headquarters of a U.S. corporation as a U.S. or as a foreign deposit? To deal with these and other problems, banks have evolved variable and often arbitrary rules of thumb.

56. My argument that costs at home may benefit international lending seems to reverse the standard view that banks expand abroad when costs at home rise. The common example is the U.S. banks' moves to the Eurocurrency market during an era of tight money at home in 1969–1970. Clearly accurate, the example is drawn from the era when banks began to build their world networks. By the mid-1970s, those networks existed and the competitive dynamic had changed. The 1969–1970 experience demonstrates the importance of home policy to international lending in an earlier phase.

57. See, for example, Cary Reich, "Spreads: The Search for Solutions," *International Investor*, June 1978, p. 33.

58. Interviews, Europe and Japan.

59. I have classified capital expenses as costs for convenience in this example. One could legitimately treat dividends and retained earnings separately as profits.

on both sides, and the margin must meet all other costs. The margins are typically small, below 1 to 3 percentage points, and in syndicated loans they are similar for all leading banks. A lead bank can achieve above-average profitability only by reducing costs, and that is where the home comes in. The home can affect the cost of the overall transaction (such as the information costs described above), overhead costs, capital costs, translation or exchange costs, and even costs that are reduced by an implicit government guarantee.

The Limited Power of Banks

Most of these effects came about, not because banks gained independence from their home by becoming transnational, but because of the banks' intricate role in the home economy. Some occurred for purely domestic reasons. Banks are only one of several interest groups, strong on some issues and weak on others, and they must attend to the issues that concern them.

There is no evidence that systemic cost effects such as high leveraging arise from governments' attempts to improve their banks' position in loan markets, though typically, big banks do support their home country's system.[60] Instead, governments are motivated by interests beyond the competitiveness of the financial system, as described in chapter 2. The lower costs may help compensate banks for government involvement in their lending activities. Such compensation is necessary: in Japan, for example, the banks take large portions of government debt at below-market prices. Nationally owned banks in France are expected to lend to the public sector and to distressed areas of political importance.

The banks' acquisition of privileged relations with home firms is a complex story. To the extent these relations give banks more independence from their home government than they would otherwise have, autonomy results from national forces exerted over decades rather than from a transnational aspect of the banks' operations.

60. The Japanese banks, for example, are the single largest contributors to the governing party, whereas the nationalized French banks engage actively in bureaucratic politics. Stephen Bronte, *Japanese Finance: Markets and Institutions* (London: Euromoney Publications, 1983), p. 13. In France, prior to nationalization, the private banks appear to have helped the private sector evade restrictions that were essential for the system to remain self-contained.

In the export credit war among industrial countries the banks are more like soldiers than generals. They do little to help formulate the basic policies of their home government. A country's aggressive export credit program represents a broader government commitment to promote trade. Support comes from domestic groups whose interests are vitally affected: the exporting firms, their employees, and their suppliers. Banks do, however, help promising customers move reluctant agencies, such as a finance ministry, with all available means of persuasion commensurate to the likely return. The prospect of aid lures banks into the political process. They actively mobilize allies inside and outside the government to secure official aid when they believe a customer may win its deal. Lobbying for support from an existing program is far removed, however, from the idea that transnational banks manipulate their governments' policies.

A government's implicit guarantee of its big banks is the result, not of the transnational status of the big banks, but of their position in the *home* financial system. Other implicit assurances tend to be based on broader systemic rationales than on the international action of the banks. For example, Japanese banks see the participation of the Industrial Bank of Japan in a project as a guarantee. The government's rationale is, of course, to promote the development needs of the nation, but the broader the implicit guarantee, the greater the benefit to home banks when competing with other banks at home and abroad.

In short, whether one considers home policies that change costs through systemic action or policies that work more directly, the banks receive them as greater costs or benefits. The banks are neither powerful transnationals nor passive instruments of national policy.

Protection at Home

The government's ability to protect home markets offers an important opportunity, since a protected home base gives banks a competitive advantage in international lending. This ties them more closely to their home. For the advantage to be real, domestic competitors must not destroy it through competition. Among the countries that protect their banks, France restricts competition through credit allocation and Japan carefully balances the needs of the banks and other intermediaries through interest ceilings. The important point in such cases is that protection can be a highly political issue, and controls must be carefully negotiated among various interest groups over a long period of time.

In their own markets all governments protect banks—even banks from other countries—against some forms of competition, if only by regulating standards for banking. One would expect the home, if of special importance, to provide substantially more protection for its own banks than they can receive elsewhere. Again, the effect hinges on the mix between volume (the size of the protected base relative to the bank's total business) and scope (the extent of the protection). As we saw above, the sheer volume of a bank's business at home overshadows its business in other countries that might provide protection.

The real question concerns the extent of protection at home in the G-5 countries. Markets are protected in two main ways: banks may be protected from foreign competitors and banks may enjoy protection for their special relations with domestic borrowers.

Protection from Foreign Competitors

At first blush, it would appear that the G-5 markets are not protected. In each G-5 country many foreign banks do business locally. Their market shares are low, averaging 13 percent of the assets of deposit-taking banks in the G-5 countries, but that alone does not suggest protection because national markets do not integrate at once. To identify protection, one must look for a growing supply of foreign banks without a commensurate growth in market share. We find this pattern in Japan. Although the number of foreign-bank offices has increased considerably in the last ten years, their share of the domestic market has remained at about 3 percent.[61] Access to Japan's financial services market has become a matter of diplomatic contention in recent years, also suggesting protection.

Among the G-5 countries the degree of foreign penetration varies widely, as do the supporting government policies. The source of protection is another matter. Banks from the G-5 countries typically find it difficult to break into one another's home markets.[62] The difficulty does not always stem from home government policy. Chase

61. Interviews with foreign bankers in Tokyo. Data for the 1970s have not been published, although they have been shown to individual foreign bankers there.

62. Interviews in all G-5 countries.

Manhattan Bank attributes its failed efforts to enter the German retail banking market in the 1970s to the market power of the big German banks.[63] Elsewhere, official policy seems to be the main factor. In France, the method of monetary management discriminates against new entrants. There is no simple explanation for the flat market share of foreign banks in Japan, but Japanese banking is a highly managed system.

Protection of Privileged Relations

One major source of a big bank's competitive strength is its close ties with major firms in its home country. Often extending over decades, sometimes broadened to include equity interests in the firm as well as loans to it, these ties make it hard for competing banks to take business simply by underpricing. In several of the G-5 countries, however, the legitimacy of the ties themselves are challenged, not by competing banks, but by groups outside the financial community.

The growth and volume of international lending by the big banks periodically inflame domestic political debate about the allocation of credit at home. The banks are denounced, particularly in times of tight money and economic hardship, for lending abroad rather than to those in need at home. The attack quickly expands to include the banks' ties with their large corporate clients at home. Critics often assert that the big banks lend in a way that cripples the country's industrial growth and competitiveness. By financing established firms and foreigners, the banks are said to be ignoring the dynamic and innovative small business. In the United Kingdom, for example, Lord Lever of the Labour party advanced this argument in 1980, and the same view was expressed in Germany, France, and Japan.[64] One part of the proposed solution in West Germany and Japan has been an attempt to reduce the banks' equity in companies to which they lend.[65]

63. Interviews, West Germany, 1980 and 1983.
64. Lord Lever and George Edwards, "Banking on Britain," *Sunday Times* pamphlet (London, 1980). The Labour party argued thus during the 1970s. See also D. Vittas and R. Brown, *Bank Lending and Industrial Investment: A Response to Recent Criticisms* (London: Banking Information Service, 1982).
65. Other responses are joint ventures by government and the banks that are supposed to finance the credit-poor sectors. The Deutsche Wagnis Finanzierungs Gesellschaft in Germany, Sofinnova in France, and the Industrial and Commercial Finance Corporation in the United Kingdom are examples.

Banks typically try to avoid meeting these political challenges head-on. They stall, make small changes, and try to influence opinion. Because the controversy extends beyond the financial system, however, the banks' power is relatively limited. The outcome varies by country.

In both areas of protection—from foreign banks and from challenges to privileged relations with firms—the political process usually draws players from only a narrow band on the political spectrum: the banks, others in the financial system, and the home government. The banks, if international markets are important to them, must try to balance protection at home with reciprocity abroad. Others in the financial system, such as securities companies, are concerned with preserving their own power and prerogatives against the banks. For the home government, the interests of the banks are merely one part of the political equation; other issues include management of the monetary system, control over cross-border flows, the structure of the financial system, and control over economic policy in a broader sense.

As long as the political debate stays within the financial system, bargaining among the players is relatively manageable. The process here resembles that seen in chapter 3, when regulators asserted their sole responsibility for the financial system. Thus when the threat to protection comes from foreign players, which is the case for protected home markets, the big banks are better able to maintain the barriers. When the threat comes from other domestic groups, however, which is the case for the protected customer base, the big banks are in a weaker position and must rely on broader political affiliations.

Certain home governments protect markets and customer relationships of their big banks. Their actions reflect formal and tacit alliances rather than the banks' independence and power. In France, the government owns its banks, so independence does not describe the relation. In Japan, the banks' international operations are too small a share of total assets (15 percent at most) to grant them independence. In Germany, protected ties with firms existed for over a century, surviving the destruction of the German banks' international networks during both world wars.

The Regulation of International Lending

Much of the argument that banks are transnationals independent of government authority centers on the multiplicity of legal jurisdictions in which banks do business. Given fungible money, inventive financiers, and financial havens, the argument holds, the banks operate as free agents outside the jurisdiction of any one nation's laws. The implication is clear: a government cannot restrict the international operations of banks against their will. This view may reflect the limited power of many host countries, but it vastly underrates the power of the home countries.

The home is the one jurisdiction that can regulate the international operations of its banks. When the Basle Concordat placed ultimate lender-of-last-resort responsibility with the home country, it was merely acknowledging the existing lines of authority. No government other than the home is in a position to get a complete view of the banks' worldwide operations. Moreover, this authority is more than a legal nicety: the big banks' interests in their home country are, as we have seen, so strong and so interrelated that the banks cannot extricate themselves. As former Federal Reserve Board chairman Arthur Burns has said, the U.S. regulatory system prompts competition in laxity, in part because banks can switch regulators. Ties at home are so strong, however, that the big banks do not switch citizenship.

Most G-5 banks are subject to a complicated set of rules that shape international lending in terms of safety and soundness, structure, tax, credit allocation, lending in the home currency, antitrust laws, and restrictions on the types of services banks can provide. We have here more than Glendower's empty command.[66] The Bank of England is attentive to the prudential aspects of cross-border loans by British banks. U.S. and Japanese authorities regulate the number of new foreign branches their banks may open. French authorities effectively prohibit their banks from lending francs across borders for most purposes. It is certainly true that the G-5 governments have not enforced all laws, but the circumstances of each asserted lapse must be carefully reviewed, as the case of the U.S. 10 percent rule shows.

The extent to which big banks are able to minimize home regulation varies widely among the G-5 countries. Most of the countries do, however, have the authority and the power to regulate the international lending of their big banks. In one way or another, all G-5

---

66. "I can call spirits from the vasty deep," says Owen Glendower in *Henry IV Part I* (3, 1). "Why, so can I. But will they come when you do call for them?" is Hotspur's reply.

governments exercise this authority over the entire international operations of their own banks more effectively than can any other jurisdiction.

The Threat of Imminent Loss

The most effective anchor to the home country is the role of the home government as lender of last resort. Each country looks after its own banks. Each also has de facto responsibility for debtor countries that are important to it: West Germany for Poland, for example, or the United States for Mexico (see chapter 7). Bankers can "read" the system in advance: they know that in a crisis they can turn to the home government, and they know not to burn their bridges in advance of crisis. Indeed, they cannot turn elsewhere. To put it crudely, only their home government will bail them out. This is hardly the stance of an independent, transnational firm.

Faced with the threat of a large and imminent loss on loans to a foreign country, the big banks turn for help with rescheduling to other interested parties at home: the other lending banks and the government. The big banks have two goals in these circumstances: to deal with the immediate prospect of loss, and to preserve or augment their competitive position in the long run. In seeking government action, the banks must ensure that policymakers see a danger to the home country. Often the danger is obvious even to the most myopic, and so the banks need take no direct action to convince officials that a crisis exists. Their earlier lending has already affected the system in which policymakers operate and reflects their own reading of the government's strategy.

In the face of imminent loss, the big banks can turn to three political arenas: interbank politics, bailout politics, and the politics of competitive positioning. In each arena the banks need the help of their home government.

Interbank Politics

In rescheduling, an effort is made to keep small banks in the game— a matter of no small concern to big banks. Interbank politics draws the home government in when, from its perspective, important state interests must be represented. The task of the big banks is to demonstrate that these interests are affected by the crisis. The home government, despite its great concern about the stability of the financial system, will be even more active in interbank politics when the debtor country is strategically important. The special involvement of the U.S. government in Mexico's rescheduling and of the West German government in the reschedulings for Poland and Yugoslavia exemplifies the home's role in interbank politics.

Bailout Politics

Any hint of a bailout—the government's providing public funds that allow the banks to avoid the consequences of ill-judged loans—stirs the political caldron at home, particularly in the United States. When the danger is geographically close, government expenditure is easier to justify. Even a threat to the international financial system is important less for its effect on the system as a whole than for its consequences at home.

The big banks have pursued a twofold strategy for bringing in government funds. First is the now familiar emphasis on maintaining control over the process of decision making: keep the policy debate within the financial system. Second is the natural inclination to shift the costs or trade-offs to those outside the financial system. Banks want debate about the fact and scope of assistance to take place among them, their regulators, and the treasury; the common interests of the participants discourage awkward questions about responsibility for the crisis. In Japan and Europe, debate has in fact stayed within these groups. Banks shift costs outside the financial system both at the level of the debtor country and at the systemic level. Each of the G-5 governments, for example, provides aid to the country in distress or to multilateral institutions rather than to banks. The banks benefit from this practice, which focuses political attention away from the lenders. Banks from different countries have had varying success with this strategy.

The Politics of Competitive Positioning

So much of rescheduling requires banks to cooperate that it may seem grotesque to identify a politics of competitive positioning designed to secure the bank's place when the dust settles. Yet a crisis offers opportunities to the agile bank. Effective leadership during the crisis enhances a big bank's reputation afterward. Market standing reduces costs, on the liability side, as depositors demand smaller risk premiums, and increases the opportunity for fee income as borrowers turn to the leaders to take action, for example, by assembling syndicates. The home government, after all, plays a part in legitimizing leaders; the more highly structured the home financial market, the greater the role. In Japan, the Bank of Tokyo has played the main leadership role because of its close relation to the Finance Ministry. One might suppose that the home government plays a neutral role among banks, but in practice stronger banks can use the regulatory system to erode the position of weaker banks. Tighter prudential rules, for example, are a competitive weapon. When U.S. regulators in effect require banks to make on-site inspection for country analysis, they exclude many smaller U.S. banks from the international loan market.

Summary

Implicit or explicit, systemic or direct, the alliances that banks forge with their home government have at least two phases. Interest in the crisis phase today should not obscure the importance of the lending phase yesterday or tomorrow. Home policy can provide a low-cost base and protection for banks, increasing profitability. The home market is such a large part of the business of big banks that even slightly lower costs and protection can have a strong effect. The home is the market that is willing to protect its banks. Banque Nationale de Paris cannot expect the Japanese Ministry of Finance to protect BNP, for example, but even if the ministry did so in Japan, the effect on the bank's overall earnings would be insignificant. The effect of French government protection would be major. The home also helps direct the flow of credit abroad through incentives to lend in certain ways, such as export credit and implicit guarantees, and through the selective application of prudential rules.

The home plays a special role during and in anticipation of crises. Only the home government will bail out a bank directly. This is the home government's ultimate weapon in dealing with its banks, and can mean potent benefits in the lending phase. Such weapons are important, for the home is the one central jurisdiction that can regulate the international operations of banks.

Banks are one of many groups competing for home government help; they sometimes win and sometimes lose. Their success hinges on their ability to identify their own needs with a broader purpose that motivates their home government. The relation between home government and its big banks is not easy, but the government is far from subordinate to the big banks.

That the home government has qualitatively greater influence than others over its big banks' international lending makes sense. The home has the greatest opportunity to influence costs and to control credit allocation, and it also plays an important role in the banks' international business strategy. The market considers the natural origin of a bank important, and this attitude reinforces the banks' ties with their home countries.

Differences Among the G-5 Nations

In much of this discussion I have treated bank-government relations in the G-5 countries as essentially similar. In fact, there are important differences and they affect the international lending of the banks and the stability of the world financial system as a whole.

If one were dealing with transnational banks, one would expect them to win and use government resources in ways not linked to their home countries. If big banks were truly transnational, one would not expect them to have similar portfolios, and the differences among the portfolios would result from the banks' business strategies rather than their nationality. Nor would one expect to see big differences in the extent of their freedom from regulation or the help they get when threatened with imminent loss. In practice, however, the differences are large.

Cost Structures

Cost structures differ among G-5 countries, as exemplified by leveraging (a systemic cost) and export credits (a form of resource allocation). In both cases Japanese and French banks make one group, German and U.S. banks a second. British banks are closer to the former group on export credit, closer to the latter on leveraging.

These groups reflect basic differences in government policy in the five countries. In some countries banks can leverage their equity a great deal, in others much less, and the differences have a dramatic effect on asset growth. In 1982, for example, one dollar of equity would support $80 of assets for French banks and $44 for Japanese

162

banks, compared with $22 for U.K. and U.S. banks and $34 for German banks.[67] As a result, a bank from Japan or France could lend more than other banks in world markets on a smaller equity base or could lend the same amount at narrower margins. Increased lending contributed to the rapid growth of bank credit in the 1970s; narrower margins contributed to intense price competition.

The export credit policies of home governments vary widely, and the differences affect the international lending of a bank in several ways. In particular, they determine, to the extent that they help the banks' home customers win bids, which country's banks will supply collateral finance. In this way these differences can influence the flow of credit. Subsidies have gone mainly to developing countries and Eastern Europe, thus encouraging banks to lend to these groups of countries.

Home Protection

Foreign banks hold considerably different shares of the domestic markets in the G-5 countries (see Table 4–2). Japan is an extreme case: the market share of foreign banks in Japan is less than one-third of the share of foreign banks in West Germany, the closest country. Such differences reflect official policies, shaped in part by the needs and pressures of the home banks and in part by other government concerns.

Barriers to market entry are most pervasive in Japan (see chapter 2). The Japanese Finance Ministry has closely controlled its borders to maintain a domestic financial system that promotes industrial competitiveness. The interests of the Japanese city banks have been consistent with the Finance Ministry's goal of closed markets: over 85 percent of the city banks' earnings at home come from highly seg-

---

67. *Euromoney*, June 1983, pp. S6–12. As a result of accounting differences, the comparison of debt to equity is rough. Other comparisons find the same ranking. See "The Top 500," *Banker*, June 1982, p. 177. A more systematic approach that is not sufficiently disaggregated for this analysis is R. Revell, *Cost and Margins in Banking: An International Survey* (Paris: OECD, 1980). In Japan, where no bank has failed since World War II, a complex web of official policy and industry structure reduces risk and permits higher leverage. In France, where the state as dominant shareholder does not require market returns on its equity investment and the government offers subsidized rediscounting for favored credit, structure has an even more direct impact on the cost of capital for the banks.

TABLE 4–2. Market Share of Foreign Banks in G-5 Host Countries, 1982–1983

	U.K.	France	U.S.	Germany	Japan
Assets: *Foreign banks as a share of:*					
All deposit banks	21%	17%	14%	10%	3%
Largest banks	52	33	30	27	7
Loans: *Foreign banks as a share of:*					
All deposit banks	23	18	16	11	3
Largest banks	52	34	30	29	8
Largest banks are:	Clearer Big 3 (5 banks)		10 large Big 3 NYC banks		12 city banks

These comparisons are rough. For example, the United Kingdom shows only sterling loans and assets; the United States shows 1,738 commercial banks with assets over $100 million; Japan shows other ordinary banks (city banks, long-term credit banks, and regional banks), but adding other deposit-taking banks would reduce the foreign banks' share by only 1 percent; France excludes *banques d'affaires* even though they can take deposits.

SOURCE: Central bank bulletin of each country, except for controller of banks in France. Data are as of the end of December 1982 for the United Kingdom, February 1983 for Japan, June 1983 for the United States, July 1983 for Germany, and January 5, 1983 for France.

mented domestic markets to which they want to retain privileged access.[68] As a result Japan, alone among the G-5 countries, still has "a substantial lack of national treatment and equality of competitive opportunity in practice for U.S. and foreign banks" operating in the country, according to the U.S. government.[69]

More subtle forms of protection are found in France and West Germany. France controlled the money supply through the *encadrement* system of ceilings on the growth of credit. The effect was to limit every bank to the market share it had when the system went into effect in the mid-1970s.[70] From their pivotal position in the financial system, the big German banks can discipline newcomers greedy for market share.[71]

London's longstanding role as the world's premier financial center encouraged both the government and the big banks to protect domestic markets less. The largest British banks are international, and they depend on substantial foreign earnings. They are inclined to encourage reciprocity at home, even though to do so could increase competition in the lucrative, inefficient domestic market. Barriers remain strong, however, in matters critical to the informal management of banking and monetary policy in the United Kingdom, among them control of

---

68. Bronte, *Japanese Finance*, pp. 67ff.

69. Department of the Treasury, "Report to Congress on Foreign Government Treatment of U.S. Commercial Banking Organizations," Washington, D.C., September 17, 1979, p. 77. Only in the last few years have restrictions on foreign banks in Japan been reduced. Many survive. Many foreign branches "were required to submit pledges not to solicit local deposits," making them subject to Bank of Japan quotas on currency swaps (p. 75). They have had to obtain advance approval for yen loans to non-Japanese, unlike the big banks with foreign-exchange licenses. They have been limited in their ability to expand their branch networks. Foreign banks are not part of the syndicate that can trade in government securities. They can issue certificates of deposit for up to 30 percent of their yen assets, whereas domestic banks' CD issues may reach 75 percent of capital.

70. Because of the long-term decline in the exchange rate of the French franc, foreign banks were reluctant to increase their capital, the only way to raise one's market share within this corset. Some negotiation with the authorities is possible, but a dramatic increase in share was not.

71. See, for example, John Zysman, *Governments, Markets, and Growth: Financial Systems and the Politics of Industrial Change* (Ithaca, N.Y.: Cornell University Press, 1983). Chase Manhattan Bank's failed effort to establish a retail base in Germany is an example.

the London and Scottish clearing banks.[72] Despite the efforts of the British Foreign Office and Board of Trade, for example, the Bank of England thwarted an attempt by the Hong Kong and Shanghai Banking Corporation to take control of one clearer, the Royal Bank of Scotland, in 1981.

In the United States, government has long followed a policy of limiting the power of the big banks. Among other constraints, banks have been prohibited from crossing state lines in their operations. In the 1970s, however, the big banks began aggressive political action to challenge these barriers. In their quest to open their own national market the banks have allied themselves with some regulators (notably, the comptroller of the currency) and with foreign banks against the smaller, regional U.S. banks.

Home Regulation and Overseas Lending

In their attempts to escape regulation by moving overseas, big banks from the G-5 countries have had very different experiences. As described in chapter 3, the European banks have much more independence abroad than banks from either Japan or the United States.

The Threat of Imminent Loss

When threatened by imminent loss, truly transnational banks should receive no special treatment from any government, not even from that of their home country. We know, however, that no G-5 government has agreed to provide lender-of-last-resort support to a bank from another country. We also know that each G-5 government has agreed to support its own banks.[73] Differences among governments are differences of nuance. The German government presents the appearance of arm's-length relations; so does the U.S. government, but that did

72. See, for example, William Hall, "Bank of England Seeks Stronger Financial Sector Merger Controls," *Financial Times*, September 23, 1981, p. 1. More recently the Bank of England has instructed foreign banks not to break into the sterling market by underpricing in the acceptance credit market, which is where the bank "conducts its daily money market operations." "The Bank Squeezes the Bankers," *Banker*, June 1983, p. 13.

73. The effort by the Italian authorities to escape the terms of the Basle Concordat at least suggests that governments outside the G-5 may not subscribe to it wholeheartedly.

not prevent U.S. authorities from assisting large depositors in the case of Continental Illinois.

Conclusions

There are substantial differences among banks in the extent to which they obtain and use home government resources, thereby forging an alliance at home, and these differences have important competitive effects. Nationality should be an important factor in the portfolio differences among big banks, and the causes behind the differences extend beyond simple bank regulation and macroeconomic policies.

I have examined four areas in which home government policies affect the banks' cross-border lending: cost structure, barriers to entry or mobility by foreign banks, regulation of cross-border lending, and protection from imminent loss. To the extent the banks themselves seek or acquiesce in the treatment they receive, they assign different priorities to the four areas.

- The big German banks rate freedom from regulation above the other goals; self-help is a principle that dominates all goals, underlying the banks' role in the whole West German economy.
- The big British banks couple freedom from regulation with protection of home markets and are less preoccupied with reducing costs or the threat of imminent loss. The City of London benefits the British economy, so protection cannot be excessive, yet some protection is necessary to meet the needs of the clearing banks as domestic financial institutions.
- The Japanese city banks repeatedly place least emphasis on freedom from regulation in their international lending, by choice or by necessity. They look instead to their government for protection, lower costs, and safety from imminent loss.
- The big French banks seem to focus on government help in reducing costs and guarding against loss, but they receive freedom from regulation by default.
- The big U.S. banks subordinate independence to a larger goal: reduction of barriers within their own country. They use international credit markets as one of several means to this end.

167

These various priorities represent major political trade-offs. Japanese banks, for example, are the most regulated in their international lending but also the most protected and most assisted by various cost advantages. Government assistance may represent, at least in part, compensation for tighter controls. These trade-offs are the major costs and benefits of the alliances between banks and their government that worked effectively in the Sicartsa negotiations.

Analysis of the banks' global lending suggests the tenacity of what could be called economic nationalism in a world economy that is increasingly integrated. Since the banks are not the independent Eurobank in the global markets of the liberal model, they must be able to forge the alliances at home. Since they are not simply government dominated, they have room to forge the alliances. The corporate interests of a bank may profitably lie with the home strategy, though home government action is only one strand, albeit a strong one, of the home's ties. Despite the entry of major multinational banks into international markets, the banks remain bound to their home countries by many institutional links—structural, cultural, even stylistic—that benefit them economically.

The general implications of this view are clear. If the home really plays such an important role in international debt, we should expect structural and policy changes at home to affect the flow of international debt. Perhaps one way to increase the flow of private credit across borders is through change in the home countries of the intermediaries.

Several refinements to this interpretation should be noted. First, players other than the G-5 governments and the major banks have a role. Big debtors have leverage and borrowing countries can manage their economies to attract or repel credit. Home government policy must, however, be conducive to the flow of new credit. Second, politics and economics are linked in banking. Banking is so highly regulated within national markets that a pure market model does not adequately explain lending behavior, even though banks in the G-5 countries maximize profits. Third, politics at home is more than a matter of Walter Wriston talking to George Shultz. The bureaucratic politics of contending ministries, the interest group politics of banks and other blocs, the so-called high politics of secretaries of state and defense—all frame home government policy.[74]

74. For a typology of relevant political issues see John T. Wooley, "Political Factors in Monetary Policy," in Donald R. Hodgman, ed., *The Political Economy*

In earlier chapters I examined the impact of the home government on lending activities in which home interests were high: trade finance. But not all lending draws such attention. What of activities of lower priority to the home or activities that seem more obviously global? During the 1970s, perhaps the most conspicuous example was loan syndication. Lead banks from many countries formed syndicates of banks from the four corners of the earth. Surely these lenders were independent of home influence.

of Monetary Policy: National and International Aspects (Boston: Federal Reserve Bank of Boston, 1983), p. 177.

5

Leaders Among Banks: International Syndication and the Home Country

Banks syndicated loans worth hundreds of billions of dollars between 1970 and 1982, when the market slowed. In the heady years from 1979 to 1982, one source reported $520 billion in syndicated loans.[1] Syndication was the vehicle for a massive expansion in world credit that fueled economic growth after the oil shocks of the 1970s. Without a way for the banks to pool their resources, the balance-of-payments deficits could not have been financed. Syndication then quite naturally earns the blame for permitting the debt problems of the 1980s.

Long familiar as a device for grouping underwriters, the novelty of syndication in the 1970s was that commercial banks from many countries took the borrower's paper for their own account. One or several banks would lead.

> The syndicate leader performs four rather separate functions . . . sourcing, structuring, selling, and servicing. . . . [The manager's] loyalty is owed equally to the borrower and to the participating banks, and he must balance delicately the interests of both parties while working in an atmosphere of full disclosure. . . . The participating banks may rely to a certain extent on the integrity and reputation of the lead manager.[2]

1. Euromoney Syndication Guide, *Euromoney International Loan Annual, 1984* (London: Euromoney Publications, 1984), p. 2.
2. Robert N. Bee, "Syndication," in F. John Mathis, ed., *Offshore Lending by U.S. Commercial Banks*, 2d ed. (Washington, D.C.: Bankers Association for Foreign Trade, 1981), pp. 177, 179.

As a major lending activity, syndication is a prism that refracts global and home forces on the lead banks. Neither the liberal nor the mercantilist account of bank-government relations does justice to the complexity of this market. At first glance, nationality would seem less important here than for trade finance. One would expect the home's role to be limited and the home government to stay in the background, consistent with the liberal view. Yet the home's impact turns out to be strong and, in the countries I examine in depth, the government plays a key role. In contrast to the mercantilist view, the banks act in their own self-interest rather than in response to direct government command, even in France. Self-interest is defined in Germany by the oligopolistic structure of the home banking industry and in France by the introverted rivalry of the big French banks. The joint action of banks and home government in this setting is more in the nature of alliance than command.

The forces at home that helped direct banks' trade finance (chapter 2), that guided the regulation of banks' international credit (chapter 3), and that shaped their business strategies (chapter 4) are at work on banks in this market. Even in this global market, the governments' policies toward the banks fit the broader home strategy and the home decision-making process plays an important role. In Germany, this process is the formal separation of government from banks in the context of the oligopoly. In France, it is the bureaucratic politics of a largely state-owned system.

In this chapter I first describe the major aspects of syndication,[3] then examine how twenty-eight major banks from the G-5 countries allocated their loans geographically (see Table 5–1). To delve deeper into the home's impact on the banks' syndications, I examine first the strategies of German banks, which are remarkably alike in geographic markets and pricing, then turn to the banks from each of the other G-5 countries.

Syndication: A Complex, Global Service

Syndication is a service that, in the abstract, ought to respond more to global than to home forces. Home forces should matter to any loan

3. For an exhaustive study of Eurosyndication from 1976 to 1984 that describes how the market works in more detail, see I. D. Bond, *The Syndicated Credits Market* (London: Bank of England, 1985).

TABLE 5–1. Twenty-eight Major Banks* by Home Country

United States	Germany
BankAmerica Corp	Deutsche Bank, A.G.
Citicorp	Dresdner Bank, A.G.
Chase Manhattan Corp	Commerzbank, A.G.
Manufacturers Hanover Corp	France
J.P. Morgan & Co.	Banque National de Paris
Chemical Bank Corp	Credit Lyonnais, S.A.
Bankers Trust Company	Société Générale, S.A.
Continental Illinois Corp	Banque Paribas
First Chicago Corp	United Kingdom
Japan	Barclays Bank
Bank of Tokyo Ltd	Lloyds Bank
Industrial Bank of Japan Ltd	National Westminster Bank
Fuji Bank Ltd	Midland Bank
Sumitomo Bank Ltd	Standard Chartered Bank
Mitsubishi Bank Ltd	
Sanwa Bank Ltd	
Dai-Ichi Kangyo Bank Ltd	

* These banks were the major syndicate leaders up to 1982.

in which the government or firms in the home country have a clear interest, which would be true for loans that finance trade or are made to borrowers important to the home. Homes forces should also matter if the home can influence the transaction (see Figure 5–1). The home exercises far less influence over syndicated loans than over, say, project finance, as in the Sicartsa example, because syndication more often involves general purpose finance and a standard document. Thus the home's influence should be present in syndication, but theoretically should not outweigh the influence of global forces. In fact, the home is powerful.

The Requisite Skills of a Lead Bank

In the 1970s, the syndication of medium-term loans in the Eurocurrency market involved three sets of players: a borrower, like Sicartsa; a group of participating banks that loaned the borrower the money;

FIGURE 5–1. Factors Affecting the Home's Impact on Different International Credit Activities

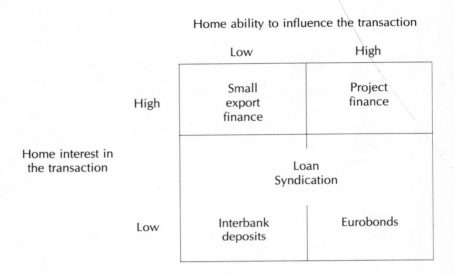

and a lead bank (or several) that arranged the loan by negotiating its terms with the borrower, assembling participants who would lend at those terms, and managing the paper work. Each bank loaned directly to the borrower, who usually paid all lenders a floating interest rate computed according to a common formula of a fixed spread added quarterly to the cost of funds in the London interbank market. The leader also earned fees for its services.

To lead a syndicate, a bank must have ties with other banks, firms, and governments, outstanding loans to the borrower or the borrower's country, and network, skills, and a track record. In the Sicartsa financings, the eventual leaders of the syndicates demonstrated more of these qualities than their rivals: the Bank of Tokyo used its experience and ties to the Japanese government to displace the newer Sanwa Bank, which was the Japanese supplier's house bank. Lloyds Bank drew on its experience and network in Mexico to displace National Westminster Bank and on its deposit base to displace the merchant bank Lazard Frères. In Sicartsa, the winning strategies reflected the banks' own goals, of course, but also the needs of their home governments, the Mexican borrower, and their home exporters. In syndications generally, exporters play a smaller role and another group of players takes the stage: the participating banks.[4] Lead banks face two kinds of buyers: participants and borrowers. To understand the lead banks' strategies in this market, one must know their buyers' needs and how syndication meets those needs.

Syndication became popular because, compared to other types of finance, it adds value by lowering costs, reducing risk, enhancing revenue, and opening markets. Consider how it worked in the Sicartsa financing. Costs fell for the borrower and the banks. The banks in a group could advance larger loans than any one bank acting alone, thus sharing scale economies. The borrower benefited from economies of scale in marketing, legal fees, and other transaction costs.[5] The participating banks benefited from scale economies in credit analysis, transaction costs (one bank can act for many), and monitoring the borrower's performance.[6] The individual lenders spread the risk, which further reduced the risk for each by deterring default: that is, simply by their large number, the banks involved could restrict the access of a delinquent Sicartsa or Mexican government to other sources of finance.[7] Lead banks enhanced their revenues by earning manage-

---

4. Outside of trade-related loans, home governments and exporters play a less direct role. Their needs will not be considered here.

5. Most authors agree on this advantage. See Bee, "Syndication," p. 177; T. H. Donaldson, *International Lending by Commercial Banks* (New York: John Wiley, 1979), p. 68; Azizali F. Mohammed and Fabrizio Saccomanni, "Short-term Banking and Eurocurrency Credits to Developing Countries," in *IMF Staff Papers*, Vol. XX No. 3, November 1973, pp. 612, 622–623; R. M. Pecchioli, *The Internationalization of Banking* (Paris: OECD, 1983), p. 32; Marcia L. Stigum and Rene O. Branch, Jr., *Managing Bank Assets and Liabilities* (Homewood, Ill.: Dow Jones-Irwin, 1983), p. 133; and Eugene L. Versluysen, *The Political Economy of International Finance* (New York: St. Martin's Press, 1981), p. 17. Hereafter, these works are cited by last name of author.

6. See Pecchioli, p. 32.

7. See Bee, p. 177; Donaldson, p. 68; and Pecchioli, p. 32.

ment fees in addition to the interest paid on the loan.[8] Finally, banks found that markets would open or expand for them from the publicity they receive in the financial press and among other banks when they lead or participate in syndicates.[9] Borrowers may receive one set of benefits and participating banks another, but the benefits overlap and call for related traits in the lead banks.

Borrowers choosing a lead bank consider its reputation, its special skills, and its ability to help them through bad times. Garcia Torres considered each of these. First, like other borrowers, he wanted a leader with a solid reputation among banks for professional, efficient service, so he could go to the market with a low-cost loan that would be acceptable to other good banks. A good showing would then enhance his position when he next approached the market. Second, Garcia Torres needed a lead bank skilled in project finance. Borrowers in general consider the lead bank's expertise if they need an uncommon type of financing or if the loan is for such industries as "shipping, real estate, aircraft, and highly complex industrial credits such as plastics, pharmaceuticals, and electronics."[10] Third, Garcia Torres considered what Sicartsa's needs would be if Mexico's position in financial markets should worsen. Generally, if during the life of the loan the borrower encounters problems meeting the terms, it will want a lead bank that is "imaginative enough to recognize constructive actions . . . and carry the syndicate."[11]

The participating banks need a lead bank that can identify the "creditworthy borrower," set a "competitive interest rate," design covenants appropriate to the borrower, and generally act with integrity.[12] To meet these needs the lead bank must be able to evaluate and track the borrower's performance, for which special industry or country skills and inside information are useful. The participants expect the lead bank to be able to read the market accurately when setting rates. Participating banks see the leader's integrity in its track record, while its visible and continued activity in the market assures them that the lead bank will live up to its reputation in the future.

---

8. See Bee, p. 177, and Benjamin J. Cohen, *Banks and the Balance of Payments* (Montclair, N.J.: Allanheld, Osman, 1981), p. 101.

9. Bee, pp. 177–178.

10. Bee, p. 180.

11. Donaldson, p. 80.

12. Bee, p. 179.

In sum, a lead bank needs experience in syndication, an established reputation, a network of relations with other banks, and the capacity to analyze the credit, the borrower, and the country. The lead bank may also need the capacity to absorb any part of the loan that it does not sell to other banks, as Bank of America and others had to do in May 1982 when smaller banks were reluctant to participate in a Bank of America syndicate for the Mexican government. A leader would benefit from a presence near the borrower, as Lloyds had in Mexico. Versatility in these areas gives the lead bank a competitive edge. Syndication itself has an edge over other methods of intermediation because the lead banks can tailor the loan contract for a transaction or for a borrower that cannot approach public markets while at the same time making the transaction accessible to other banks that lend with less information than that available to the leader.

The Behavior of Lead Banks in Eurosyndication

International banks become known for certain lending policies, often in ways that reflect their broader business strategy. The qualities the banks share cross national lines, and thus create strategic groups that are transnational. This is why even in highly integrated markets the banks would not hold homogenous portfolios. To help it win the Sicartsa mandate, Lloyds Bank relied on its known skills in project finance, its long history and close ties in Mexico, and its deposit base. Lloyds used one of three strategies available to lead banks: the other two are a low-cost, low-price strategy and a first-mover strategy.[13]

Many well-known international banks exemplify these three strategies. Many banks differentiate: some, like Morgan Guaranty Trust Company and Deutsche Bank, stress quality; others, like Chase Manhattan Bank and Société Générale, stress industry expertise; and those like Lloyds emphasize their knowledge of the borrower or the underlying transaction to be financed. Examples of the second strategy are the Japanese and French banks, known for low pricing in the late

13. Here I speak of general tendencies. Experienced syndicators, especially in the largest banks, did not all set a formal, detailed strategy to which they then hewed unswervingly. In this fast-moving market, mandates were tested and agreed on sometimes in a matter of days. The able syndicator was flexible. Still, in looking at the banks over a period of time, one finds patterns.

1970s. Many banks used this strategy to buy market share in overseas markets. Some persisted, bundling services, pricing on their total relationship with the borrower rather than the transaction alone. Banks following the third strategy—first mover—are known for opening markets or devising innovative financial techniques. Citicorp is often associated with this strategy. Bankers Trust Company claims to have led the first Eurocredit syndication in 1968. These banks use novelty to claim high returns. They move fast; successful innovators remain alone in this industry scarcely longer than the twenty-four-hour mayfly lives.

National origin influences the choice of syndication strategies largely through the structure of the home financial system.[14] The home's financial system gives lead banks certain broad specialties when its laws define their powers as commercial, merchant, or specialized banks. In Japan, for example, the geographic focus and pricing by the specialized banks (Bank of Tokyo and Industrial Bank of Japan) differ radically from that of the city banks. The nature of competition at home can generate oligopolistic reaction in the syndicated loan market. The Big Three German banks seem to have matched each other's moves in the syndication market, for example.

Each of the three strategies needs different resources and faces different barriers, so if the home influence is weak and the market highly integrated, one should find groups of banks from several G-5 countries with a common strategy. These groups would be transnational. On the other hand, if the banks' national origin is important, these transnational groups should be weak and banks from the same home country should exhibit common traits.[15] Against this polarity,

14. The home could have an influence in various other ways, but does not appear to do so. Trade finance is influenced by the strategy of the home government, by ties with home firms that affect the banks' perceptions of risk and return, and by the home country's competitiveness, hence the banks' customers' international performance. The home government and home firms are less interested in syndication than in trade finance.

15. I adapt here Porter's concept of strategic groups to link banks with similar performance in pricing. See Michael Porter, *Competitive Strategy*, (New York: Free Press, 1980). One qualification is in order. There is no reason to expect banks from the same home to adopt identical strategies. Quite the contrary: to distinguish themselves, even banks from oligopolistic home markets may follow different strategies. Cartel members could divide the world by regions or allocate markets or customers. On the other hand, members of a tacit or weak cartel are likely to match each other's moves.

I examine data about the geographic market shares of the syndicated loans of twenty-eight banks. The loans are the outcomes of the banks' strategies.

Geographic Focus in Syndication

The twenty-eight lead banks' regional concentration reveals durable national as well as transnational forces. An important factor is the structure of the home banking system. The banks demonstrate distinct national characteristics. French, German, Japanese, and U.S. banks clearly concentrated their leadership on different regions of the world. Together, they led almost 85 percent of the $273 billion in loans syndicated by the twenty-eight banks from 1979 to 1982.[16]

These are the banks that locate and bring borrowers to market. Their activities are extremely important, for their own large portfolios and for those of hundreds of participating banks. The leaders' choice of potential borrowers largely decides the borrowers' access to the Eurocredit market and the participating banks' access to borrowers.[17]

The 1979–1982 period spans the time from the second oil shock to the Latin American debt crisis, a distinct era in loan syndication. During this period, syndications averaged $130 billion a year, with a low of $88 billion in 1980 and a high of $181 billion in 1981. The twenty-eight banks accounted for 53 percent of the total. The U.S. banks dominated, leading $155 billion. The British and Japanese banks each led just over $40 billion, while the French led $22 billion. The German banks, which pulled back during this period, led syndicates of only $14 billion.

16. The source is Euromoney Syndication Guide, *Euromoney International Loan Annual, 1984* (London: Euromoney Publications, 1984). It gives total lead and co-lead managements by the 200 largest leaders, measured in dollars, and regional lead and co-lead managements by the largest 50 banks. Most of the 28 banks I compare were in the top 50 in each region, though more so in 1982 than 1979. In a world where some loans are secret, this source seems reasonably complete and accurate. Its compilers seek two sources for each loan. Their data base was originally promoted by one of the largest U.S. banks, has existed since the later 1970s, and is used by many banks today. They assign to each sole lead bank the full value of the loan. Each co-lead receives an equal share, which distorts the data somewhat.

17. M. S. Mendelsohn describes the process by which large and small banks with very different interests entered syndicates during this period in *Money on the Move* (New York: McGraw-Hill, 1980), pp. 88–91.

My goal is to determine the relative importance of various regions to the individual banks over the four years. This means I am not interested in simple market share: it is well known, for example, that the U.S. banks lead in each regional market. Instead, to identify each bank's regional emphasis and to suggest the regions where each bank has a competitive edge, I relate the bank's market share in each region to its market share in all syndications. I do the same with all banks from the same country. For example, the Big Three German banks led 4.9 percent of all syndicates over the 1979–1982 period, but only 1.5 percent of all syndicates to North America and fully 25.9 percent of all to Eastern Europe. If the German banks' share of all syndicates is 1.00, then their relative share of syndicates to North America is 0.31 (1.5 divided by 4.9) and to Eastern Europe is 5.24. In addition to these two regions, I consider Pacific Asia, North America, and OPEC, as well as the OECD countries and developing countries generally (see Figure 5–2).

The three concentric circles index the share of market: the edge of the inner circle is the bank's market share for all syndications, the edge of the second is twice that share, and the edge of the third is three times. The German banks' share in Eastern Europe is 5.24 times its overall share. The banks' share in North America is below one-third (actually 0.31) its overall share. To see the German banks' relative regional emphasis, join the market share points. The Germans led relatively more loans in Eastern Europe and OPEC. Their position as leaders of syndicates for borrowers in developing countries was average. They led relatively fewer loans in industrial countries.

In comparing the twenty-eight banks, one can explore the regional emphases of banks from each of the G-5 countries. If banks are transnational, one should not find clusters by home country of banks with similar regional positions. In fact, many such clusters appear. The home country is so important that banks from the same country often have above-average relative market shares either in the home country itself or in regions that are important to the home. Banks from the same home may or may not have similar relative shares in various regions, depending on whether they choose to differentiate themselves along regional lines.

Home Country Distinctions

There are distinct national differences. First, compare countries by simple market share in each region and the total dollar volume of the

FIGURE 5–2. The Measure of a Lead Bank's Relative Market Share

Measure of Relative Market Share:
1 = Average for All Loans

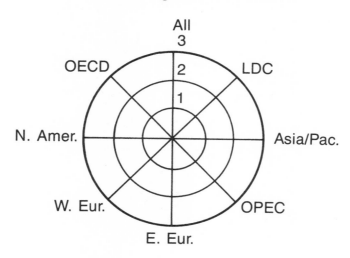

Relative Market Share
The Big Three German Banks

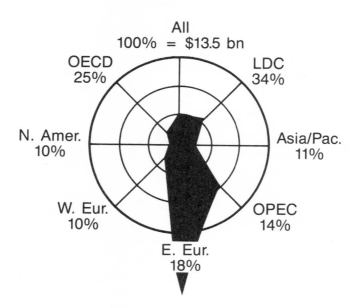

FIGURE 5–3. *Relative Regional Market Share by Home Country (1979–1982)*

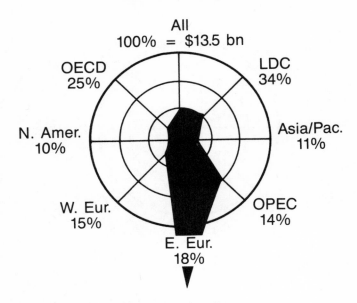

**German Banks:
Eastern Europe**

All
100% = $13.5 bn

OECD
25%

LDC
34%

N. Amer.
10%

Asia/Pac.
11%

W. Eur.
15%

OPEC
14%

E. Eur.
18%

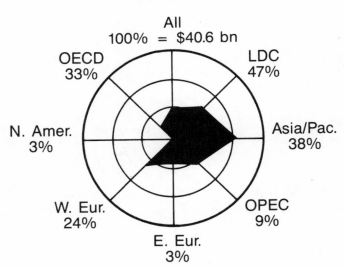

**Japanese Banks:
Asia & OPEC**

All
100% = $40.6 bn

OECD
33%

LDC
47%

N. Amer.
3%

Asia/Pac.
38%

W. Eur.
24%

OPEC
9%

E. Eur.
3%

(cont.)

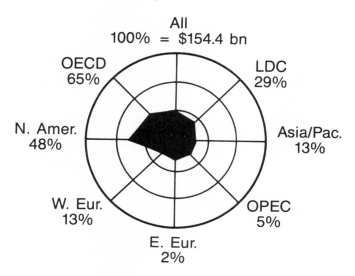

U.S. Banks:
W. Europe, OPEC, Asia

All
100% = $154.4 bn

OECD
65%

LDC
29%

N. Amer.
48%

Asia/Pac.
13%

W. Eur.
13%

OPEC
5%

E. Eur.
2%

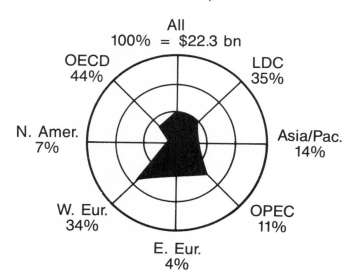

French Banks:
West & East Europe, OPEC

All
100% = $22.3 bn

OECD
44%

LDC
35%

N. Amer.
7%

Asia/Pac.
14%

W. Eur.
34%

OPEC
11%

E. Eur.
4%

Fig. 5–3 (cont.)

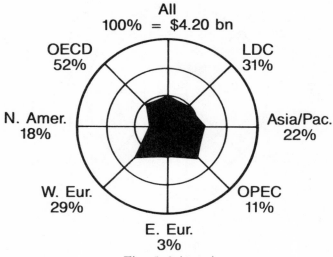

U.K. Banks:
W. Europe, OPEC, Asia

All
100% = $4.20 bn

OECD 52%

LDC 31%

N. Amer. 18%

Asia/Pac. 22%

W. Eur. 29%

OPEC 11%

E. Eur. 3%

Fig. 5–3 (cont.)

syndicates those banks led over four years (see Figure 5–3). Grouping banks by the same home country, one sees that the most extreme set is the German banks. Their relative share of loans to Eastern Europe was 5.24 times their average, and their share to OPEC was 1.90. Both regions had close ties to Germany, Eastern Europe for reasons of history and culture as well as trade and national security, OPEC as the object of Germany's export thrust. In Eastern Europe, the German banks led 25.9 percent of all syndicates, but elsewhere their market share was low, averaging only 4.9 percent overall. At first glance, their below-average share for Western Europe may seem odd, since so much German trade is within that region. But compared with trade with other regions, little of the trade with Europe requires medium-term syndicated credit.

U.S. banks concentrated in North America, where their market share was 1.53 times their average. No other region reached 1.00. In North America, the U.S. banks swept up 86.0 percent of the lead managements, dominating this market as they assembled megaloans to finance mammoth corporate mergers and acquisitions. Their ties to their home companies and their dollar base gave them a competitive advantage the non-U.S. banks could not match. The U.K. banks held only 8.8 percent of the North American market, while the French,

German, and even Japanese banks—despite the growing Japanese capital surpluses—each held barely 1.5 percent. On average, the U.S. banks led 56.6 percent of all syndicates, far ahead of the nearest contenders, the U.K. banks with 15.4 percent and the Japanese with 14.9 percent. As a group, the U.S. banks were helping finance the growing U.S. current-account deficit during this period.

Japanese banks' regional leadership policy was the opposite of that of the U.S. banks. The Japanese banks held above-average shares first and foremost in Pacific Asia but also in OPEC. They were far below their average—14.9 percent of all loans—in North America, somewhat less so in Eastern Europe. It is as though, ceding the strongholds of the American and German banks, they decided to focus on their own backyard. In Pacific Asia, the Japanese led 31.7 percent of the syndicates, and although they did not displace the U.S. banks' 40.4 percent, they drew very close in an area that U.S. banks, U.S. firms, and their home government also consider important. The Japanese banks did this during a period in which their international lending was initially restrained by their own Finance Ministry.

The French banks focused on Western Europe, where their relative market share was 1.82. In this they are unlike the German banks, which led relatively less in Western Europe. For the French banks, Western Europe probably meant France, since during this period they led many syndicates for French borrowers. If so, the French banks were helping finance their own country's current-account deficit. Like the German banks, as part of their country's export push the French banks also led relatively more syndicates to OPEC. This is an area in which credit is used to promote exports, as are the other regions where French banks had a share slightly above average: Eastern Europe and the developing countries (probably Africa and Latin America, given the low share in Asia). French bankers have noted that during the 1970s the shift in their cross-border portfolios toward Eurocredits entailed a shift away from commercial finance.[18] It appears that after the second oil shock they reverted to a closer link between Eurosyndications and commercial loans.

Compared with the others, the U.K. banks are much less geographically focused. In part, this may be the result of the high level of aggregation; one might define a clearer focus by, for example, breaking out the former colonies scattered across Asia and Africa. But in part

18. Interviews, Paris, 1980.

the greater uniformity of relative share reflects the differences among the five U.K. banks. Since the overseas banks had grown in different regions, it should not be surprising to discover the Asian focus of a Standard Chartered (2.11), for example, offset by the low leadership of a Barclays (0.88). Compared with banks from the other countries, the U.K. banks emerge as second or third in relative emphasis in each region: second to France in Western Europe, second to Japan in Pacific Asia, a distant second to the United States in North America, and third in Eastern Europe, OPEC, and developing countries in general.

In sum, when one groups banks by country, the regional focus of four of the G-5 stands out in sharp relief. The impact of national forces appears quite strong and that of the transnational forces weak. As my analysis of the U.K. banks shows, however, differences among banks from one country are obscured by grouping them. In Japan, the two quasi-public banks accounted for almost three-fifths of the Japanese syndicates. Because these two alone led 26 percent of all Asia syndicates of the twenty-eight banks, they skewed the Japanese group as a whole toward that region. Since the big banks can swamp the smaller, it is essential to look at the positions of the twenty-eight different banks.

Syndication

Almost all of the twenty-eight banks competed in each region and therefore in a sense with each other around the world. In North America, only two Japanese banks, a U.K. bank, and a French bank were absent as leaders. In Western Europe and in Eastern Europe, a U.S. bank was absent. But the range of market share was enormous, from Deutsche Bank's 19.3 percent in Eastern Europe to Sanwa Bank's 0.1 percent in North America. Of interest here is the degree to which banks varied from the norm.

To compare the twenty-eight banks, I grouped them according to the regions they emphasize in their lending (see Figure 5–4). The banks from most countries had markedly different regional policies. Only the three German banks are close. Banks from Japan, the United Kingdom, and the United States may be found in several regions. This is not unexpected, since the banks from the same home often try to differentiate themselves from one another. The result is that banks cluster in five or six areas, and only the Western Europe-OPEC axis contains banks from many countries.

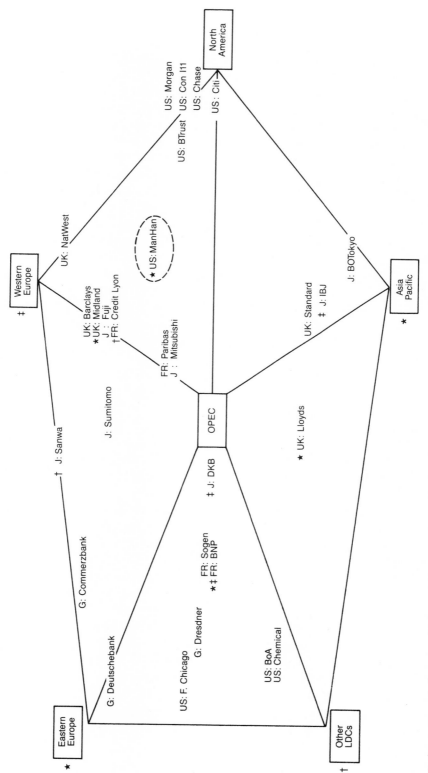

FIGURE 5–4. Regions Emphasized by 28 Banks

Banks are grouped close to or far from a designated region according to the emphasis they place on that region. OPEC is placed at the center because it was a major or secondary region for many banks during the period examined (1979–1982). Some banks have above-average relative shares in more than two regions; they appear off the connecting lines or are marked to indicate the other region.

Several of the regional groupings are bastions for banks from only one country. The cluster of banks in North America consists solely of five from the United States. Only two U.S. banks led predominately to developing countries outside Asia. The three German banks were the real force in Eastern Europe; First Chicago led 14 percent of the loans in 1979, then effectively dropped out as the German banks increased their share to 68 percent by 1982.

The transnational groups of banks center around Western Europe, OPEC, and Pacific Asia. Here, too, banks cluster by home country.

- Three British banks emphasize Western Europe.
- The two other British banks are in OPEC and the Pacific Asia areas.
- Two French banks are concentrated in Western Europe and OPEC.
- The two other French banks are in Eastern Europe and OPEC.
- Two Japanese banks are concentrated in Pacific Asia. These are the two quasi-official banks, the Bank of Tokyo and the Industrial Bank of Japan.
- The five city banks from Japan are somewhat looser but are still concentrated in Western Europe, Eastern Europe, and OPEC.

Given a market with few apparent barriers to mobility, the overlap of big banks of different nationality is to be expected. The national clusters are intriguing and suggest the continued power of the home country.

One anomaly deserves note. No bank chose to focus on both Pacific Asia and North America. This gap was not the result of regional exclusivity by the U.S. banks dominating North American syndicates. Of the six, five also served a second region: for Morgan Guaranty and Continental Illinois, it was Western Europe; for Citicorp, OPEC; and for Bankers Trust and Manufacturers Hanover, Eastern Europe. Nor was the gap the result of the Latin American debt crisis, which flowered in late 1982. If, as some think, economic forces will continue to bind North America and Pacific Asia, the gap suggests the U.S. banks' strategists overlooked important opportunities.

The interplay of home forces that led to these national groups is apparent in a closer look at some of the groups. Leadership and specialization at home are directly related to the banks' relative regional focus. In this sense, the structure of the home banking system influences the strategies of banks that lead Eurocredit syndicates. To demonstrate how this works, I explore the broader role of banks in more detail by home country.

German Banks: Making the Alliance Work

The Big Three German banks hail from a country whose government distances itself from them with great formality, and therefore their home should affect them least in international credit markets. Yet they are remarkably similar in geographic focus and in their pricing of loans. Their mutual retreat from Eurocurrency syndication is a story of matched moves back to Germany.

In fact, at work here is a tacit alliance between the banks and their home government that placed the German banks in a stronger competitive position internationally by the mid-1980s. The German government played an important role, manipulating the banks' environment. The financial structure through which these policies worked gave a direction to the banks' response. The government and bank were able to take preventive action rather than await the debt crisis.

Deutsche Bank was the leader that shifted the other banks to Germany and its backyard, Eastern Europe. Between 1979 and 1981, Deutsche Bank cut its share of all syndicates from 4.5 percent to 1.1 percent. It reversed from an expansionary strategy barely five years old, one apparently forced upon it by the other big German banks and tied to German commercial interests. Its rivals' weaknesses offered the conservative Deutsche Bank a chance to retrench, which it readily grasped. Caught in a shake-up, the other two banks followed Deutsche Bank back home.

The Shift from Eurosyndication

Deutsche Bank came late to the syndication market, though it was the sixth most active bank in 1979 and ultimately led $6.4 billion in Eurocredits between 1979 and 1982, 50 percent more than Dresdner Bank and 140 percent more than Commerzbank. According to Wilfried Guth, one of Deutsche Bank's two cospokesmen, "In the late 1960s and early 1970s, Mr. Abs, the chairman of the supervisory board, saw the Euromarket as very dangerous." So the bank entered with caution, yet with "no plan toward the Euromarkets. We just followed the demand."[19] In the early 1970s, Deutsche Bank participated in its first Eurocredit. Not until 1974 did it become an active leader, for a $600 million credit to finance a pipeline for the USSR. It next managed a $300 million loan to Mexico in 1975. After that, "Our Eurocredit business exploded. . . . We consciously sought Eurosyndications and managements then. We were invited by big U.S. banks to manage," said a senior officer. Deutsche Bank's slow entry here mirrored its cautious reentry into international banking in general after World War II.

Not Deutsche Bank but Dresdner Bank blazed the trail overseas for German banks after the war. "When we went abroad," said a Dresdner Bank senior vice-president, "we led the German banks. We were the first in Luxembourg, London, Singapore, Chicago, Los Angeles." In Luxembourg, for example, Dresdner's innovation in 1967 was to open Compagnie Luxembourgeiose de Bank, a wholly owned subsidiary that could even lend back to borrowers in Germany without subjecting the parent to the strict capital limits governing at home. Deutsche Bank and Commerzbank joined soon.[20] Not until 1976, however, did Deutsche Bank open a London branch. Its slow start affected even its commercial financing: an official of the bank estimated in 1980 that its share of the export finance market had fallen substantially from the 50 percent it held in 1965.

By the end of 1978, Deutsche Bank had caught and surpassed its two major competitors. Its 81 offices abroad exceeded Dresdner's 72 and Commerzbank's 66.[21] In a short space of time Deutsche became an international force, though the numbers somewhat exaggerate the German banks' foreign presence. Deutsche Bank was represented in forty-five countries, half of them developing, but often its interest was less than 10 percent or simply took the form of a representative office. Nevertheless, the bank now had the global network that would help it lead Eurocredit syndications.

19. Unless a source is otherwise given, the interviews quoted in this section took place in Frankfurt in September 1980 or May and June 1983, in Tokyo in October 1982 and May 1983, and in Mexico City in August 1982.

20. See Carol Parker, "The Lure of Luxembourg," *The Banker*, May 1977, p. 37.

21. Frederick Kempe, "Third Time Very, Very Lucky," *Euromoney*, February 1979, p. 79.

Deutsche Bank tied Eurocredit syndicates closely to German commerce. "Most of our international lending is commercially related, not financial," said a Deutsche Bank official. Other German bankers echoed him. At Commerzbank, a member of the managing board said, "The catalogue of priorities we have in this bank would list in first place helping our German customers finance their exports. Second, consideration would then be given to assisting non-German customers who export to other countries."[22] At Dresdner Bank, a country loan officer said, "We consider first the interest of the German client and German exports." His boss added, "A bank can easily fill its country limit to 75 percent with existing export finance or [project-related] credits with long lead times." The manager of one of the biggest American banks in Frankfurt concluded that "before a German bank gives away country risk in a syndicated loan, it will give it for trade credit." The syndicated loan to finance exports resolves the conflict.

The German bankers' focus on trade finance is more than just a convenient strategy; it reflects a state of mind very different from that of a banker from, for example, the United States. Speaking of a syndicate for the Quintette coal project in Canada,[23] a Deutsche Bank officer justified his bank's lead management on the basis that the project posed "no threat to German coal producers, since Ruhrkohl sets German coal prices." Twenty-five years earlier, Deutsche Bank's concern for home clients prompted it to open an office in Brazil after German firms complained that the German banks were late entering the country, despite the influx of German direct investment. Nor is this just a postwar phenomenon. At the turn of the century, the major German banks, including Deutsche Bank, followed their customers abroad. The move led them to, among other places, Eastern Europe, where eighty years later they concentrated their efforts.

Deutsche Bank and Dresdner Bank appear to share the opportunity and responsibility of lending to Eastern Europe. Dresdner led in Poland, where, for example, it "managed the last major Polish syndicated loan, an issue of more than $500 million, in December 1980."[24]

22. Wolfgang Jahn, cited in Harvey D. Shapiro, "German Banking Goes Back to Basics," *Institutional Investor* (International Edition), June 1981, p. 139.
23. See the discussion of Quintette in chapter 2.
24. Frederick Kempe, "Dresdner Bank Chief, after Weathering Loan Disasters, Faces Government Probe," *The Wall Street Journal*, January 18, 1983, p. 56.

Dresdner also led in the USSR, where it had "for all intents and purposes been the Soviet Union's German bank."[25] Deutsche led in Romania, East Germany, and Yugoslavia, as subsequent rescheduling showed. Their strong interests in Eastern Europe prompted them to return there several years after withdrawing from the syndication market. In November 1984, Deutsche Bank led a syndicate for the East German export-financing bank; initially set at $150 million, the loan was raised to $400 million as banks oversubscribed to the issue.[26] It is hard to imagine Deutsche Bank doing the same for Latin American borrowers.

Reticent at entry, Deutsche Bank led the German banks' pullback from syndications. Its strategic decision occurred about February 1981, perhaps earlier,[27] and by June 1981 the other big German banks had followed suit. They acted for several reasons. In part, simple business policy dictated the retreat. German banks needed to digest the fruits of their rapid expansion after 1976. Having sought volume growth, they now chose to emphasize profitability. Syndication alone did not offer the mix of yields provided by straight trade finance, namely, bid bonds, performance bonds, letters of credit, remittances, and foreign exchange, as well as the credit itself. But this explanation, standing on its own, glosses over the trouble the big banks faced at home.

In addition, the government urged retreat. As early as 1980 the Bundesbank urged the banks to change their growth policy. Its report "accused German banks of acting as if 'expansion is more important than profit.'"[28] The central bank was addressing the problems in Dresdner Bank and Commerzbank. Both had badly mismatched the maturities of their assets and liabilities. In 1977 and 1978, low interest rates attracted long-term borrowers but only short-term savers. Hav-

25. "German Banking: A Special Report," *Institutional Investor* (International Edition), July 1977, p. 68.

26. "East Germany Secures New $400 Million Loan from Western Bankers," *The Wall Street Journal*, November 26, 1984, p. 7.

27. Dr. Wilfried Guth said that as early as 1979 his bank was sensitive to the declining margins (Harvey D. Shapiro, "German Banking Goes Back to Basics," *Institutional Investor* [International Edition], June 1981, p. 139), but in February 1979 Hans-Otto Thierbach, a member of his managing board, said, "We are confident that there will be many opportunities for Deutsche Bank in international lending" in "the Third and Fourth World" (Kempe, "Third time").

28. Shapiro, "German Banking Goes Back to Basics."

ing financed long-term loans with short-term deposits, the banks got caught in a squeeze when interest rates rose in 1979. They were obliged to write down their bond portfolios to the lower of book or market.

Of the three, Commerzbank was most exposed, its mismatched portfolio reaching DM 25 billion, or almost $14 billion, "at the peak."[29] Dresdner Bank's misfortune extended further.[30] The poor performance of both banks forced them to cut dividends. Commerzbank paid none in 1980, 1981, or 1982. Dresdner, having paid dividends of DM 9 for each share with a nominal value of DM 50 in 1979, paid only DM 6 in 1980, and DM 4 in 1981 and 1982. During this time, Deutsche Bank raised its dividend from DM 10 in 1980 to DM 11 in 1982, on the same DM 50 share, turning the screws on its unfortunate rivals.

The three banks responded to the shocks at home with a remarkable cohesion that suggests the oligopoly's strength and support from the German government. All built reserves against bad debts, Deutsche Bank setting the pace. An example of their united front is that each decided its Luxembourg subsidiary would pay it no dividends but build provisions instead, and the government helped with this. Having encouraged the banks to raise provisions to as much as 40 percent in certain cases, the government allowed tax deductions for five years pending actual loss.[31] The weak banks also sold some of their shares in client firms.[32]

29. Stewart Fleming, "Operating Earnings Surge at Commerzbank," *Financial Times*, March 24, 1983, p. 21.

30. Beyond mismatching, it lost at gold trading (it had, for example, "bought 95 percent of a U.S. Treasury gold auction in August [1981] as gold prices were setting new records almost every day") and from more domestic bankruptcies than other German banks (Dresdner was AEG Telefunken's *hausbank*, for example). Kempe, "Dresdner Chief." Senior management problems plagued the bank from the mid-1970s. Terrorists killed its chief executive, Jurgen Pronto, in 1977. His replacement, Dr. Hans Friedrichs, a former economic minister, found his background in politics distanced him from the Frankfurt banking community. He ultimately resigned in 1984 during a political scandal.

31. See Stewart Fleming, "Commerzbank to Set Aside DM 500m Bad Debt Provisions," *Financial Times*, November 30, 1983.

32. The domestic shake-up of the early 1980s is a familiar pattern in German banking. To continue paying dividends in 1980–1983, Dresdner Bank sold large blocks of equity in such German firms as Metallgesellschaft, a major chemicals, metals, and transport firm, in Kaufhof, the second largest department store, and in Bilfinger und Berger, the construction group. See "Dresdner Bank's Shares

The German government saved the banks. As it eased interest rates, their fall created a profitable gap for the banks between the higher earning assets and the newly cheaper liabilities. The funding gap gave all three banks the earnings with which to fund provisions. In 1981, for example, a discount rate of 7.0 percent and a money market rate of 11.5 percent gave German banks a 4.5 percent spread. By 1983, Deutsche Bank claimed that its provisions extended to 20 to 40 percent of its loans to all endangered countries and 100 percent of those to Poland and Yugoslavia. The banks, having slowed their international lending early, kept their exposure in the troubled countries low, making it easier to reach this high rate of provisions.

Deutsche Bank's leadership in the retreat home is palpable, and its leadership at home is also apparent. Its vast deposit base gives it a major role in setting margins for the big banks. In March 1983, for example, its cospokesman, Dr. Wilhelm Christian, signaled the end of gapping that allowed the banks to increase their reserves.[33] The other banks do not march in lock step, but they move with care.[34] Their concern about Deutsche Bank's actions extends beyond Ger-

---

Rise as DM 4 Dividend is Announced," *Financial Times*, December 3, 1982, p. 21. The sales marked an important shift in Dresdner's industrial holdings. These interests trace back to the early days of industrialization and help explain the banks' close ties to German firms today. The banks' holdings arose from dislocations much more severe than those in the 1980s. When many companies collapsed in the depression of 1873, the banks took up their stock. Later, in the process of underwriting the issue of company stock, the banks also acquired substantial shares in major firms and placed representatives on the boards of directors. The companies themselves had supplied much of the savings deposited with the banks. That the buyers of Dresdner's interests in the early 1980s were from America and Africa rather than Germany may seem to suggest that the German cohesion is weakening. Deutsche, however, the most powerful bank, was not forced to sell. It is too soon to announce the demise of the German banks' industrial power.

33. See Stewart Fleming, "Deutsche Bank Trebles Provisions," *Financial Times*, March 31, 1983, p. 19.

34. One example occurred in 1981. Commerzbank's president, Walter Seipp, ignored Dr. Guth's public opposition and bought a quarter share in Philipp Holzmann, Germany's largest contractor, which Deutsche Bank controlled. Later, Seipp sold Deutsche Bank his bank's interest in a regional savings bank over which Guth had wanted to consolidate his control for a long time. See Darrell Delamaide, "Walter Seipp's Last Laugh," *Institutional Investor* (International Edition), October 1983, p. 83.

many's borders.[35] Leadership abroad is a function of leadership at home.

For international lending, the important question is the nature of Deutsche Bank's leadership: why it chose to follow others abroad but lead them back. The common explanation is that the bank had been badly burned by expropriations in the past.[36] Twice burned, thrice shy, perhaps, but since the other German banks were also twice burned, one must still ask why Deutsche Bank followed them abroad instead of leading. Part of the answer lies in Deutsche Bank's position as market leader at home, part in the bank's administrative structure.

As the dominant bank, Deutsche Bank acted like leaders in other concentrated industries by favoring the status quo.[37] Thus, it was cautious during the expansion. In the downturn, by raising its dividends, the bank took care to further entrench its own position, but it did not use its market power to endanger its competitors. Instead, Deutsche Bank helped return the industry to stability. In other industries, this is often called statesmanship when it is not called anticompetitive. In banking, people generally see stability as a public good.

The second explanation for Deutsche Bank's conservatism in international markets is its administrative structure. Unlike the other big German banks, Deutsche Bank is run by more than one chief executive officer. Its collective leadership builds in a consultative approach that reacts slowly to change. The practice of having two men speak for the managing board began in 1967, when Hermann J. Abs retired.

35. In November 1979, according to a senior officer, Dresdner decided margins were too narrow for it to participate in a jumbo loan to Brazil. "When we heard Deutsche Bank, as the Brazilian government's number one [German] bank, decided not to participate, the decision was easier for us."

36. In earlier eras, Deutsche Bank had led. In Brazil, it set up the German-American Bank as a subsidiary at the turn of the century, Dresdner Bank following with the Bank Deutsche Sudamerikanischer in 1906. Then came the First World War and Deutsche Bank lost its overseas network. During the 1930s, it established close links with the Nazi party, expanding fast to recover its dominant position in Eastern Europe. Instead, it lost its network again in World War II.

37. Although one might legitimately argue that the German financial sector is not concentrated because of the universal powers of the many different institutions, here I describe international lending, which the Big Three dominated. According to some estimates, they accounted for as much as two-thirds of international lending from Germany during the period under discussion.

Although there is obviously a hierarchy, the bank reinforces the notion of shared responsibility in several ways, some symbolic, others operational.[38] Given the decentralized organization that is predominately domestic, small wonder the bank's policies abroad were conservative.

Germany shaped its banks' leadership role in the market for Euro-syndication. Deutsche Bank emerged as a bank firmly grounded in the German market and a leader of the Big Three more dominant in 1985 than it seems to have been in 1975. The structure of the home financial system played an important role in Deutsche Bank's leadership. Using taxes and guidance, the German government helped its banks recover from their vulnerable position of 1979–1980, but expected them to be more cautious internationally. Given their ties to German firms, the banks were not inclined to stop supporting German exports. As a result, observers see few fundamental differences in the international strategies of the Big Three banks, although Deutsche Bank clearly implemented its strategy in a much more competent manner. The size of the German market and its declining profitability mean the Big Three will return to international lending more actively. When that happens, however, they probably will be no less tied to Germany than they have been in the past decade.

Here is a subtle and complex alliance among banks and their home governments. It is tacit, not explicit. It builds on the interests of all the players: the government's need for stability and concerns for Eastern Europe, the banks' need for growth and market share, and their shared interest in the export performance of German firms. It requires both sets of players to bear certain costs: the government and country through the monetary policy and the banks in their losses and retreat. The effect was to give German banks a position more secure than that of other banks as the debt crisis deepened in the mid-1980s.

---

38. Deutsche Bank lists the members of the managing board alphabetically. It makes each member responsible for business in one region of Germany, at least, as well as some broader function. As a result, no one member is responsible for all international business. It requires all board decisions to be unanimous. And only board members attend the meetings; a junior member takes the notes. See Jonathan Carr, "Deutsche Bank: The Art of Understatement" and "An Enviable Ability to Pick the Plums," *Financial Times*, July 15, 1985, and April 4, 1985, p. 23; "Changing the Guard at Deutsche Bank," *Institutional Investor* (International Edition), April 1985, p. 76; and John Tabliabue, "Tradition of Deutsche Bank," *New York Times*, April 18, 1983, p. D7.

Pricing of Eurosyndicates by German Banks

Coherent in geographic focus, and marked by similar retreat from the market, the Big Three German banks are almost alike in their pricing of syndicates. Even the difference is explained by their home country. Deutsche Bank and Commerzbank track one another in average pricing over several years. Dresdner Bank's pattern, unique among all lead banks studied, reflects its role in various reschedulings.

The statistics behind these conclusions are the spread and maturities of the loans the leaders syndicated. The data rank banks that led or co-led ten or more floating-rate loans, using the London interbank offered rate (LIBOR), in each of the years 1978, 1980, 1981, and 1982.[39] Each year *Euromoney* calculated the average weighted spread over LIBOR and the average maturity of loans made by each bank, and arrayed as many as one hundred banks against the average spread and maturity.[40] To trace the pricing by each bank as it evolved in relation to the twenty-seven others and to the average for all leaders, I reformulated the data.

By measuring the average spread and average maturity of each lead bank's loans during the year, I compare each bank to the group average and compare the bank's movement to the group average over four years (see Figure 5–5 for the basic matrix). I organize banks into four basic groups: banks that led loans with above-average spreads and below-average maturities; banks that led loans with both spreads and maturities above average; banks that led loans with below-average spreads but longer than average maturities; and banks that led syndicates whose loans carried lower spreads and shorter maturities than the average. The reader is cautioned not to draw conclusions about relative risk from these data;[41] the chart traces relative movement, not risk.

39. Data for 1979 were omitted, since many banks changed in the middle of the year as the second oil shock occurred and the change muddies conclusions about pricing for the whole year. Some banks did not lead ten or more syndicates in 1978 or in 1982.

40. *Euromoney* weighted the spreads according to the loan volume. See Nigel Bance, *Euromoney*, August 1979, p. 14; March 1981, p. 14; March 1982, p. 23; and April 1983, p. 25.

41. The data suggest characteristics of the borrowers but are too ambiguous to allow firm conclusions. Borrowers high and to the left in Quadrant I are probably high-risk borrowers, since they pay wide spreads for very short-term funds. The reverse might be true for those in Quadrant III, who may be blue-

FIGURE 5–5. The Spread-Maturity Matrix for Lead Banks

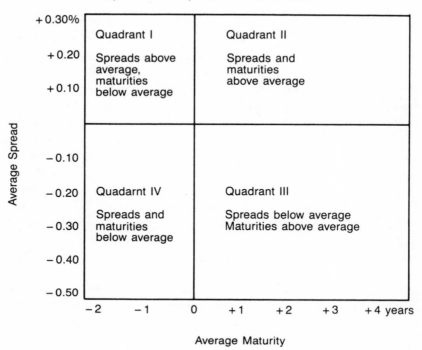

Consider a specific example (Figure 5–6). Deutsche Bank and Commerzbank began in 1978 with spreads[42] just below average and maturities barely one year past the mean. By 1980, after the second oil

chip firms or governments that pay less for above-average maturities. But they may also be the borrowers at least one rung below the blue chips, borrowers that more aggressive banks are introducing to the least costly part of the market. So one cannot be categorical even about borrowers in Quadrant III. Borrowers along a 45 degree line through the center may be of equal risk, since as the line rises, the higher spread would simply reflect the longer maturity.

42. Since the data show spreads but not fees, they do not report all the returns to the lead banks. Fees seem to vary directly with spreads, however, so the higher spreads probably also carry higher fees. Over hundreds of loans reported here, the weighted spreads probably show most banks correctly in relation to one another.

FIGURE 5–6. German Banks' Pricing:
Deutsche Bank (○) and Commerzbank (◇)

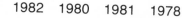

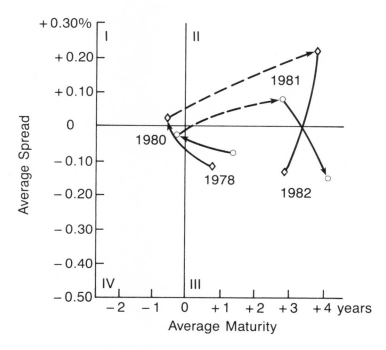

shock, both had shortened their maturities, as one would expect of banks in a crisis, and both sought spreads slightly higher than the average. More important, both moved closer to the average· for the year. In 1981, both had dramatically longer maturities against the average, and Commerzbank's spread dramatically increased. In 1982, both dropped back to smaller spreads but above-average maturities.

These two German banks moved in tandem over the four years. Further conclusions about common strategies must be guarded.[43] The

43. *Euromoney* labeled banks according to quadrant: those in I are panthers. Those in II are pioneers, presumably trailblazers who discover exotic new borrowers. In III are gunslingers, who "price aggressively over longer periods," and in IV are sheep. Although these labels are colorful, they oversimplify the banks' strategies in this market. "Tracking the Lead Banks: Who's Competing the Hardest?" *Euromoney*, August 1979, p. 14.

data show outcomes rather than intentions. They also show averages for regions, industries, prices, and maturities. For Deutsche Bank and Commerzbank, which had shifted back to Germany, a plausible story is that by 1982 they were both leading syndicates mainly for borrowers actively involved in buying from German firms or with some other German connection. The educated guess is that they were indeed focusing on the best borrowers, as they announced they would in 1980.[44] Dresdner Bank was different.

Dresdner Bank's unique path is explained by factors at home. Its shift (see Figure 5–7) from dead center in 1978 to very high spreads at slightly shorter maturities radically separates it from its Frankfurt

FIGURE 5–7. Dresdner Bank

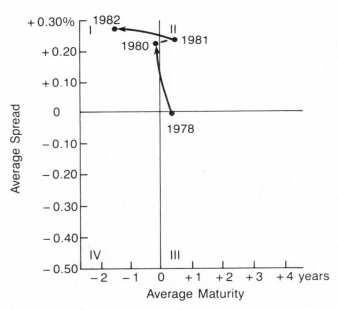

44. These data are averages. In individual transactions, such as leading syndicates for developing countries buying German exports, Germany's Big Three may have been quite aggressive.

200

confreres and, indeed, from the rest of the twenty-eight banks, none of which took this path. During this period, Dresdner Bank led the reschedulings for Eastern European countries such as Poland and for troubled German firms. Reschedulings often impose higher spreads and sometimes involve shorter than average maturities. Dresdner's role predates the massive reschedulings in Latin America and other developing countries after 1982, which would explain its different showing.

The Home Dynamic in Syndication

Grouped by home country, many of the other twenty-eight banks also show common patterns of pricing and geographic focus, such as the big banks from Japan, the United States, and the United Kingdom. Patterns common to banks from the same country suggest that forces at home shape the syndications. Here I seek only the common patterns. To discern possible reasons for similar patterns, I also speculate about the nature of the forces at work. Apparently the forces differ among the home countries. Japanese banks have converged in their pricing; regulatory forces appear to explain this. U.S. banks form distinct subgroups, but regulation seems less a direct cause here than in Japan. Instead, the banks' different positions in their home market seem to be the controlling factor. British banks vary in pricing and geographic emphasis, apparently a result of their history as British banks in the empire. This earlier role, which accounts for much of their international strategy, seems to affect syndication, too. Three patterns, two strong and one weak, are apparently explained by forces at home: direct regulation, market position, and early history.

Japanese Banks: Convergence from Wide Differences

In 1978, the four lead banks from Japan were more widely dispersed on prices than banks from any other home country (see Figure 5–8). Bank of Tokyo, the specialist in foreign-exchange transactions with a hundred-year history, had above-average spreads and maturities (Figure 5–9). The Industrial Bank of Japan, specializing in project finance,

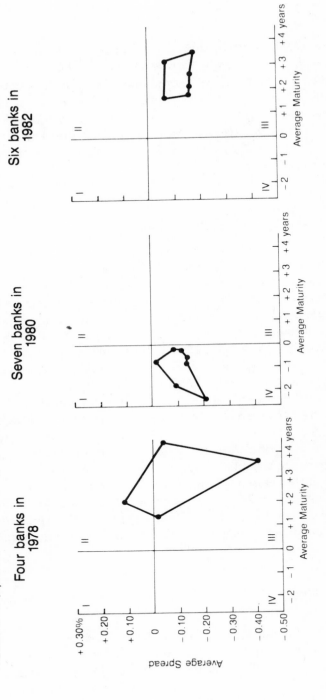

FIGURE 5–8. Japanese Banks: Pricing by Year

FIGURE 5–9. Specialized Banks

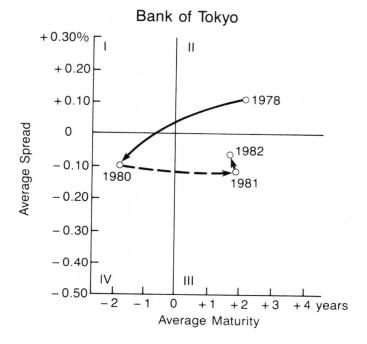

Bank of Tokyo

Industrial Bank of Japan

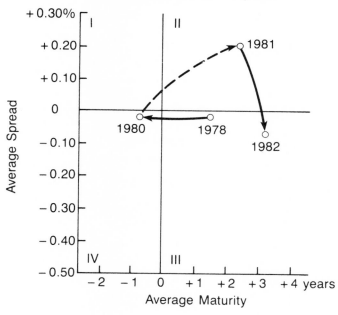

FIGURE 5–10. City Banks

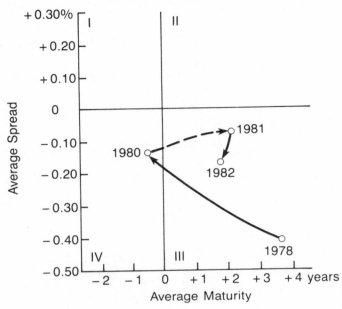

Sumitomo Bank

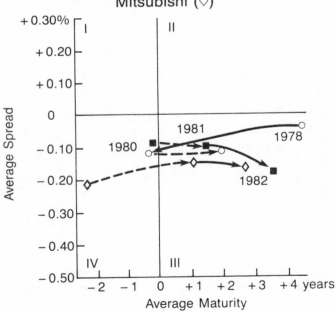

Dai-Ichi Kangyo (○), Fuji (■) Mitsubishi (◇)

was close to average. Dai-Ichi Kangyo Bank, the largest in Japan because of a merger in 1970, but a much smaller world player than Bank of Tokyo, showed average spreads for the longest maturities, while Sumitomo Bank was apparently earning its aggressive reputation by offering loans with the lowest spreads for very long maturities (Figure 5–10).

The cause of the early disparities seems to rest in the laws governing Japan's financial system. By law, two of the four banks have special functions. The disparity in pricing among them, and between them and the two city banks, is no more a surprise than the difference in geographic focus between the two groups of banks. The two specialized banks also focused their lending in Asia (see Figure 5–4). The city banks concentrated in Western Europe and OPEC.

By 1982, all Japanese banks[45] were leading loans with below-average spreads and above-average maturities.[46] Their action on spreads was remarkably consistent. In the four years recorded here, only twice was a Japanese bank above the average spread line, and these were the specialists, Bank of Tokyo and Industrial Bank of Japan, rather than the city banks. One way to interpret the data is that all Japanese banks were pricing aggressively compared to the average for all banks.[47] If this is accurate, it fits the banks' reputation in the Euromarkets for very competitive pricing.

The likely explanation for this trend is Japanese policy. During this period, the Finance Ministry restrained Japanese banks for two reasons. First, the 1979–1980 oil shock seemed to require that the banks reduce their cross-border exposure. Second, foreign banks and gov-

45. Fuji Bank and Mitsubishi Bank had joined the ranks of the top lead banks and DKB, always more domestically inclined, had retired. Of the 7 Japanese banks in the group of 28, only Sanwa Bank did not lead or co-lead at least 10 syndicates in any year.

46. During this period the Finance Ministry limited Japanese banks' participation in syndicates to 33 percent of the loan value, or 50 percent if the loan was led by Japanese banks. This ceiling became a target, since many non-Japanese syndicators would build their loan around a 33 percent block from Japan. To do so required getting one or more Japanese banks to arrange the Japan portion, so Japanese banks came to dominate the lists of managers and comanagers, as opposed to lead managers. The distinction is important for this chapter: Lead managers actively select borrowers, managers simply arrange participants.

47. Another interpretation is that all loaned to Japanese borrowers of good standing who were able to pay below-average spreads for above-average maturities.

ernments had begun to criticize Japanese banks for aggressive pricing. In 1982, all six banks were closer together than at any time in the past (Figure 5–8) and closer than any other banks grouped by home country. By comparison, the German (and French) banks moved further apart during this period, and the U.S. banks formed distinct groups.

U.S. Banks: Distinct Pricing Groups

There are three distinct pricing groups of U.S. banks. First, the Big Three—Citibank, Bank of America, and Chase Manhattan Bank—along with Morgan Guaranty Trust Company follow one pattern. This pattern is of tremendous significance for the syndication market because these four U.S. banks led 42 percent of the loans syndicated by the top twenty-eight banks. Their common pricing pattern, coupled with the New York banks' common focus on North America, set the tone for the market. All four began in 1978 with above-average spreads and maturities; all are known to have held out during this period against declining spreads. All then shift to below-average maturities in 1980, then again have above-average spreads and maturities, and then end with below-average spreads and above-average maturities (see Figure 5–11). None of the other twenty-eight banks follows this path.

Two other sets of U.S. banks are quite different. Bankers Trust Company and Chemical Bank begin with below-average spreads and above-average maturities. In 1980, both have a different relative mix of prices, only to return to their starting position by 1982 (see Figure 5–12). One possible interpretation is that they tested a different product mix after the second oil shock. This testing would fit their known efforts to change their lending strategies during this period.

In contrast to both other U.S. groups are the two Chicago banks, Continental Illinois Bank and First National Bank of Chicago. They sit on the borders. Only in 1982, when Continental Illinois was no longer a major lead bank, did First Chicago achieve above-average spreads and maturities. The pair is interesting on several counts. None of the other twenty-eight banks hugs the mean so closely for so long. As the two major banks in Chicago, both served similar markets there. Their common pricing pattern suggests that as their environment shifted, the two shadowed each other's moves around the norm. Yet

FIGURE 5-11. Citibank (◇), Bank of America (■), Chase (☆), Morgan (○)

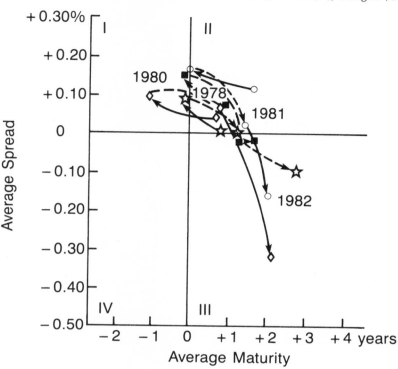

they had very different geographic focuses (see Figure 5–4) and they had different reputations in the syndication markets.[48] We can tentatively reconcile the conflict: under pressure at home during this period, senior officers in both banks set a course that limited the options of the London syndicate managers.[49] Rather than oligopolists matching one another's moves, both were subject to similar pressures in part because of their common home base.

In sum, there are three groups with distinct pricing patterns among the nine U.S. banks. Only Manufacturers Hanover is in a league by

48. Interviews, London, November 1985.
49. Interviews in London in November 1985 support this interpretation.

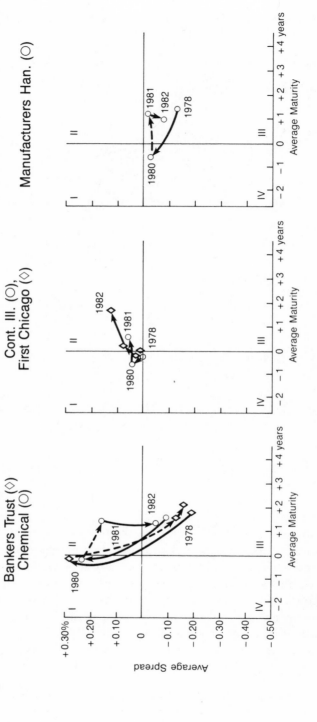

FIGURE 5-12.

itself (Figure 5–12).[50] These banks offer a strong contrast with the Japanese banks' pattern of convergence.

U.K. Banks: Diversity Abroad from a Historical Role

Common patterns are less discernible among the U.K. banks. It is true that three of the five U.K. banks priced their loans in a similar pattern over the four years (Figure 5–13). The geographic patterns, however, are less strong; while three British banks concentrated on Western Europe, two focused on OPEC and one focused more on North America. The other two banks emphasized Pacific Asia and OPEC.

The roles of the banks in the British financial system may explain the diversity in both measures. This explanation is clearest for Standard Chartered Bank, the only one that runs counter to the national pattern in pricing. In 1978, Standard appears to have priced very conservatively with short maturities and low spreads; then as most other banks reduced their maturities during the early years after the second oil shock, Standard took longer though still below-average maturities. Only in 1981 and 1982 did Standard join the others in having below-average spreads and above-average maturities.

By origin an overseas bank, Standard traces its early history to Africa, notably South Africa, and through the Chartered Bank to Asia. Never part of the inner circle in London, Standard continues to operate predominately abroad. It is scarcely surprising that its pricing behavior should differ from that of the others and that its geographic focus should be the developing countries. Standard Chartered is also the only one of the five that is not one of the key clearing banks.

Three of the clearers—Lloyds, Midland, and NatWest—showed similar pricing patterns. They dominated British syndicates: from 1979 through 1982, Lloyds and NatWest led 60 percent of the U.K. loans and Midland led 14 percent. Clearers differ from other British financial institutions in their nationwide branch systems, administration of "the national payments system by clearing cheques," and retail

---

50. Its consistent near or below average spread and minimal shifts despite the big changes in the world economy from 1978 to 1982 distinguish it from the other groups of U.S. banks.

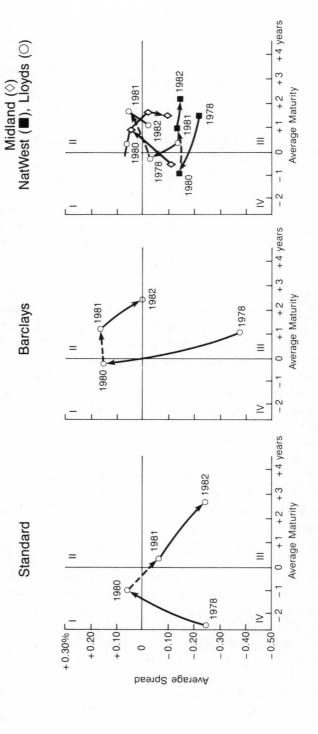

FIGURE 5-13.

banking.[51] Theirs is a long history of cooperation as clearers at home and diversity abroad. Lloyds Bank, for example, prospered alone in Latin America for over a century. During these four years, Lloyds had the reputation of being the strongest British lead manager, more aggressive and better represented among big borrowers in Latin America and Asia. It is small wonder that Lloyds focused its syndications on Latin America and other developing countries (see Figure 5–4). NatWest and Midland were newcomers that expanded their role during the period, hence their different geographic focus.

The fourth clearer, however, resembles banks from the United States, not the United Kingdom, hinting of a transnational group. Barclays Bank, responsible for 18 percent of the U.K. leads, followed a pricing circuit similar in direction to the others, but with so much more apparent movement on spreads that Barclays seems to have behaved like Bankers Trust and Chemical. In geographic focus, despite its colonial network, Barclays led more to Western Europe, like the newcomers.

In sum, there are common patterns among banks from the same country that distinguish them from banks from other countries. The apparent causes stem from the structure of the home financial system: the legal framework in Japan, the big banks' dominance in U.S. commercial and industrial loans, the regional markets in the United States, and the specialization that arose from Britain's colonial history. Not every bank's performance can be explained in this way. Barclays Bank is an example. Nor are these factors the only ones at work. A detailed review of French banks emphasizes the importance of bureaucratic politics.

The French Banks: Market Rivalry and Bureaucratic Politics

The French banks are a study in contrasts with the German. In pricing and geographic focus, the French banks are much more diverse than the German, though the reverse might seem more likely. All French roads lead to Paris: the government owns the banks. In Germany, the links between the banks in Frankfurt and the government in Bonn are much less formal.

51. Economists Advisory Group, *The British and German Banking System* (London: Anglo-German Foundation, 1981), p. 9.

Among the French banks there are two areas of geographic focus and a single direction in pricing. Credit Lyonnais and Paribas emphasize Western Europe and OPEC, while BNP and Société Générale emphasize Eastern Europe and OPEC (see Figure 5–4). All four followed the same path in pricing over the four years (Figure 5–14). In 1978, all but Paribas (which is absent that year) had below-average spreads and above-average maturities. All shift to average maturities or below in 1980, then lengthen their spreads and maturities in 1981. All reduce spreads while maintaining above-average maturities in 1982 (when Société Générale drops out). As a group of banks from the same country, the French banks distinguish themselves by their pattern from both the distinct shifts of the U.S. banks and the convergence of the Japanese banks.

The French banks' syndication strategies differed. The pricing patterns are an example. Although the banks moved in similar directions, each bank's positions are indeed different. Part of the reason is the nature of competition in France. Though state owned and presumably subject to the same guidance, these banks must try to differentiate themselves from each other for competitive purposes at home. Considering the range of alternatives, such as that of the Chicago banks or the Bank of Tokyo, the differences are modest.

More is at work than simple market forces at home, however. Precisely because they are state owned, their syndication strategies reflect the government impact in two ways. The first is commonly noted: the French banks are part of their government's national strategy. The second is more subtle, informal, and often missed: as part of a vast bureaucracy, French bankers must adjust even their syndication activities to the demands of complex bureaucratic politics. I turn now to a closer look at the second impact.

Maurice Armand guided Credit Lyonnais's syndication unit to become the fifth largest among those of the twenty-eight banks in 1980; it had been in the top ten the year before. The contrast with the other French banks, all of which together led less than Credit Lyonnais in 1979, is striking.[52] Armand's unit gained an international stature that

52. Many reasons prompt one to expect basic similarity, at least among France's Big Three banks. After all, they have had the same shareholder since 1946 when they were nationalized. The government used them, as part of the commanding heights of the economy, to channel savings to priority industries. Following reforms in 1966 to open the banking system, the three competed more

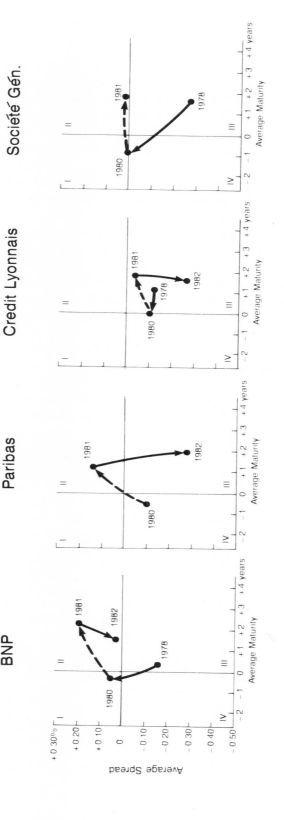

FIGURE 5–14.

eclipsed the others. Credit Lyonnais's high early rank as a syndicator rested naturally on the shoulders of a bank that had been preeminent worldwide before 1914.[53] In the 1960s, it had set out to regain its lost standing.[54] Moving faster than its home competitors, by the end of the decade Credit Lyonnais had set in place the most complete and prestigious international network of all French banks.[55]

After mid-1981, Credit Lyonnais ceded its high standing by choice. A continuing stop-go approach to policy afflicted the bank because of entrenched internal interests and the short terms of its presidents. Beginning in the 1960s, first one chief executive and then another in rapid succession attacked but failed to end bureaucratic infighting that split the bank. In 1967, Marcel Wiriath gave Charles de Gaulle his resignation as president of the bank after failing to resolve deep conflicts between his most senior aides. François Bloch-Laine, a senior civil servant, replaced Wiriath but left in 1974 after failing to change Credit Lyonnais' strategy or to reorganize the bank and trim its staff. Jacques Chaine was president for barely two years before he was assassinated. His successor, Claude Pierre-Brossolette, previously the *chef du cabinet* of President Giscard, let Maurice Armand's unit flourish and resumed Bloch-Laine's policy of staff reductions to cut costs. But Pierre-Brossolette survived only six months beyond his mentor's defeat at the polls by the Socialists. This time the French president

---

actively at home, but the national bureaucracy in Paris continued to play a key role. The new Socialist government, after June 1981, politicized the banks still more at home. All this suggests the Big Three march to the beat of the same drum. Banque Paribas, or Banque de Paris et des Pays-Bas as it was earlier known, was not nationalized until 1981. A *banque d'affaires*, it operated under different statutory authority until 1966, and afterward it continued to act as an investment bank.

53. During the reign of Napoleon III, it had opened its first foreign branches, in Spain, Egypt, Switzerland, and the United Kingdom. Vivian Lewis, "France's Nationalized Banks—A Whiff of Re-privatisation," *The Banker*, July 1980, pp. 43, 45. It then lost many loans in the USSR after 1917, failed to grow between the wars, and gave up much of its foreign network after World War II to finance domestic French needs.

54. Unless otherwise noted, the quotations are from interviews in France and with French bankers abroad. The interviews took place in Paris in 1980, 1982, and 1983; in London in 1982; in New York after 1978; in San Francisco in 1983; in Tokyo in 1983; and in Mexico City in 1982.

55. Pierre Beaudeux, "Le match des banques nationalisées," *L'Expansion*, May 23–June 5, 1980, p. 109.

appointed someone from within Credit Lyonnais as its president. Jean Deflassieux, previously responsible for the bank's international operations, took over in February 1982, though his star had been rising since the mid-1981 elections. Close to new Prime Minister Pierre Mauroy, Deflassieux had been a member of the Socialists' steering committee for economic and banking policies before Mitterrand took office. Deflassieux halted Armand's activities.[56]

Armand and Deflassieux came from different traditions in Credit Lyonnais, though both were international bankers. Armand had built his syndication unit on what many bankers call pure financial lending, loans independent of trade. Under him, Credit Lyonnais won its reputation as "the most aggressive continental bank in the Eurocurrency market." As one reporter said at the time, "There is no country where they are not making their weight felt."[57] Armand rapidly built the bank's Eurocredit portfolio, which by 1980 amounted to about $5 to $6 billion. This helped the bank increase net profits 60 percent and assets 22 percent in 1980. Since lending in foreign currencies in France was outside the limits on domestic credit, it alone grew 68 percent in 1980.[58]

Deflassieux rose through another wing of the strife-ridden bank's bureaucracy. He had been in charge of the bank's international commercial loans, then, as head of the international division, Armand's boss. Mostly in francs, the commercial loans came to four or five times Armand's financial portfolio. Their weight reflects the Giscard government's use of credit to promote trade. When Mitterrand took office, however, the government's policy swung inward. Deflassieux became "an opponent of some of the more exuberant Lyonnais Eurobankers. [He purged] the international finance department . . . [and] cut back its own lead management."[59] Credit Lyonnais pulled back as the market boomed in 1981 and early 1982, when the twenty-eight banks led loans of $105 and $71 billion, up from $40 billion in 1980

---

56. See ibid., and David Marsh, "The Practical Dilemma of a French Socialist Banker," *Financial Times*, April 6, 1984, p. 2.

57. Ellen Pearlman, "Overreaching in Paris," *Institutional Investor* (International Edition), May 1981, p. 47.

58. David White, "Credit Lyonnais Profits up 60% Despite Controls," *Financial Times*, April 3, 1981, p. 21.

59. Vivian Lewis, "France's Big Three: A Sudden Burst of Youthful Activity," *The Banker*, June 1984, p. 45. Armand's illness during this period temporarily removed him from the fray.

and $56 billion in 1979. As Paribas and BNP took part in this general expansion, Credit Lyonnais reduced its loans from about $2.3 billion in 1979 and 1980 to $2.0 billion in 1981 and $1.2 billion in 1982.

Bureaucratic politics using national strategy as a cover shortened Armand's career as a syndicator. Deflassieux argued that the bank's place in the financial world was at stake. He called for the bank to retrench, raising its reserves against the extravagances of the past. In 1982, he allowed profits to fall 34 percent so reserves on loans to problem countries could triple.[60] Citing an urgent need to strengthen the bank's balance sheet, Deflassieux told the banking world, "What I am seeking for my successor is for the bank to survive."[61] Credit Lyonnais had chronic problems, but since the French government stands behind the bank, Deflassieux's words seem to ring with hyperbole. True, when the new Socialist government fueled the French economy, it relied on the banks to help finance the expansion by raising funds abroad. Credit Lyonnais's international standing was important for the country, but it is not obvious that the relatively small share of its assets devoted to pure financial loans was a lethal threat. Moreover, Credit Lyonnais's leading emphasized Western Europe, not the area of great danger. Indeed, as Credit Lyonnais cut back on its Eurosyndications, other French banks raised theirs, hardly what one would expect if the French government wanted to reduce nonessential dollar lending by its big banks.

In Credit Lyonnais's strategic change, bureaucratic politics in the bank dovetailed with national strategy. Armand was vulnerable precisely because the pure financial loans he led were not obviously linked to French commerce. The conditions that permitted Deflassieux to end Armand's role and slow the bank's syndications existed because of the way the French financial system works: the stop-go policies were endemic to a bank whose chief executive was changed often, usually by the nation's president.

BNP surpassed Credit Lyonnais in syndicates in 1982. Gerard Prache, Armand's counterpart at BNP, actively marketed the bank's services worldwide, building its syndications steadily from $338 million in 1979 to $1.7 billion in 1981, then easing slightly to $1.2 billion

60. "Credit Lyonnais," *International Bank Report*, Vol. 16, No. 7, April 13, 1984, p. 107, and "Credit Lyonnais Lifts Profits after Increasing Write-offs," *Financial Times*, April 6, 1984, p. 1.
61. Lewis, "France's Big Three."

in 1982. His fierce rivalry with Credit Lyonnais was part of a broader goal set by BNP's first president, to catch and surpass France's historical international leader. In his market, Prache succeeded.

BNP's ambition and success grew out of its nativity. The bank was formed in 1966 when two banks merged, one a "grand bank, with a British style that was aristocratic and international and with very distinguished but not very profitable ties with large, old firms," and the other "a bank whose directors were not invited to the old established clubs and whose clientele was medium-sized business."[62] The merger forced BNP's managers to consolidate; in so doing, they overcame the bureaucratic inertia of Credit Lyonnais. The merger forced BNP to work harder for the business of French firms; some of the larger firms were not prepared to let the new bank alone have, for example, the 35 percent of their business that would result by adding the shares of the two predecessors. The new bank benefited from a continuity in leadership that eluded Credit Lyonnais. The BNP director general in 1966, Pierre Ledoux, became its president in 1971. Jacques Calvet replaced him and was in turn replaced by Réné Thomas in 1982, a twenty-five-year veteran of the bank.

President Ledoux decided that BNP would be a universal bank and set out to master the Eurocurrency market. His need to invest, and high administrative expenses precluded a low-cost strategy. His strategy led BNP beyond operations common to the Big Three, to commodity finance, for example. It prompted BNP to buy Bank of the West, entering the California market in 1980 through this small bank active in high-technology finance. In the early 1980s, BNP began to emphasize profitability more than in the past, setting return-on-investment targets within the bank. The overall strategy appears to have paid off: alone among the Big Three, BNP was able to show rising net after-tax profits after Mitterrand took office.[63] That the banks fix their profits by negotiating with the government qualifies this achievement, however.

Part of the BNP strategy was to be everywhere, unlike its rivals in France. According to Calvet, "We do not wish to be everywhere . . . we are everywhere."[64] Its global network did surpass Credit Lyonnais's in 1976, though BNP actually favored English-speaking mar-

62. Beaudeux, "Le match des banques," p. 109.
63. Lewis, "France's Big Three."
64. Beaudeux, "Le match des banques."

kets, such as New York, California, Australia (where it had gone to finance the wool imported by northern France almost one hundred years earlier), Hong Kong and Singapore in Southeast Asia, and Nigeria in black Africa. Credit Lyonnais was stronger in Europe, including Spain, and in parts of Latin America. In Brazil, only Lyonnais had a subsidiary with local branches when the country closed its doors to new foreign commercial banks in 1963. Société Générale had been strong in Germany since before World War I and in the Mideast, where it was second only to the French investment banks. Clearly the Big Three differentiate themselves internationally, like British banks, by their geographic presence.

This differentiation by network carries over, in part, to the French banks' syndications. BNP's stated go-everywhere policy fits its interest in many regions: OPEC, Eastern Europe, Asia, and developing countries. Only BNP emphasizes syndicates in Asia, where it alone had a network before 1976. Société Générale's position in the Mideast coincides with its emphasis on OPEC syndicates, whereas its ties with Germany and Russia dating back to the nineteenth century help explain its emphasis on Eastern Europe. Credit Lyonnais, with a stronger European network, emphasizes syndicates in Western Europe far more than in any other region. The regional congruence of network and syndicates is not, however, universal. All four banks are weak in North America, where even BNP's superior network helped little against the American giants.

For the French banks (and, I argue, banks from other countries), the syndication strategies primarily reflect their broader rivalry with other banks from their home country. In the words of one of the Big Three syndicators, "We only compete with French banks." In practice, this means they compete for French business. The French banks' foreign networks are integral to their broader rivalry. Each network, by focusing on a distinct part of the world, differentiates its bank from other French banks. The syndicators use a similar regional approach. By building on the networks and by otherwise focusing on different regions, the syndicator differentiates his bank from other French banks, as opposed to banks from other countries.

The Big Three French banks had three different strategies for international credit. BNP chose to compete in all product and geographic markets as a universal bank (relative to other French banks). Riven by factions and without effective leadership, Credit Lyonnais lacked clear direction over the long term. Société Générale adopted a third approach in the mid-1970s, a low-cost strategy that accepted higher risk in order to allow the bank to pass BNP while achieving profitability above the average for French banks. At home, Sogen was more efficient than the other two, while focusing on major industrial clients. Abroad, syndication fit Sogen's strategy well. Syndication keeps costs low, since a small staff can manage billions of dollars in this wholesale market. Even when margins are thin, it allows the bank to build assets.

The Big Three compete on assets, measuring their relative performance by asset growth rather than earnings. The opportunity for greater profitability comes in the attitude toward risk. Sogen accepted higher risk in its choice of borrowers and in its decision to act more like an underwriter than a mere leader of Eurocredit syndicates. From 1979 to 1982, at least, the bank emphasized borrowers in the riskier regions—Eastern Europe, OPEC, and developing countries outside Asia. The bank went beyond most lead banks, who normally promised to make their best effort to find participating banks but accepted no obligation to advance the credit themselves if others did not come forward. Sogen, which led the Big Three in managing Eurobond issues, said it made "firm commitments for large amounts. . . . We are willing to buy paper for ourselves because the new-issue business has become an integral part of running and refinancing your own portfolio. It's a totally new concept. . . . The key is reciprocity. . . . When you do three, five, or ten *lead* managements, you get invited afterwards."[65] Such a policy can turn sticky if buyers do not appear.[66]

Sogen could implement this strategy because, more than either of the other banks, it had continuous leadership. Maurice Laure held sway first as general manager and then as president, from 1967 to 1981. He revitalized Sogen, gradually centralizing power in his own office, turning to computers to track hundreds of profit centers (215 in 1980).[67] Laure first attacked the domestic side, until 1973, then turned to the international fiefdoms in Treasury and Foreign Exchange. Having set up a Eurocredit department in 1972, he merged

65. David Cudaback, "Thunder out of Paris," *Institutional Investor* (International Edition), May 1980, p. 99.

66. For example, when Sogen's president on a visit to Mexico is reported to have personally promised the government that his bank would lead a $500 million syndicate, only to learn that the other French banks would not come in, Sogen had to pick up the entire loan itself. Interview, Paris, 1983.

67. Beaudeux, "Le match des banques," p. 109.

it with the Eurobond operation in 1976. The new International Finance Department joined a sister unit for international commercial credit to form an international division like that at Credit Lyonnais. Its first chief lasted barely two years, but his successor, Bernard Lorain, whose father once chaired Sogen, stayed in office from December 1978 on. His unit had moderate independence, being empowered to make loans up to $50 million. It led $2.8 billion during 1979 and 1980, making Sogen second in leaderships only to Credit Lyonnais ($4.5 billion), but its International Finance Department was not caught up in a revulsion against Eurocredits, as was Armand's at Lyonnais. Lorain himself survived the transition to a new president in 1981, when Jacques Mayoux took office. As Mayoux shifted Sogen more toward investment banking, Eurocredit syndications fell off, down from $1.5 billion in 1980 to only $0.9 billion in 1982.

Among the French Big Three, the impact of the government seems remarkably indirect, and yet also bureaucratic. As seen in chapter 4, home strategy is effected largely by manipulating the market, providing incentives for the banks with devices like the discounted refinancing of export credits. Even Mitterrand, whose government actively intervened in individual decisions at home, left the big banks independent of government directive in international markets in order to strengthen their position in those markets. Many government committees continued to be involved in international matters that affected the banks, but they tended to play a role when a specific state interest—such as credit to promote exports—was involved.

Though indirect, government influence permeates the big banks' own senior and middle management. Here is the source of the bank-government alliance. A French banker, speaking of Eurosyndications, said, "Ours is a *people* business. The difference between banks comes down to one or two men, whether its Armand at the Lyonnais, Prache at BNP, Hass and Brunet at Paribas."[68] In one form or another, many of the individuals who lead the banks came from an official post. Many trained in the Finance Ministry as *inspecteurs de finance*. They include Sogen's long-lived chairman, Maurice Laure, his general manager, Marc Vienot, and successor, Jacques Mayoux. Paribas's chairman from 1970 to 1978, Jacques de Fouchier, began his career as an *inspecteur*, as did BNP's René Thomas. If they arrived at the top of the bank's management, it was a reward for even more august careers

68. Cudaback, "Thunder."

in government. Laure had been director of Credit National, and Mayoux, while heading Credit Agricole earlier, helped Prime Minister Barre frame a program of bank reform. At Credit Lyonnais, François Bloch-Laine had been a civil servant, Claude Pierre-Brossolette was Giscard's *chef du cabinet*, and Jean Deflassieux, though a Lyonnais careerist, was a senior adviser to the Socialist shadow cabinet. At BNP, Jacques Wahl, the head of international, had been France's executive director to the IMF and World Bank, then another of Giscard's chiefs of staff. In fact, one person reported that among the top commercial banks and Credit Agricole during Giscard's tenure, the chief executives of all but one had been in Giscard's cabinet or with him when he was finance minister. The practice was not limited to the Big Three. Paribas's CEO from 1978 to 1981, Pierre Moussa, was assistant to Premier Mendès-France's minister of overseas territories, and then to President de Gaulle's minister of public works and transport, before heading the World Bank's Africa department. Moussa's successor, Jean-Yves Haberer, came direct from the Trésor, the most prestigious unit in the Finance Ministry.

In sum, two important factors in the syndication strategies of the French banks turn out to be rivalry among the Big Three and bureaucratic politics within the banks. The rivalry at home extends abroad; witness the efforts by Sogen to catch up with BNP as BNP tries to catch up with Lyonnais. The Big Three measure their success against the needs of their shareholders, of course, and against each other. Nothing suggests their competition with non-French banks is irrelevant, but it is distinctly secondary. This phenomenon is not unique to France, but the specifics are, and the French financial system accounts for them. The syndication strategies go back to 1967, just after France got a new banking law and the Big Three appeared with new management. A change in syndication strategy that affected the entire market, notably, dropping Armand, occurred as part of a new CEO's effort to get control of his bank. That CEO took office because of French government policy.

The importance of bureaucratic politics is vividly illustrated by the Armand-Deflassieux encounter, but it extends far beyond individual personalities. A porous boundary between government and the senior management of the banks allows the politics of French officialdom to seep into the banks. Bureaucratic politics is common to all large organizations, of course, and the practice of moving from government to senior bank management, though most pronounced in France, exists in Japan, the United Kingdom, and even Germany, where Dresdner Bank's chairman was formerly a cabinet member. Despite the government's ownership of French banks, France emerges not as unique but as simply further along the same spectrum.

Conclusion

Lead banks in the Eurosyndication market would seem to be relatively independent of their home country. The market is international; the home government and major firms have only a qualified interest in the market's activities. Such a view is mistaken.

The home exerts an influence even in such a market. Evidence of home influence abounds at two levels of analysis. At the aggregate level, one finds distinct geographic thrusts for each home country and common pricing patterns among banks from the same country. At the bank level, one finds that the evolving strategies of German and French banks reinforce the home's potency in this supposedly global market.

Other forces than the home are at work, of course. The pricing of the twenty-eight banks also reveals the role of integrating market forces. First, not all banks from the same home country behaved the same way. Second, all but four of the twenty-eight banks described a clockwise shift over the years. Third, several patterns were similar for banks from different countries, suggesting transnational groups. One group would be four banks that appear to have experimented. In response to conditions after the oil shock of 1979–1980, Bankers Trust Company, Chemical Bank, the Banque Nationale de Paris (BNP), and Barclays Bank made radical shifts from below-average to above-average spreads. A second group would include four that specialize in merchant banking: the Industrial Bank of Japan, Banque Paribas, and the two German banks, Deutsche Bank and Commerzbank, all of which have similar pricing patterns. This second group suggests that banks that, like merchant banks, have similar special powers or functions follow similar pricing policies even though they are from different countries. A third transnational group would be narrower. Two banks with reputations for being aggressive in the late 1970s—Sumitomo Bank and Credit Lyonnais—moved dramatically but stayed entirely where one would expect to find aggressive banks. Despite these three groups, however, a comparison of banks by home country seems to explain much of the banks' pricing behavior.

Certain important differences that are related to the banks' country of origin suggest durable national forces. Each year banks from the same home country tended to cluster, the most pronounced cluster being among Japanese banks. The patterns differed among countries. U.S. banks priced in stark contrast to those based in France and Japan. Over time, the Japanese converged. All French banks followed a similar circuit. Even British banks moved together. Competitors in the same group at home seem to follow similar pricing policies in syndicating loans. Three of the four British clearers, the top four banks in the United States, the two Chicago banks, and two of the Big Three German banks priced in ways that were remarkably similar within the group but distinct in comparison with other banks. The city banks from Japan, though following somewhat different paths, never ventured into above-average pricing. Within individual countries, distinct groups formed and common shifts occurred.

In chapter 4 I described two ways to understand the relations of big banks and their home governments. In the liberal view, MNCs are relatively independent; in the mercantilist, they are subject to their home government. Each of these traditional views was flawed when applied to the banks. The relation was more complex than simple independence or hierarchy. Mutually reinforcing interests opened the possibility that both could work as allies. This chapter bears out that view.

Even when banks lead Eurosyndications, an activity that in the abstract would seem to allow independence, the home is potent. Although banks' portfolios are secret, data describing their geographic focus and pricing trends undermine the liberal view. Yet the accounts of the German and French banks' Eurosyndication strategies undermined the simple mercantilist view. The structure of each home banking system played a major role in the banks' strategic decisions. In Germany, the oligopolists matched each other's moves. In France, bureaucratic politics shaped the banks' senior management, who framed strategy in the Eurosyndication market. Still, both home governments played an important role directly and indirectly. Germany's government publicly encouraged banks to withdraw from the market and used its interest rate policy to ease the pressure on the banks so they could build reserves. France's government used personal ties among senior bankers and civil servants, as well as the systemic policies described in chapters 2 and 4. The two governments acted not because the banks forced them but in their own interests.

The syndication market was a cornerstone of international banking during the 1970s. Its sheer volume, $520 billion between 1979 and 1982, and its rapid growth drew the attention of many. It attracted hundreds of banks, some would say like moths, given the aftermath. There is a tendency to condemn the banks for this gush of credit, much to developing countries that could neither absorb the funds nor generate foreign exchange to repay. The banks bear responsibility, but are not alone. It should be clear, in addition, that even as the lead banks formed syndicates, they acted in an environment in which forces from their own home country helped shape their choices. It is small wonder that when the crises came, the banks turned to their homes for help. The process of alliances at work on national level at the time of initial lending was at work in the crisis. The economic nationalism that had helped guide banks' loans to developing countries persisted as problems arose.

6

When the Buck Stopped:
The 1982–1983 Collapse

Mexico broke the back of lending to developing countries. Announcing in August 1982 that it could not service its debt, it was soon joined by many other countries. By October 1983, twenty-seven countries had rescheduled their debt to banks or were in the process of doing so, and more did so thereafter.[1] These twenty-seven countries owed banks $239 billion.[2] Sixteen of these countries were Latin American; the four largest, Mexico, Brazil, Venezuela, and Argentina, owed banks $176 billion, or 74 percent of the total. These same four owed the nine largest U.S. banks alone $39 billion, or 130 percent of the banks' total capital.[3] Salomon Brothers understated the case when it said earlier in 1983 that "an intensive case of the jitters has pervaded the $2 trillion Eurocurrency market."[4]

Hundreds of banks faced the prospect of default. A small number of big banks had led the rest into this predicament. Why had the others chosen to follow? They knew little about the borrowers from direct experience. Instead, they had relied on the lead banks, who

1. E. Brau and R. C. Williams, "Recent Multilateral Debt Restructurings with Official and Bank Creditors," International Monetary Fund Occasional Paper No. 25, December 1983, Table 11, p. 30.

2. Ibid., Table 6, p. 11.

3. Thomas H. Hanley et al., *A Review of Bank Performance: 1984 Edition* (New York: Salomon Brothers, 1984), Figure 45, p. 70. The nine largest banks are those studied in chapter 5 (see the Appendix).

4. Thomas H. Hanley et al., *A Review of Bank Performance: 1983 Edition* (New York: Salomon Brothers, 1983), p. 6.

had rejected any responsibility for information about the borrower. By failing to agree as a practical matter about this responsibility, banks failed to allocate risk clearly. This increased the instability in lending. Banks resolved the immediate problem by falling back on relationships at home. The solution reflects another form of alliance built around the home, the alliance between big bank and small bank from the same country.

Banks, their home governments, and the borrowers laid the groundwork for the crisis over the previous decade. The proximate cause of the crisis is another matter. In this chapter I add to the conventional analysis of immediate causes another factor: instability in the dominant form of intermediation, the syndicate. Mexico, the precipitating case, was one of the major syndicated borrowers. Banks' exposure there was exceptional, for reasons examined in the last part of this chapter.

The Conventional Reasons for the 1982–1983 Debt Crisis

Each major group gets some credit for the 1982–1983 debt crisis. In the debate about responsibility that often ends by assigning blame, the stakes are high. At heart this is a debate over who is to bear what may be a monumental cost.

Most observers round up the usual suspects: the borrowers, the banks, and the major industrial governments. The borrowers mismanaged the resources made available by credit that was not abnormally large by historic standards.[5] They were thus vulnerable to unexpected external shocks. The banks loaned for the many causes—from macroeconomic to interbank competition—described in earlier chapters. The banks believed they did not need to monitor the effect of their lending on each borrowing country because they understood the system: since all major sources were party to the loans, the borrower would have no choice other than to comply with the terms of the agreement. If a borrower chose not to honor its commitments, it could turn to no other source for funds. As the later shocks hit the borrowers, however, the banks contracted liquidity just as borrowers needed more. The policy of the G-5 governments helped create the shocks.

5. See World Bank, *World Development Report, 1985* (New York: Oxford University Press, 1985).

"This whole debt crisis business could have been avoided if the Treasury had been doing its job," a New York lawyer said.[6] In this view, if the secretary of the treasury, Donald Regan, had listened to warnings from his staff as well as from the Mexican finance minister, the United States could have acted sooner and averted the crisis by helping Mexico through a period of illiquidity. With Mexico liquid, the conflagration would not have spread. Few others blame a single person for the 1982–1983 debt crisis. Certainly the U.S. government's failure went beyond individuals like Secretary Regan. Government has had, since at least 1960, an ad hoc approach to foreign economic policy that scuttles preventive action.[7] Until the crisis loomed, the leader of the free world was busy with other problems. This argument of U.S. responsibility, however, ignores the factors that depleted Mexico's reserves, many under Mexico's control. The cupboard need not have been bare when it was.

Borrowers encountered serious debt problems as their need for credit rapidly outstripped their ability to earn foreign exchange. They reached this point by mismanaging their own economies and their foreign debt. There was domestic mismanagement in three related areas: output, exchange rates, and trade. Venezuela's "combination of expansive public policies and a recessionary private economy" was typical:[8] demand management and government spending for nonproductive purposes fed inflation. The countries failed to devalue fast enough as domestic prices soared.[9] This affected each country's external balance in two ways: imports grew much faster than exports,[10] and as residents foresaw the economy deteriorating further, capital left the countries in massive amounts.[11]

6. Joseph Kraft, *The Mexican Rescue* (New York: Group of Thirty, 1984), p. 4.

7. John H. Makin, *The Global Debt Crisis* (New York: Basic Books, 1984), p. 7.

8. Thomas O. Enders and Richard P. Mattione, *Latin America: The Crisis of Debt and Growth* (Washington, D.C.: The Brookings Institution, 1984), p. 27.

9. Inter-American Development Bank, *Economic and Social Progress in Latin America: External Debt—Crisis and Adjustment* (Washington, D.C.: Inter-American Development Bank, 1985) (hereafter cited as the "IDB Report").

10. Richard Williams et al., "International Capital Markets: Developments and Prospects, 1983," International Monetary Fund Occasional Paper No. 23, July 1983, p. 27 (hereafter cited by author).

11. The World Bank estimates that between 1979 and 1982, capital flight from Venezuela, Argentina, and Mexico was $67.7 billion, or 67 percent of gross

The borrowing countries mismanaged their debt by putting it to bad use and by accepting dangerous terms, which made them vulnerable to unforeseen changes in their environment. A country that takes foreign loans need not invest those funds in projects that earn foreign exchange, provided the economy as a whole can generate external earnings at the same rate that debt service grows. The problem countries failed to meet this proviso. They invested excessive amounts in grandiose but inefficient projects and frittered more away in graft. They allowed consumption to grow as investment stagnated.[12] They accepted risky conditions when they borrowed. They mismatched maturities, using medium-term and even short-term funds to finance long-term projects. A seven-year Eurosyndication would finance a dam that would not begin to pay its way even in local currency for ten years or more.[13] As interest rates rose, the countries shifted to shorter-term loans so as not to be locked into high rates.[14] The borrowers were dangerously exposed if for some reason banks should want to reduce their exposure.[15]

Policy failure in the borrowing countries made them vulnerable to the unanticipated shocks, largely from outside the financial system, that disturbed the precarious balance borrowers had achieved. There were four such shocks: the second oil price rise, the deflation and recession of 1980–1982, the decline in commodity prices, and the Falkland Islands War. It is important to this argument that the shocks were unanticipated.[16] If the lenders or borrowers had assessed the probability of such events well, they could have discounted the effect when pricing the loan.[17]

---

capital inflows. These three countries had the most serious problem. World Bank, *World Development Report, 1985*, p. 64.

12. Cline disputes this, pointing out that outside of Venezuela, Argentina, and Mexico most countries' rates of savings and investment rose during the 1970s. He acknowledges, however, that in the four years leading up to the crisis new external debt mainly serviced existing debt. And of course, the exceptions are three of the four largest debtors. William R. Cline, *International Debt* (Washington, D.C.: Institute for International Economics, 1984), p. 16.

13. See Enders and Mattione, *Latin America*, p. 31, and Kraft, *Mexican Rescue*, p. 33.

14. See Makin, *Crisis*, pp. 215–216.

15. These generalizations do not, of course, apply equally to every country. For example, the maturity profile of Brazil's debt was much longer than Mexico's.

16. See Cline, *International Debt*, p. 17.

17. See Donald R. Lessard, "North-South Finance: The Implications of Overreliance on Bank Credit," Working Paper 1463–83, Alfred P. Sloan School of Management, Massachusetts Institute of Technology, August 1983.

The second oil price shock created an imbalance in the borrowers' economies that was never corrected.[18] Following in rapid order came the dramatic shift in U.S. monetary policy, the recession of 1980–1982, and a sudden rise in interest rates that had been negative in real terms.[19] High interest rates hurt highly leveraged borrowers severely. The collapse of world commodity prices cut the earnings of borrowers in Latin America and Africa, who, unlike Asian borrowers, largely exported commodities.[20] Finally, the war in the Falkland Islands hurt Argentina's standing in international credit markets. The timing of the war was unfortunate, since it underlined the borrowers' vulnerability.

One cannot look solely to the borrowers and the shocks that disturbed their equilibrium to explain the crisis. After all, lenders as well as borrowers could have anticipated external shocks, if not in the specifics at least as a general principle. All parties to the debt could have responded more effectively to the shocks. The lenders reacted ad hoc, not having planned for external shocks despite their large exposure.

By the second oil shock in 1979, banks were already well exposed in many developing countries. Macroeconomic policy in industrial countries and the oil shocks created demand for bank credit by generating payments imbalances in need of finance. The developing countries offered higher returns than those available in banks' traditional markets. The banking industry, recently transformed by multinationalization and new procedures for lending, was well positioned to provide credit to developing countries. Even without this structural change, international banks were predisposed to euphoric lending, particularly as competition among them grew. Primed for the trade-finance wars of the 1970s, the banks marched into battle and their exposure grew.

After the second oil shock, the banks gradually cut back new funds flowing to the borrowers until much of the flow simply serviced existing debt.[21] They did this in part because each bank has limits,

18. Cline says the oil price hikes were the major exogenous shocks, *International Debt*, p. 8.

19. Ibid., p. 1; IDB Report, p. 5; Makin, *Crisis*, pp. 7 and 203; and Williams et al., p. 27.

20. See Cline, *International Debt*, p. 18; Makin, *Crisis*, p. 8; and Williams et al., p. 27. Enders and Mattione, however, find that changing terms of trade were not so important. *Latin America*, p. 21.

21. See IDB Report, p. 5.

prudential if not legal, to its exposure in any one borrower.[22] Since such limits are often flexible, the major problem seems to have been confidence, alternately called psychology[23] or herding.[24]

By 1982, lenders had lost confidence in Latin American countries, in part because of recent trends in the world financial system. A series of prominent borrowers had encountered problems. In the United States, the failures of Drysdale Government Securities in May and Penn Square National Bank in July undermined depositors' confidence in the domestic banking system and some of the leading banks. Elsewhere, there was a similar result after the discovery of irregularities at Banco Ambrosiano and the list of countries with debt problems grew.[25] When Mexico, assumed to be among the strongest of borrowers, could not service its debt, the banks without offices in Latin America, lacking reliable information about borrowers there,[26] generalized to other countries in the region.[27] They curtailed new credit to borrowers in the entire region with a speed that was "abrupt" when compared with earlier lending to troubled countries.[28]

This summary of the conventional explanations for the debt crisis of 1982–1983 suggests the weakness of such lending by banks. Lessard notes that instability of this sort is built into a system in which banks lend for general rather than specific purposes. If banks made true project loans, with export receipts paid directly to the creditor, rather than turning to the debtor's government should the borrower fail, risk would rest where it belonged, with investors outside the country who, by virtue of their size and diverse portfolios, would be better able than the borrowing country to bear the risk.[29] Lessard points to the *use* of the loan to explain the system's instability. I would add another serious problem that involves the *form* of the credit.

Instability reflecting a basic lack of confidence among the banks was built into the dominant form of lending to these countries, syndica-

22. Enders and Mattione, *Latin America*, p. 13.
23. Cline, *International Debt*, p. 17.
24. Enders and Mattione, *Latin America*, p. 15.
25. See Cline, *International Debt*, pp. 1 and 17; Makin, *Crisis*, pp. 222–223; and Williams et al., p. 3.
26. Michael Moffitt, *The World's Money* (New York: Simon and Schuster, 1983), p. 226–227.
27. Williams et al., p. 27.
28. Cline, *International Debt*, p. 18.
29. Lessard, "North-South Finance."

tion. Explicit language in the contracts to the contrary notwithstanding, the lead banks and participating banks did not really agree about who was responsible when borrowers encountered problems. A fuzzy allocation of risk among the lenders marred syndication from its start and exacerbated the herding in 1982.

Syndication: The Conflicting Interests of Lead Banks and Participants

In a clause standard to most syndicated Eurocurrency agreements, the lead manager disclaims responsibility to the participants.

> *Section 9.4. Responsibility of the Agent and Managers.*
>
> *Neither the Agent nor any Manager shall be responsible* to the Lenders [the participating banks] *for the validity*, effectiveness, enforceability or sufficiency *of* this Agreement or the Notes or *any document delivered* hereunder or *in connection herewith* or for the accuracy or completeness of any statement made at any time or in any manner to the Agent or any of the Lenders by or on behalf of the Borrower or the Guarantor or be obliged to ascertain or inquire as to the performance or observance of any of the terms, conditions, covenants or agreements contained herein or as to the use of the proceeds of the Loans
>
> [emphasis added].

No airline would expect a passenger to agree in advance to excuse the pilot's negligence. Yet the syndicate leader invites other banks to participate in a multimillion-dollar loan to a distant borrower about which the others know little, and then disclaims legal responsibility for the "validity . . . or sufficiency of . . . any document," including the prospectus it probably wrote. The lead bank also disclaims responsibility "for the accuracy or completeness of any statement made . . . on behalf of the Borrower," including statements by those in the lead bank who sold the loan to the participating banks. It is as though all the passengers were expected to have pilots' licenses.

Language of this sort is common in financings in the United States, where all investors are sophisticated and the securities law protects them. Each is assumed to be able to weigh risk and return if accurate data are available. In a syndicated loan, the participating banks' data about the borrower are often much more meager than the lead bank's, yet the leader specifies—and the participants agree—that the participants be treated as the leader's equal. How is this possible? In this conundrum lies much of the recent instability in international lending, since ability to tap the vast pool of participating banks was a precondition to the enormous flow of funds to borrowing countries during the 1970s. Leadership without responsibility is unusual enough to merit attention.

Syndicate managers normally approached participants as near equals. A manager with a major U.S. bank described his procedure for attracting or identifying participants in the late 1970s.

> First we would get a good, big Japanese bank to speak for one-third of the syndicate [by arranging for banks in Japan to participate]. Second, we checked on reciprocity—who feeds us business. Third, we went to other banks with whom we had good relationships, even major competitors. Fourth, we offered the loan to banks that in our experience had placing power or could meet any special documentary requirements like waiver of sovereign immunity. Then we turned to banks with an "eat" appetite, like those from the Middle East. And finally, we looked for banks that we knew had a preference for the country and still had room under their country limit.

It would have been operationally impossible for the leader of a $100 million syndicate to determine whether prospective participants were competent to judge the borrower. It would have been foolhardy to accept responsibility if they were not. It could have been costly to acknowledge responsibility for the accuracy of the selling and loan documents. Hence the disclaimer; without it, the lead bank could not have assembled the syndicate. Yet it was common knowledge that many participating banks made loans relying on the lead bank.

The conflict between the leader and the participants over information and liability is inherent in their relationship, but is more profound for some banks than for others. For big banks, like many of the twenty-eight examined in chapter 5, the conflict is less severe; some are often as capable as the leader to judge risk because they have equal access to information. The smaller and less experienced the participating bank, the more it will face a conflict. But the line between big and small, sophisticated and naive, is not obvious. Even the twenty-eight banks are unequal. Other differences among the banks exacerbate the conflict of interest. The lead bank's bigger share of the loan ties it more closely to the borrower than do the stakes of the small participants.[30] The lead bank may be willing to accept a lower spread than the smaller banks would prefer. The big lead bank probably has a lower cost of funds than the smaller banks.[31] As a manager earning fees and possibly also as a bank servicing the borrower in other ways, a leader benefits from the entire relationship, not just the loan.

One cannot finesse this conflict of interests. One writer tries, saying that the lead bank's primary obligation is to the borrower, since the lead bank starts by getting the borrower's mandate.[32] This observer ignores complex interbank ties: cooperation in earlier syndicates and correspondent relations may predate the mandate by years. Lloyds used the Sicartsa loan to reward banks for participating in an earlier, less lucrative syndicate. Others argue that syndication itself renders decisions about a borrower's creditworthiness less important, so that the smaller bank would presumably not need wholly accurate data or a full disclosure. In this view, the insurance principle of portfolio diversification relaxes the lending principle of creditworthiness.[33] Certainly the banks lending to Sicartsa did little independent credit analysis. But diversification is illusory when instead of making one $100 million loan to a borrower, the bank makes ten $10 million loans to that borrower through ten syndicates. The illusion evaporates when country risk unites many supposedly disparate borrowers, which happened in Mexico in August 1982. In practice, the opportunities to diversify were too few.

Given the conflict, there are two views of the lead bank's obligation to participants. One applies only a due diligence and gross negligence

---

30. M. S. Mendelsohn, *Money on the Move* (New York: McGraw-Hill, 1980), p. 90. Of course, the proper measure of a bank's stake in the borrower should not be the absolute amount of its exposure, but that exposure's share of the bank's capital. Some of the smaller Texas banks' exposure to Mexican borrowers was small compared with that of the big U.S. money center banks, but still a large share of their capital, making them sensitive to the borrowers' performance and needs.

31. Yoon S. Park and Jack Zwick, *International Banking in Theory and Practice* (Reading, Mass.: Addison-Wesley, 1985), p. 105.

32. Mendelsohn, *Money on the Move*, p. 85.

33. Mohammed and Saccomanni, p. 622 (see chapter 5, note 5).

test. Here, the lead bank is a neutral conduit whose duty at most is to see that the information be "free from any distortions, omissions, or gross negligence."[34] The participating banks can expect the leader only to exercise due diligence. Found in the U.S. Securities and Exchange Commission's antifraud law, this flexible standard varies with the lead bank's activity, becoming stronger as involvement increases.[35] The lead bank is safe. It can rely on the borrower's statements and need not "inquire . . . beyond [its] actual knowledge."[36] Not surprisingly, given its heritage, this view is associated with U.S. banks.[37] U.S. lead banks, lacking an analogue to the Securities Act, turn logically to a full disclaimer. Yet this may be inappropriate to the relation between lead and participating banks.

The European and Japanese view is that participating banks will, must, and should rely on the lead bank to a certain extent. According to a London banker, in Europe this view derives from the small number of banks in each country and from the house bank practice. All recognize that the house bank has inside information it will not share, but all expect this inside position to inform the lead bank's dealings with the other banks, toward whom it accepts some responsibility.[38] The alliance of bank and firm spills over to create an alliance of bank and bank. This does differ from the U.S. practice, but even in the United States, in practice small banks sometimes rely on the leader.[39]

The home plays an important role here. When participating banks follow lead banks, they must rely on existing, continuous relations with those banks to ensure that the leaders will not misdirect them. Although the growth of international banking established more continuity in relations among banks from different home countries, by far the greater continuity and stronger ties are still in relations among banks from the same home country. It is not by chance that the

34. Park and Zwick, *International Banking*, pp. 97 and 103.
35. Reade H. Ryan, Jr., "International Bank Loan Syndications and Participations," in Robert S. Rendell, ed., *International Financial Law* (London: Euromoney Publications, 1980), p. 25.
36. Mendelsohn, *Money on the Move*, p. 85.
37. Donaldson, pp. 70–71 (chapter 5, note 5).
38. Donaldson, p. 71.
39. See Park and Zwick, *International Banking*, p. 95, and Mohammed and Saccomanni, p. 622.

experienced syndicator said he went first to "a good, big Japanese bank" to arrange the 33 percent Japanese portion of the syndicate. The potential participating banks in Japan relied on their continuous relations with the "good, big Japanese bank." Thus, as we will see in the next chapter, in a crisis the home country becomes the central device for managing the solution.

This discussion raises serious questions about the role of international law in transactions of this sort. Loan contracts place the risk on participating banks, but during the debt crises lead banks did not escape responsibility. Legally unaccountable, they remained practically bound. The big banks' exposure gave them a major stake in the outcome, of course. Moreover, the language of the contract fell away before the strength of the ties binding banks from the same home country. One must ask why private contract law, instead of trying to shift risk, does not address the underlying business responsibilities of the parties in a simple, direct way. Perhaps the solution rests in treating syndication as a partnership, for legal purposes. Rather than basing Eurocredit agreements on U.S. underwriting contracts, the lenders would agree to recognize the joint risk of the partners and simply establish a standard of good faith for the lead manager.

The question remains why a smaller, less informed bank would participate in loans it was not qualified to judge when it could not rely as a matter of law on the lead bank? In theory, this is merely the riskier loan in the small bank's diversified portfolio. If this is true, then the smaller banks would not have tried so vigorously to escape debt restructurings; the price of the loan would have reflected the risk. Other explanations, based on the smaller banks' ignorance and greed, may have a kernel of truth but are not sufficient.[40] Large banks have no monopoly on wisdom.

This discussion suggests another form of tacit alliance at the home level, one among banks. In addition, all lenders anticipated help from a lender of last resort (see chapter 7). The story goes far beyond simple intervention by central banks. It helps explain one of the most extreme cases of lending in the period before the 1982–1983 crisis, Mexico.

---

40. See, for example, Darity's critique of institutional weaknesses to explain loan pushing by banks. William Darity, Jr., "Did the Commercial Banks Push Loans on the LDC's?" in Michael Claudon, ed., *World Debt Crisis* (Cambridge, Mass.: Ballinger, 1986), pp. 199, 212ff.

The Extreme Case: Managing Mexico's 1982 Debt Crisis

Mexico was one of the largest borrowers of syndicated loans. Fourteen hundred banks, far more than for any other country, gave it credit. Mexico accomplished this by virtue of its importance to one of the G-5 countries, the United States. Both borrower and creditors received special treatment after the August 1982 crisis. Anticipation of this special treatment helps explain the euphoric lending to Mexico in the years before the crisis. By most measures exceptional, Mexico was still only one extreme point on a continuum rather than an isolated case.

Treatment during the Crisis

The special treatment accorded Mexico by the U.S. government contrasts with the assistance given to Brazil.[41] By many financial measures, the two countries are roughly equivalent, yet the U.S. government helped Mexico much more than Brazil. The absolute volume of funds in the first year was twice as high in Mexico as it was in Brazil (see Table 6–1). Moreover, the help came much faster.

TABLE 6–1. U.S. Help in Rescheduling: Volume and Timing in the First Phase

	Mexico	(began 8/82)	Brazil	(began 9/82)
1) *Funds:* CCC	$1.00bn	one	$0.25bn	(6/83)
Swap/BIS	1.00	weekend	1.23	(9/82)
Oil reserve	1.00	8/82	—	
Ex-Im Bank	—		—	(promised mid-1983)
2) *Pressure:*				
(a) International				
Mobilized other OECD countries		Failed to get much new money from other G-5 governments		
(b) Domestic				
Fast and thorough		Informed from beginning but no active pressure on smaller banks until after 5/83		

41. For a detailed story of the give-and-take leading to the Mexican rescue package, see Kraft, *Mexican Rescue.* His account of the negotiation's near collapse is fascinating. The fact remains, of course, that the package was assembled.

For Mexico, these funds were arranged over a weekend, compared with many months for Brazil. By a more qualitative measure, the U.S. government exerted greater pressure for Mexico than for Brazil in the rescheduling process at both the international and the domestic level. Banks' conclusions about why the U.S. government favored Mexico in 1982 will affect their lending in the future.

There are several explanations for U.S. behavior. The first is that Brazil wanted the United States to go slower. Because the Brazilians did not want to be treated like Mexicans, they did not take the route of official rescheduling. Related to this is the view that others did not recognize the Brazilian problem as fast as the Mexican. It is true that Brazil did not give even its own bankers as much information about the country's performance as it had in the past. For several years leading up to the crisis, however, Brazil's problems had been clear.[42]

The United States appears to have acquiesced in a do-little policy toward Brazil because the U.S. government was more concerned about the impact of a crisis in Mexico than in Brazil—the impact on the U.S. financial system, U.S. economic growth, and U.S. national security—even though the United States had substantial interests in both countries (see Table 6–2).

The evidence suggests three conclusions. First, the U.S. financial system was not substantially more exposed in Mexico than in Brazil at the end of 1982. The market share of U.S. banks in both countries was about the same, as was the exposure of the biggest banks, according to Salomon Brothers: lending as a share of capital was 60 percent in Mexico and 54 percent in Brazil. This is a lot of money in both countries. The differences for the U.S. financial system are not large enough to justify a substantially different response by the U.S. government. Second, differences in equity interests also do not help to explain U.S. policy. In fact, on the basis of direct U.S. investment in the two countries, the United States should have moved more quickly for Brazil. Third, U.S. domestic politics and national security policy emerge as most important. Enormous differences exist in U.S. trade with the two countries. U.S. trade with Brazil was a much

---

42. Hindsight suggests Brazil was less able than Mexico to take strong corrective action. At the time the U.S. government helped Mexico, however, the political will to act was absent in both countries. President López Portillo of Mexico opposed stringent measures in August 1982, and Brazil's government delayed imposing such measures until after elections in November 1982.

TABLE 6–2. Economic Measures of U.S. Interests (end-1982)

	Mexico	Brazil	
All U.S. Banks' Exposure			
$ Billions	$25	$19	
Market share	39%	34%	
Exposure/Capital			
Top 9 U.S. banks	60%	54%	
($ billions)	($14)	($12)	
U.S. Foreign Direct Investment			*Total*
$ Billions (stock)	$ 5.6	$ 9.0	$221
Share	2.5%	4.1%	100%
U.S. Exports			
$ Billions (Flow)	$17.8	$ 3.8	$224
Share	7.9%	1.7%	100%

SOURCES: Federal Financial Institutions Examination Council, *Statistical Release E.16*, "Country Exposure Lending Survey," various issues; IMF, *Direction of Trade Statistics Yearbook*, 1985 (Washington, D.C.: IMF, 1985); Thomas H. Hanley et al., *A Review of Bank Performance: 1983 Edition* (New York: Salomon Brothers, 1983), Figure 37.

smaller share. The clear balance in favor of Mexico on trade translates into jobs, and so into domestic political issues. If one adds to that the long border, the immigrants, the cultural connections, and worries about the threat of war in Central America to the immediate neighbors' political stability, one must conclude that close security and economic ties to Mexico shape domestic U.S. politics and explain this treatment.

These U.S. interests—security, trade, even culture—are outside the financial system. Yet they explain differences in the treatment of the two largest debtor countries, whose defaults threatened the U.S. financial system equally. Lenders to Mexico understood this long before it happened.

Anticipation by the Banks

From 1978 on, Mexico was the darling of the banking fraternity (see Table 6–3). The growth of bank assets in Mexico far exceeded that in comparable countries, whether one considers other oil-producing countries outside the Mideast, other Latin American countries, or

TABLE 6–3. Euphoric Lending: The Growth of Banks' Assets in Mexico Compared with Other Areas, 1978–1981

Bank assets in	December 1978	Percentage growth from 12/78 to:		
		12/79	12/80	12/81
Mexico	$23.3 billion	32%	76%	138%
OPEC (non-Mideast) (1,2)	31.1	28	44	51
Latin America (1)	55.9	28	58	84
Pacific Asia NICs (3)	14.8	31	66	97

(1) Excludes Mexico.
(2) Algeria, Brunei, Ecuador, Gabon, Indonesia, Nigeria, Trinidad/ Tobago, Venezuela.
(3) Malaysia, South Korea, Taiwan, Thailand.

SOURCE: Bank for International Settlements, *International Banking Statistics, 1973–1983* (Basle: BIS, 1984), Table 5.

even the newly industrializing countries of Pacific Asia. What prompted banks to pump so much credit into Mexico?

Mexico's proximity, importance, and longstanding ties to the United States appear to have encouraged banks to lend liberally at favorable rates. Other explanations are not adequate. Euphoria surrounding oil, and the associated high demand for credit to finance fast growth of output, cannot alone explain the jump in bank credit to Mexico, since loans to other high-growth, high-absorbing oil producers fell far short of this increase. That there were limited opportunities elsewhere does not explain Mexico's spectacular growth. The tarbaby effect—banks lending to protect outstanding loans—did not apply, since banks financed much more than debt service through 1981. Ignorance of other banks' lending also was not the cause, despite the claims of some banks; the high growth and increasingly short-term portion of Mexican debt was visible in public data before 1981.[43]

Banks solved some of the problems posed by lending to developing countries in ways that created more problems. Banks presented syndication as a way to spread risk, but practiced it in such a way that country risk limited diversification. Syndicates were also supposed to place risk firmly on each participating bank, but failed. Participants solved this problem by relying on alliances with lead banks from the

43. See the semiannual debt reports of the Bank for International Settlements.

same home country. As demand for credit grew, the Federal Reserve Board tightened supply. It appears that banks did not engage in contingency or scenario planning in a way that would have helped them prepare for situations other than that extrapolated from a straight-line forecast of current conditions. In a sense, they did not need to plan. They were passing the buck by betting on the system.

The impulse to lend against the security of U.S. interests implicit in the system was recognized during the years preceding the crisis in Mexico. Banks used to speak confidently of Mother Russia's umbrella over Eastern Europe. The principle applies wherever banks perceive a powerful nation's interests. As a general principle, this view is fairly well recognized in economic theory.

Most commentators do not specify the precise mechanisms by which the powerful nations act as lenders of last resort. In my view, the mechanisms themselves have profound consequences for the stability of international lending over the long run. The next chapter explores this.

7

The Lender of Last Resort, National Security, and Regional Hegemony

In the final analysis, the home is central because it steps in when debt crises loom, doing for its banks what they cannot do themselves and what others will not do for them. There is no other international lender of last resort.

Most countries now have a lender of last resort. Its job is to prevent panics that in the past crippled financial systems when bank depositors rushed to withdraw funds from banks they considered endangered. People panicked because they knew the bank lacked reserves and liquid assets to pay all depositors, and it was therefore first come, first, and perhaps only, served. Even if a bank were actually sound, the mere assumption that it was weak could start a run that would spread to other banks. To restore confidence, an agency had to promise to satisfy all legitimate demands on the troubled banks. For its promise to be credible, that agency had to have unlimited funds; in short, it had to have the power to create money. Over the years, the central bank, a part of the government, became the lender of last resort in most countries.[1] Most students of this activity use the acronym LOLR to describe it.

The same dynamic should apply to cross-border lending, but there is no single lender of last resort on the international level to do a comparable job in a crisis. A crisis occurs when a country lacks the exchange to service residents' foreign debts. That international lending

1. Charles P. Kindleberger, *Manias, Panics, and Crashes: A History of Financial Crashes* (New York: Basic Books, 1978), chap. 10.

241

has survived nearly a decade of trauma suggests, however, that something did actually function as the lender of last resort, keeping creditors from hasty withdrawals that could make the crisis worse. Who or what performs this function? We can eliminate at the outset several candidates for the international lender of last resort: the International Monetary Fund, the U.S. Federal Reserve Board (as creator of dollars, in which most cross-border loans are made), and the private banks as a group.

In my view, the job is done by the G-5 governments, operating with their big banks, according to informal conventions that allocate responsibility along regional lines because that is the way their underlying interests cluster. To save time and space, I refer to this function as the ILOLR, the international lender of last resort. The members of the ILOLR negotiate each problem case by case.

Any international lender of last resort runs up against the central political fact of the twentieth century: despite the apparent integration of the global economy, the world is organized by nations. Peru in 1976 offers an early example of the problems this creates. After the government of Peru negotiated a $386 million syndicated loan to help it restructure its problem debt in October 1976, it promptly announced the purchase of $250 million in military equipment from the Soviet Union.[2] Far from easing Peru's debt crisis, the new loan appeared to have financed imports the lenders found least desirable. Embarrassed, the governments and banks of the West—including the United States and Germany—learned a lesson for the next restructurings. They wrung from Peru's government an undertaking not to buy more military equipment. Soon after that agreement, a representative of one of the three big German banks visited a senior Peruvian official with an offer. As part of the effort to increase exports, a major German customer could provide military equipment that the German bank would finance on favorable terms. Was the government interested? "Have you forgotten our agreement not to buy that sort of thing?" asked the amazed Peruvian official.[3]

2. *Institutional Investor* (International Edition), October 1976.

3. Interview, Lima, Peru, February 1978. Then President Bermudez denied that Peru had been forced to dampen its "friendly relations with the other major power bloc." His carefully chosen words, however, do not refute the assertion that Peru had agreed to end military purchases as a condition for the help it

Not far below the surface of this vignette lurks the message of Rousseau's fable of the stag and the hare. In the fable five hungry men who cannot communicate well must hunt a stag they can catch if they all cooperate. But a hare darts by, one catches it and defects, and the stag escapes. In one view, "in cooperative action, even where all agree on the goal and have an equal interest in the project, one cannot rely on others."[4] Despite the efforts of the group to work together, the immediate needs of its members can thwart its efforts. In the case of Peru, Germany's immediate urge to export took precedence over the long-term interest of all creditors in the debtor's agreed course of recovery. The ILOLR must confront and subdue short-term interests that would destroy the group's solution.

Here I examine how the ILOLR functions in practice. My central question is how the nation-based system, built around five industrial countries, affects debt crisis management and future lending. The literature suggests three important policy questions:[5] (1) Under what circumstances will a powerful player take responsibility for the system? (2) Under such circumstances, what is the danger that individual parties will act at the expense of the group? (3) How does intervention on behalf of the system benefit more than just the immediate parties?[6]

The actions of the ILOLR raise issues that are inseparable from those of the G-5 countries' foreign or security policies. To articulate these interests, the G-5 governments have equipped their national security agencies in very different ways, which reflect the varied impact of the debt crises on the G-5 countries.

The action of the ILOLR in crisis shapes the way banks allocate credit in the long term. Simply put, despite the forces for integration, the ILOLR today ties the banks more closely to their home countries, which in turn play an important role in defining risk and return on future cross-border loans. To understand this, I examine the process

---

received. "How Peru's President Views the IMF and the Banks," *Euromoney*, March 1978, pp. 28–29.

4. Kenneth Waltz, *Man, the State, and War* (New York: Columbia University Press, 1965).

5. A substantial literature has developed these notions since the nineteenth century. The story gives a new meaning to passing the buck. I have relied on it and the reader is encouraged to explore it.

6. In the argot of the trade, these are stated as (1) When does the lender of last resort act? (2) How is the moral hazard resolved? (3) What is the public good?

by which the G-5 governments and banks have managed debt crises since the mid-1970s.

Who Acts in International Debt Crises?

Despite the ad hoc appearance of efforts to resolve the debt crises, the process involves more than just muddling through. To manage debt crises, there is a system that is decentralized to the level of states. Instead of relying on a global institution, the creditors that are party to a debt crisis coordinate their response through one of the G-5 powers and its major banks.

There is an alternate view. In this view, as a result of the increasing integration of world financial markets, the job of managing the crises is in the hands of the banks themselves and the IMF. Among private-sector entities, principally banks, the restructuring committees for each debtor country suggest a high level of integration in world finance. The Institute for International Finance (IIF), an analytic agency set up in Washington, D.C., by banks around the world, gives intimations of a still higher circle. Among creditor governments, the Paris clubs and the Bank for International Settlements, with its Cooke committee of bank regulators, provide forums for coordinated inter-government action. Among multilateral institutions, the IMF would seem to be the linchpin in a complex system.[7]

My view is that this surface cooperation masks underlying national forces of great tenacity. Syndicates and restructuring committees are organized by home country; Japan has organized its own IIF, in part to give Japanese banks more clout in the original. The Cooke committee and the Paris clubs are cautious forums for negotiating and sharing data rather than transnational actors in their own right. The strength of the IMF varies with the support of its principal share-holders, the G-5 governments. In this sense, the IMF is a player with independence at the margin, powerful when the country it deals with is not important to the G-5, such as a Sri Lanka, or when the G-5 governments are not united.[8]

---

7. Some might argue that the U.S. Federal Reserve System is the lender of last resort to the system. This argument simplifies the way in which liquidity is provided to the system, as I describe below.

8. For a view that the IMF plays a much more important role, see Charles Lipson, "The International Organization of Third World Debt," *International Organization* 35 (Autumn 1981): 603.

The real ILOLR consists of a combination of the five major industrial nations aided by their major banks. One of the G-5 governments, with one or two of its banks, usually acts as leader in a particular crisis. This leads to two questions: How is the status of leader achieved? What does the ILOLR do to keep players—creditors and borrowers—in the game?

The criteria by which a G-5 country assumes the leadership and others follow are their relative interests in the problem country. The interests may be highly specific. Poland is adjacent to Germany, for example, as Mexico is to the United States. Alternatively, the interests may be systemic, either economic or political. Poland borrowed a high proportion of German banks' capital, thus threatening the domestic financial system in Germany. Indonesia occupies a strategic geopolitical position for the United States, as Turkey does for Germany. Since the relative interests among the G-5 are most clear for countries at the extreme, who the leader will be in every case is not always obvious. It is subject to negotiation (as between the United States and Japan over Indonesia) or neglect (as in Zaire or Zambia).

Leadership is important. The more successful restructurings take place under the leadership of one of the G-5 governments. Success consists of keeping creditors and borrowers from withdrawing, and eventually returning the country to a position from which it can raise net new funds in private financial markets. By this measure, examples of success are Turkey (Germany took the lead), Egypt in 1977 (the United States took the lead, helped by Saudi Arabia), Gabon (France led), Indonesia's Pertamina in 1975 (the United States, helped by Japan), and Mexico in 1982 (the United States). The notable failures have occurred in the absence of such leadership: Zaire (which no major power led), Peru in 1977 (the banks alone tried to impose a discipline), and Brazil in 1982–1983 (the United States acquiesced in a proposal that would allow Brazil and major U.S. banks to try to organize over seven hundred private creditors without official help).[9] When a G-5 government leads, it turns to its major banks for help organizing private creditors.

Banks help to lead in a crisis according to criteria that include exposure, nationality, and strategy.[10] Presumably the banks with the

9. Some problem countries shift in status: Poland in 1978 had the active leadership of the West German government, but lost it later when it outlawed the Solidarity movement.

10. I use *leader* to denote an active player who provides policy direction as

most at stake would take the lead. Yet the largest banks rarely use the best measure of stake, loans to the problem country as a share of capital.[11] Instead, a major criterion is absolute exposure. In many cases, the bank with the largest lending to the debtor country takes the lead for banks from its home nation. The banks from the nation with the greatest exposure to the debtor country take the lead in the restructuring committee. Yet relative exposure is not the sole criterion. The bank's long-term, or strategic, interest in the country is decisive.

Banks act as leaders on two levels. On the global level, one bank, or a small group, coordinates banks from all countries. An example is Morgan Guaranty Trust Company, seeking to lead seven hundred banks to a solution in Brazil in December 1982. On the national level, in each home country one bank or a small group coordinates all banks from that country, acting as a liaison with the global leaders. An example is Bank of Tokyo coordinating the Japanese banks in any number of reschedulings. Often the lead banks from each major home country form a steering committee at the global level. In this section, I discuss global leaders.

Individual banks, as leaders, can affect the way a crisis is resolved. This is evident in the handling of the Polish crisis in 1981. In May of that year, Bank of America represented U.S. banks on the restructuring committee, which seemed to agree to a rescheduling. In June, after dissension among the U.S. banks, Bankers Trust Company replaced Bank of America, taking a tough stand against rescheduling and demanding that Poland meet many conditions of economic performance and data availability. On July 19, after the Poles made it clear they could not comply, the U.S. steering committee rebelled again and replaced Bankers Trust with Bank of America and Citibank. In October, a broad group of sixty Western banks agreed to reschedule loans due from March to December 1981, returning to the earlier position.[12] A maverick leader of the U.S. banks, themselves a small

---

well as administrative services. Not even all members of the restructuring committees are active.

11. For example, in Latin America where big U.S. banks took the lead, several large British banks had loaned a higher share of their capital than had the most exposed U.S. banks.

12. Interviews in New York, July 1981, as well as Sarah Martin, "The Secrets of the Polish Memorandum," *Euromoney*, August 1981, p. 9; and "Western

subset of all banks in Poland, had taken the lead of all banks and delayed the restructuring by months.[13]

The leaders and the other G-5 states try to keep the players in the game and provide liquidity. The jawbone gets exercise. For example, in 1983 on behalf of the Brazilian restructuring, a team from the banks, the borrower, and the IMF visited major financial centers like Tokyo, Zurich, and London and presented the proposed plan under the auspices of the central bank. On rare occasions, the state exercises its power to command, usually with a velvet glove.

The G-5 nations provide liquidity. At the aggregate level, one sees this in the way developing countries fund their current-account deficits; overall it is clear that official action has provided liquidity. If one analyzes the balance of payments of non-oil-developing countries, one finds a fundamental shift in the sources and uses of funds: since 1981, governments and official agencies have borne the greatest share of the financing burden, while the banks have benefited, reversing the pattern of the preceding eight years (see Figure 7–1). This is a roundabout way for official sources to help the banks reduce their effective exposure in the developing countries. It substitutes for direct aid to the banks.[14]

Official agencies provided liquidity, funding the withdrawal by the banks as a group after the crisis began. Commercial banks' share of the funds provided dropped from 35.7 percent in the 1973–1981 period to 14.0 percent in the years 1982–1985, while the use of funds shifted dramatically from financing the trade deficit to servicing investment by banks and others (Figure 7–1). Even if one makes the conservative assumption (as in Figure 7–1) that banks received only

---

Bankers Agree to Delay Payments on $3 Billion of Poland's Commercial Debt," *The Wall Street Journal*, October 2, 1981, p. 31.

13. An example of even longer delays in effective restructuring is the management of Brazil's crisis from September 1982 to June 1983, discussed below.

14. The "bailout" here does not reduce banks' nominal exposure in the countries. It does reduce their effective exposure. In the past, banks loaned borrowers more than enough to service outstanding debt. Now public agencies do this. Since banks' capital rises faster than their exposure in debtor nations, their effective exposure falls. Their real exposure may also fall. The most important "bailout," however, is that the official funds allow the borrower to continue servicing its debt, so the banks continue to receive interest. The banks are saved from the borrowers' potential bankruptcy.

FIGURE 7–1. Non-oil-developing Countries: Banks and the Balance of Payments

Sources of Funds   Uses of Funds

1975–81 ($724 billion)

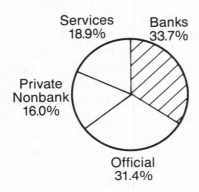

Services   Banks
18.9%   33.7%

Private
Nonbank
16.0%

Official
31.4%

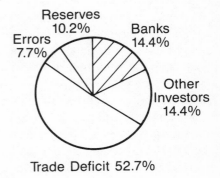

Reserves
10.2%   Banks
Errors   14.4%
7.7%

Other
Investors
14.4%

Trade Deficit 52.7%

1982–85 ($361 billion)

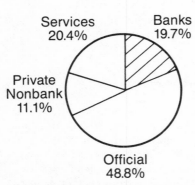

Services   Banks
20.4%   19.7%

Private
Nonbank
11.1%

Official
48.8%

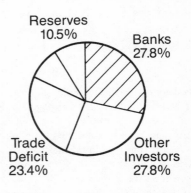

Reserves
10.5%   Banks
                27.8%

Trade   Other
Deficit   Investors
23.4%   27.8%

* Reported as "Investment income," banks and other investments are separated here 50/
  50, a conservative estimate of the banks' role.
** Official includes errors and omissions and long-term nonbank flows.
Source: IMF Staff, World Economic Outlooks (Washington, D.C.: International Monetary
Fund (May 1983), Tables 21, 25, 28; (April 1985), Tables 37, 48.

half of the investment payments, the banks supplied over twice as much as they drew during 1973–1981 but then received about 50 percent more than they supplied in 1982–1985.

Finally, the big banks provide some liquidity. Within the banks as a group, the big banks tend to increase their exposure in crisis countries slightly relative to other banks. Among U.S. banks, after 1980 the nine largest steadily lost share of Latin American credit to U.S. banks smaller than the top twenty-four. When the crisis hit Latin America, the largest U.S. banks increased their share of U.S. exposure there as many small banks reduced theirs. Although the direction of the shifts is important, however, its actual size is marginal: the small banks merely returned to their 1977 share of 19 percent, down from about 22 percent in 1981.[15] Escape is difficult.

Does the System Protect Itself from Free Riders?

The system just described is messy. One result is moral hazard: the system may encourage single players to act to the detriment of the group before, during, or after a crisis.[16] For at least a decade, the U.S. Congress and the press have cried that the banks were lending imprudently on the expectation that the government would bail them out. If this view is accurate and the system persists, we could expect to see the banks' behavior continue. Today's ILOLR, however, seems to have the commonly accepted prerequisites to reduce moral hazard: a qualified uncertainty over the long run about the role of the ILOLR and penalties for invoking its aid.

The Role of the ILOLR

Over the long run, to the extent a bank is uncertain of a bailout, its risk and costs rise and, one presumes, it hews closer to the straight and narrow path of prudent lending. To estimate the uncertainty, a banker might adopt implicit guidelines about the ILOLR. From the behavior of the major players in the debt crises of the last several years, a bank strategist could reasonably draw the following inferences about future crises:

15. Federal Reserve System, *Country Exposure Survey*, various issues.

16. Among the creditors, the single player may be a national government as well as a bank.

(a) Official aid will come, but a bank cannot be certain about the volume, timing, terms, and immediate recipient (banks or countries).

(b) The composition and leadership of the multiple ILOLR will vary among borrowing countries. In many cases a bank cannot be certain in advance about the extent of the leader's or the other members' commitment.

(c) The most exposed big banks will increase their share of credit to the problem country marginally as smaller banks pull back after the crisis. Although the outflow is limited at the aggregate level, a bank cannot judge in advance the degree to which the smaller banks will escape in particular problem countries.

(d) Since leadership among the banks will be defined not only by their relative exposure but also by their long-term interests in the country, a bank cannot be certain how dedicated other major banks will be in a debt crisis.

Each of these factors creates uncertainty over the long run. Guideline (a) is self-evident. For guideline (b), evidence of uncertainty about the ILOLR itself abounds: one multination study "found considerable controversy over what LLR facilities are, let alone which banks had access to them."[17] Guideline (c)—that small banks will reduce their exposure at the expense of the big banks—is not surprising in the abstract and is congruent with the documented behavior of banks. As to guideline (d), a bank's long-term interests in a problem country vary with bank strategy, which may shift, so even bank leadership in a crisis is unclear in advance.

There is uncertainty because the financial assistance by the multiple members in the ILOLR is indirect. Official aid goes to the debtor rather than the banks. This happens because, in varying degrees among the G-5 countries, domestic politics constrain the government from bailing out the banks directly. As a result, politics at the national level determine the aid a problem country will receive.

Since domestic politics determines aid to the debtor country, variations in the political processes in the G-5 countries create uncertainty.

17. Jack M. Guttentag and Richard J. Herring, "Uncertainty and Insolvency Exposure by International Banks," the Wharton Program in International Banking and Finance, University of Pennsylvania, November 1983, p. 31.

In Japan, the political process for assistance to developing countries is bureaucratic rather than parliamentary,[18] so when we know the administrative position, the outcome is more certain than in the United States, where legislative scrutiny can change the executive's plans after the bureaucracy works out its position.[19]

Uncertainty also arises because the interests of each G-5 country vary among debtor countries in ways that undermine a bank's ability to estimate the likelihood and volume of aid. Japan is an example. Imagine debt crises in South Korea, Indonesia, and Malaysia. Given South Korea's proximity to Japan and its long history as a recipient of substantial Japanese aid, a bank might expect Japan to take the lead if South Korea were to restructure but expectations would be less clear for Indonesia or Malaysia.[20]

Finally, the degree of uncertainty varies among the G-5 countries because traditional relations between a government and its banks vary. The best example is the contrast between Japan and the United States. In Japan, private lenders treat lending by financial institutions that are part of or close to the government as a sign that the borrower or the project has government support, increasing their certainty about help in the event of debt problems.[21] In the United States, there is no such understanding. The tradition of arm's-length relations even led U.S. banks to take the U.S. Export-Import Bank to court in 1976 in a matter related to the restructuring of Zaire's debt.[22] The U.S.

18. Japanese aid is provided by the Overseas Economic Cooperation Fund, which is not part of the general budget and is funded by the postal savings system.

19. The most recent example is the IMF quota increase, but aid funds are notoriously subject to congressional intervention.

20. For many years, Japan has provided rice to South Korea whenever the country has been unable to feed itself.

21. The troubled history of Mitsui's petrochemical project in Iran suggests that government help is not automatic, however.

22. While Zaire was in effective default on its debt, the Export-Import Bank and a group of U.S. banks tried to make a new loan conditioned on their receiving a prior claim on certain dollar receipts by the Zairoise. Excluded from this financing, Citibank and other U.S. banks sued and the dispute was eventually settled out of court. See *Citibank, N.A. v. Export-Import Bank of the United States and Manufacturers Hanover Trust Company*, U.S. District Court (S.D.N.Y.) 76 Civ. 3514, August 9, 1976, and "Two Banks Drop Suits after U.S. Ex-Im Bank Alters Zaire Loan Pact," *The Wall Street Journal*, October 14, 1976, p. 20.

government helps its banks, but the extent of the help and the circumstances under which help will be given are uncertain.

One prerequisite for an effective lender of last resort—uncertainty—exists, at least in small measure. A second prerequisite is penalties. The ILOLR must penalize those who use its aid to discourage them from relying on that assistance over the long run. A lender of last resort commonly assesses penalty rates against banks that draw on it. In the recent country debt crises, such a penalty has rarely been possible, since the borrowers rather than the banks received the help. Thus a penalty must either reduce the value of the banks' loans or increase other costs to the banks. It is not at all clear if the present ILOLR system reduces the economic value of the loans.[23] It is useful, however, to look at other costs.

The effective penalty banks pay for ILOLR help in reschedulings consists of the costs they cannot pass on. All banks bear several costs.

- Administrative costs and costs of making provisions for problem loans arise as banks negotiate acceptable terms not only with the borrowers but also with creditor governments and other banks. Multiple reschedulings are expensive.
- Opportunity costs are incurred as funds are frozen.
- Administrative and opportunity costs arise when banks lose power to their home regulators.

Of these, the final point is least noticed. The crises enable banks' regulators to consolidate their control even in areas not linked to the particulars of a crisis. In 1974, just after the first oil shock, Japan's Finance Ministry reined in its banks' overseas activities and kept firm control into the next decade. It acted because the Japanese banks faced a funding crisis in their international lending. In 1983 and again in 1984, U.S. regulators increased the capital requirements for U.S.

---

23. On whether banks lose part of the economic value of their loans when restructuring, see Jack Guttentag and Richard Herring, "What Happens When Countries Cannot Pay Their Bank Loans? The Renegotiation Process," *Journal of Comparative Business and Capital Market Law* 5 (1983): 209. In the abstract, a restructuring increases a loan's present value by making its terms more realistic while at the same time reducing the present value by lengthening the time for repayment. Data are not adequate to permit empirical analysis.

banks.[24] German regulators finally forced their banks to consolidate accounts, a major step made possible in part by the financial crisis.[25]

Other costs are a function of the home environment. For banks based in a country with a strong capital market, capital costs may rise dramatically. In the United States, bank stock prices have collapsed, in part because of the debt crisis and more so for banks highly exposed relative to capital.[26] In the other countries, capital markets are less able to distinguish among banks, since hidden reserves make it difficult to determine the effect of the debt crises.[27]

Though in total these costs can be high, the penalty evaporates if banks can pass them on. When loans are restructured, their price is no longer set simply by the forces of supply and demand. At first, after the most recent crisis, the banks were able to raise spreads as the debtors' bargaining power ebbed. Some Latin American countries became luminous profit centers in their darkest hour.[28] Spreads for Latin American countries began to fall only after the G-5 governments, led by the Federal Reserve Board, intervened.[29] Home governments constrained market forces. As a result, much of the

24. "Minimum Capital Guidelines Amendments," *Federal Reserve Bulletin*, July 1983, p. 539.

25. The German authorities proposed laws that would require banks to consolidate their accounts as early as 1975. Domestic factors also played a role in bringing the bill to law in 1984, but the world debt crisis was a stimulus (see chapter 4).

26. For example, relative to the Standard & Poor's 500, the price/earnings multiple of 12 U.S. money center banks fell from a ratio of 77.1 in June 1979, just as the second oil shock was being felt, to 45.6 in June 1983. Thomas H. Hanley and Lynne M. Christian, "Comparative Market Valuation Statistics," Bank Securities Department, Salomon Brothers, New York, August 19, 1983.

27. Both Japanese and German banks continue to carry hidden reserves. In Japan, for example, Sumitomo Bank was able to absorb the debts of the bankrupt trading company Ataka in 1975 and still declare its largest dividend at the end of the year. In Germany, Commerzbank and Dresdner Bank have been forced to show their provisions more than in the past, presumably because their reserves have not been adequate to the task. See, for example, "Dresdner Tops up Its Reserves," *Financial Times*, December 30, 1982, p. 22.

28. It is no secret that in 1983 profit centers within U.S. banks wanted responsibility for rescheduling. High margins passed the administrative costs on to the borrower and, indirectly, to creditors advancing new funds, while at the same time allowing the bank officers to reach their earnings targets.

29. Note that the Fed intervened again on behalf of a country of major economic and political importance to the United States, Mexico.

maneuvering in political arenas concerns these costs. It would appear that although the roughly 0.75 percent decline in spreads for Mexico erased the profit incentive for rescheduling, the lower spread still met the higher administrative costs, since it was 0.25 percent to 0.50 percent above pre-crisis margins. Administrative costs are easiest to pass along because they can be justified to the borrower, since in a rescheduling the lender has to do more than was anticipated at the time of the original loan.

Less easy to pass on are the other costs associated with the crises. Banks must absorb the opportunity costs of greater regulation and of having their assets frozen in countries for years to come. Placing a value on these costs is difficult, but G-5 countries with strong capital markets have done this in valuing the banks' equity, causing market-to-book values to fall.[30] Since 1982, U.S. bankers have commonly explained their unwillingness to increase cross-border exposure in many countries in terms of the adverse effect on their stock price. In other countries, where share value is less important to the bank, the finance ministries play a more direct role in building provisions against potential loan losses, which imposes costs on the banks. German banks set their own standards.

Decentralization in a Crisis

To deal with creditors that would act at the expense of the group in a financial crisis, the nation-based system shifts to more manageable groups. In a crisis involving three hundred to fourteen hundred banks from dozens of countries, most banks have a small stake in the particular problem country.[31] In the Mexican rescheduling after August

30. For the effect of the debt crisis on the stock price of U.S. banks, see Steven C. Kyle and Jeffrey D. Sachs, "Developing Country Debt and the Market Value of Large Commercial Banks," Working Paper No. 1470, National Bureau of Economic Research, Cambridge, Mass., September 1984.

31. International credit markets are highly concentrated. According to one study, "about 25 large banks based in OECD countries" make up the inner circle, accounting for some 60 percent of lead managements and over 50 percent of all bank lending. These banks could be presumed to have a stake in the system as a whole. See Paul Mentre, *The Fund, Commercial Banks, and Member Countries*, Occasional Paper 26 (Washington, D.C.: International Monetary Fund, 1984), pp. 5–6. Some bankers, drawing the circle a bit wider, refer to the Apex 40 banks. Obviously, the precise number is not important.

1982, the two banks with the largest exposure had respectively only 3.8 percent and 3.5 percent of all bank loans. Only twenty-two other banks had between 1.0 percent and 2.5 percent each.[32] At a global level, many players are potential free riders.

The system solves this problem by shifting the players from the international ocean to their smaller home ponds. There, global free riders become integral. In Mexico, Dresdner Bank of Germany had only 1 percent of loans by all banks, but 25 percent of loans by German banks. As a lead bank, it had recruited German participants for Eurosyndicates. As the second-largest bank in Germany, Dresdner was a leader with a position at home to maintain.[33] Dresdner's credibility in home markets would be affected by the success of the foreign restructuring. By the same token, Dresdner could exercise its power on smaller banks that might be less responsive to the entreaties of the U.S. banks with the largest stake in the Mexican rescue package.

That other possible forms of crisis management were not employed suggests the power of the home country as an organizing device. In the abstract, other types of decentralization were possible. For developing country debtors, one alternative would have been to organize by syndicate, relying on lead banks to do all the work; other types of lenders could have acted as blocs.[34] Industrial governments could still have been lenders of last resort, providing liquidity to the borrowers as they do now. More was needed, however. Today only the home country provides the multiple ties that keep the players in the game during a crisis.

Decentralization to the home country increases stability for several reasons.

- Home is where the oligopoly is, in banking. The Big Three in France and Germany, the Big Four in the United Kingdom,

32. This is taken from the 1983 Credit Agreement for $5 billion between the United Mexican States and Banks, Schedule 5.

33. We might say that Dresdner Bank had little choice but to cooperate, given its worldwide exposure and its interest, as a lead bank, in the stability of the market for international syndications. In fact, after its recent experience with what it might have considered the intransigence of the U.S. banks in the Polish rescheduling, it could well have adopted a tougher line.

34. This was tried in the early Brazil rescheduling and it failed.

the Big Eight in Japan all have a dominant stake in the home system.[35]

- At the national level, there are more opportunities for trade-offs among the players. Not only can they bargain about international issues, but even unrelated issues in domestic markets may be part of the deal.

- National commonalities make it easier to ride herd on the free rider: at home, bankers speak the same language, are part of the same culture, and apply the same standards for success (earnings per share or market share, for example). Leaders at home are established, permitting market discipline. Relations with the home authorities are established, increasing the predictability of official action.

Precisely this dynamic worked in the Mexican case immediately after August 1982. In the United States, for example, banks with little exposure in Mexico threatened to make waves if Mexico did not let them out fast. The big banks and the U.S. authorities pressed them to stay in. In each region of the country, a major regional bank worked to hold the smaller banks.[36] The Federal Reserve Banks did the same.[37].

The Environment for the ILOLR

Implicit in much of the writing about the ILOLR is a notion of the environment drawn from the liberal model of the world described in chapter 4. The ILOLR is often drawn from the Anglo-American experience. The underlying model assumes a market of some depth in which the lender of last resort intervenes on the liability side of the balance sheet, providing liquidity that keeps the players in the game. Banks and other creditors can and will withdraw from this market, so the way to keep them in is to maintain confidence. The lender of last resort can provide liquidity either to the banks directly (in which case the national central bank acts) or to the borrowers themselves (in

35. Even in the United States, with over 14,000 banks, the largest nine banks account for a major share of the market.
36. In the big U.S. market, regional banks play a coordinating role that is analogous to that of the major banks in other countries.
37. Interviews, Boston, New York, and Washington, D.C., 1982–1984.

which case the national treasury is often the actor). This view is deficient.

For banks from Japan, France, and to a certain extent Germany, other factors in the environment affect crisis management by the lender of last resort. French banks are state owned, Japan's are subject to tight supervision, and both Japan's and Germany's have intimate ties to groups of major companies. This is an environment in which institutional ties—between banks and governments or banks and firms or among banks—perform an important function in crisis management. The alliances described in earlier chapters prove to be essential in difficult times. More than a free market is at work. The Anglo-American model does not fit the other major countries.[38]

In this situation, the players whose interests lie in preserving stability exercise both market and political power, to keep all players in.[39] In part, this is an economic calculus: the threat of future pain can stem precipitate withdrawal. The future costs of withdrawing—including opportunity costs—exceed the immediate cost of staying in through the debt crisis.[40] In addition, the players simply may not see exit as an option. The techniques available to keep players in the game are much more varied than those in the market model. At the national level, the main power rests with hierarchies of players built around the central government and the major banks. The government can exercise its power of command (overtly or subtly through administrative guidance) as well as manipulate liquidity. The big banks can draw on a network of existing relationships with smaller banks that transcends the crisis.

Limitations of This Decentralized System

National ties shore up cooperation and confidence, but the multifaceted nature of the nation-based ILOLR also contains destabilizing

38. This is so despite the bailout of large depositors in Continental Illinois Bank in 1984. The help, highly debated in public, required nothing in return from the large depositors, who, in the event, followed market dictates and left the bank. In Japan, group members would be expected to stay with the bank.

39. This is Hirschman's concept of voice. "Voice . . . is . . . any attempt to change, rather than to escape from, an objectionable state of affairs." Albert O. Hirschman, *Exit, Voice, and Loyalty* (Cambridge, Mass.: Harvard University Press, 1970), p. 30.

40. Recall that the Japanese banks, for example, derived only 15 percent of their revenues from international operations.

elements. Weaknesses are inherent in the form of decentralization. Most important, this system of crisis management gives individual players an opportunity to take advantage of the group over the long run. Banks and national governments recognize and anticipate the system's effects. Thus banks loaned to countries likely to have the support of a G-5 government and particularly to those supported by the banks' home government. U.S. banks have had a greater market share in regions that are important to the United States for political and economic reasons—Latin America and Pacific Asia (see Table 7–1). The specific countries, major Eurocurrency borrowers in the past, were strategically important by virtue of their size, resources, or location—South Korea, the Philippines, and Indonesia in Pacific Asia; Brazil, Argentina, and Mexico in Latin America. They were also among the fastest growing, most industrial, and apparently best managed of developing countries. Both political and economic factors make the countries important.

Second, not all banking activities readily lend themselves to this nation-based system. The prime example has been the interbank market for Eurocurrency deposits; some would add the markets for Eurobonds and floating-rate notes. Much more integrated globally, these markets are less susceptible to the kind of hierarchical organization common in syndicated loan markets. For some lenders and their home governments, these markets are more important than the medium-term or sovereign risk markets of syndicated lending, particularly for developing countries. A vivid example is the conflict over the rescheduling of short-term loans to Brazil. The interbank focus of Swiss and some other European banks led them to object to rescheduling proposals that seemed to attack the integrity of their major market. One observer called their hostility "almost religious."[41] In the same spirit, the Bank of England, spokesman for another major banking center, opposed a proposal by U.S. bankers to freeze foreign deposits with Brazilian banks early in 1983.[42]

A third weakness arises because so much lending by non-U.S. banks is denominated in dollars, which only the U.S. authorities can create.

41. Peter Montagnon, "Brazil's Creditor Banks Meet for More Negotiations," *Financial Times*, May 9, 1983, p. 17.

42. This risk differs from the problem of "the proliferation in participants that has introduced second- and third-tier banks . . . to the system," as described in *Risks in International Bank Lending* (New York: Group of Thirty, 1982), p. 20.

TABLE 7–1. U.S. Banks' Market Share of Loans in Developing Countries and Eastern Europe

Regions	U.S. share over 40%	U.S. share 30%–39%	U.S. share below 30%
As of June 30, 1979			
Latin America	31.1%	20.3%	0.1%
Pacific Asia	13.6	4.8	—
South Asia	—	0.2	0.8
Middle East	0.2	0.8	3.8
Africa: Anglophone	0.1	—	3.3
Africa: Francophone	—	0.1	4.2
Western Europe (1)	—	4.1	6.5
Eastern Europe	—	—	6.4
Total	45.0% (2)	30.3%	25.1
As of December 31, 1982			
Latin America	19.7%	37.5%	0.2%
Pacific Asia	13.3	2.9	—
South Asia	—	0.6	0.7
Middle East	—	1.6	1.5
Africa: Anglophone	0.1	0.2	3.8
Africa: Francophone	—	—	1.9
Western Europe (1)	—	1.1	9.4
Eastern Europe	—	—	3.2
Total	33.1%	43.9%	20.7%

(1) Developing countries in Europe are Greece, Spain, Portugal, Yugoslavia.
(2) This means that 45.0 percent of all U.S. banks' claims are in countries where the U.S. market share (i.e., the U.S. share of all cross-border loans) exceeds 40 percent. A cross-border loan is a loan to a borrower in a country other than that of the lender's country of residence.

Despite the various concordats, it is not clear that authorities outside the United States accept their sole responsibility as lender of last resort for their banks when the loans must be funded in dollars.[43] The risk is to the system as well as the particular government: if a home government fails to restrain its banks' dollar lending to the limits of its own dollar reserves and secure lines of dollar credit, the banks may readily create more credit than the system can manage.

Another weakness exists from the perspective of the debtor nations. Some receive much help, others very little. If an Egypt had debt problems, it would quickly attract the attention of G-5 nations. If a Sri Lanka had similar problems, it would not get similar help.

What Are the Benefits of This System?

From the perspective of the G-5 nations, who manage the ILOLR, what are its benefits? So far, in this chapter I have assumed that the world at large benefits from more *international financial stability* than we would otherwise have.[44] Yet there are two other obvious systemic functions the ILOLR could perform. One is to promote *economic growth*. The ILOLR may promote the growth of developing countries[45] in the interest of the G-5 nations or the growth of the G-5 countries themselves.[46] The other is *power maximization*.[47] Perhaps

43. Interviews, Paris. Guttentag and Herring touch on this issue when they point out that the LLR "should have resources which, if not unlimited, are well in excess of the largest needs that it is likely to face in a crisis." Jack Guttentag and Richard Herring, "The Lender of Last Resort Function in an International Context," Essays in International Finance, No. 151, Princeton University, May 1983. Dean and Giddy refer to the problem indirectly. James W. Dean and Ian H. Giddy, *Averting International Banking Crises*, Monograph Series in Finance and Economics, 1981–1, Graduate School of Business Administration, New York University, p. 34.

44. This view is implicit in the work of many economists. See Kindleberger, *Manias*, and Dean and Giddy, *Averting Crises*, for example.

45. See, for example, Pedro-Pablo Kucsinski, "Latin American Debt: Act Two," *Foreign Affairs*, Vol. 62, No. 1, Fall 1983, p. 17.

46. See the arguments that the recessions in developing countries hurt U.S. trade. William E. Brock, "Trade and Debt: The Vital Linkage," *Foreign Affairs*, Vol. 62, No. 5, Summer 1984, p. 1037.

47. This view is implicit in the analysis of Carlos F. Diaz-Alejandro and Edmar Lisboa Bacha, "International Financial Intermediation: A Long and Tropical View," Essays in International Finance, No. 147, Princeton University, May 1982.

the ILOLR benefits the security interests of the G-5 governments. For each of these, however, the ILOLR is deficient. In my view, a fourth function gives the true systemic benefit: *maintenance of the political and economic status quo*. This ILOLR is inherently conservative.

The nature of the systemic benefits and their overall mix should affect lending by the banks. For example, suppose the only benefit is the stability of the financial system; to fit such a system, banks would be well advised to lend on the traditional "good security" that a lender of last resort is supposed to demand of banks. On the other hand, if economic growth alone is maximized, banks should lend to countries that are well managed, regardless of external shocks. If the ILOLR promotes only security interests, banks should make a careful study of those interests before they lend.

International Financial Stability

The benefit of the ILOLR is not to reduce the extremes in the cycle of international financial flows. The ILOLR now addresses the troughs but ignores the peaks: it protects against the downswing in the cycle without discouraging euphoric lending on the upswing. The ILOLR manages the crisis so that the trough of the cycle is shallower than it might be otherwise and possibly shorter as well (see Figure 7–2). In a crisis, the decentralized system permits the bigger players to keep others in. One should recall, however, that the overall effect of this system is to permit banks to lend under an official umbrella. Over the long run, no mechanisms deflate euphoria; the G-5 governments only act as an ILOLR when a crisis looms. This ILOLR system lacks the capability to prevent individual players from anticipating and taking advantage of its existence. A lender of last resort is supposed to provide liquidity in crisis yet not offer so much help that during normal times lenders take on more risk and force the lender of last resort to act. The decentralized ILOLR, unfortunately, helps create a crisis by not adequately discouraging lenders from pulling it in, then acts to resolve the crisis.

Economic Growth

If the benefit of the ILOLR is to promote growth in output, the system now does not push far in that direction. It crudely distinguishes among countries' economic performance but offers no way to

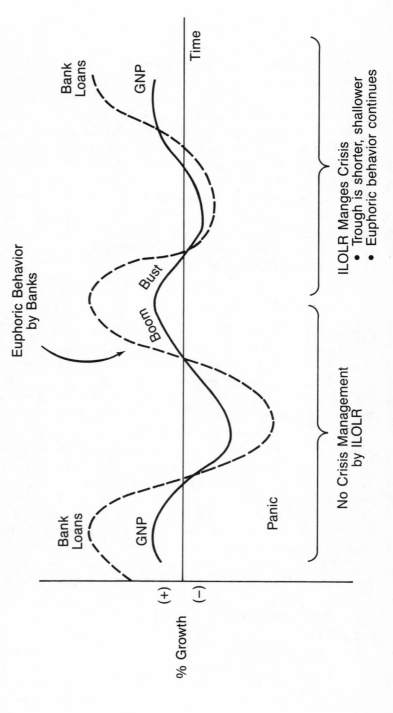

FIGURE 7-2. Cross-border International Lending in a Boom-Bust World:
The Limited Impact of the ILOLR

spark growth. One might say, however, that the existence of the ILOLR encourages gradual adjustment to disequilibria. The standard example is the oil shock and the so-called petrodollar recycling. Without the tacit support of the ILOLR, banks would have been loath to lend to oil-importing countries. Here again, however, is the short-term fix without the long-term solution. The IMF's adjustment measures rest on macroeconomic policies, giving limited attention to underlying structural problems.

Power Maximization

The ILOLR could augment the political power of G-5 countries. A long tradition supports this function. In the late 1870s, former U.S. president Ulysses S. Grant advised the emperor of Japan to eschew foreign debt.

> Look at Egypt, Spain, and Turkey . . . and consider their pitiable condition. . . . Some nations like to lend money to poor nations very much. By this means they flaunt their authority and cajole the poor nation. The purpose of lending money is to get political power for themselves.[48]

It is debatable whether, over the long run, the management of recent debt crises reduced the power of problem countries.[49] Today, however, in contrast to the colonial scramble of the 1870s, the ILOLR does not shift the balance of power among individual G-5 nations. Instead, it emphasizes the relative importance of various G-5 nations in different regions: the United States in Latin America and, with Japan, in Pacific Asia; Germany in Eastern Europe; France and the United Kingdom in former colonies; and a mix in strategic countries around the Mediterranean. In this sense, it reinforces a regional hegemony among the G-5 powers.

These three jobs for the ILOLR may conflict. U.S. national security interests mean the United States has not wanted the ILOLR to push Mexico to address its problems of corruption even if that is needed

---

48. Kamekichi Takahashi, *The Rise and Development of Japan's Modern Economy* (Tokyo: Jiji, 1969), pp. 185–86, quoted in B. Scott, J. Rosenbloom, and A. Sproat, *Japan: 1865–1978* (Boston: Harvard Business School, 1979), p. 37.
49. Large debtors often have power in dealing with their creditors.

for long-term growth and stability. The goal of export-led growth prompted G-5 countries to use credit to promote sales to developing countries, thus adding to the instability of the financial system (the anecdote about the German banks in Peru near the beginning of this chapter is an example). Obviously, as debtor countries adjust, deflation slows their growth to a standstill. This suggests that economic growth in developing countries has the lowest priority among issues of security, growth in the G-5 countries, and financial stability. This ILOLR preserves the status quo, its goal being to maintain the existing political and economic balance.

System Maintenance

The ILOLR is a device for maintenance of a system that extends far beyond finance. This partly answers the question: What are the benefits? Behavior that is anomalous in the international financial system may make more sense when viewed in a broader context. The G-5 countries seek to maintain a set of political and economic relations in which finance is only part. A multiheaded ILOLR with such a broad mandate cannot coordinate beyond the simplest operations; carefully determining penalties is beyond its abilities. An ILOLR that even contributes to financial instability does not necessarily carry within it the seeds of its own destruction. Without arguing that instability itself brings political advantages, it is possible to say that the costs of financial instability may be offset by other benefits.

The ILOLR does not extend beyond maintenance, however. Although the G-5 countries may augment their power over debtor countries, the G-5 do not seem to use the crises to economic advantage against each other. For example, one might expect Japan to continue its strategy promoting exports to developing countries through the activities of the ILOLR. In practice, Japan drastically limited the credit its Export-Import Bank could extend to countries in trouble. The G-5 also do not appear to have tried to change the political balance. The U.S. government rejected proposals emanating from its Defense Department to press Moscow by declaring Poland in default, for example.[50] Indeed, little direction is given.

50. See Benjamin J. Cohen, "International Debt and Linkage Strategies: Some Foreign-Policy Implications for the United States," *International Organization* 39 (Autumn 1985): 699.

By seeing the ILOLR as a form of system maintenance, one can explain several anomalies in the G-5 governments' approach to the debt crises. Having promoted bank lending to many of the countries that eventually defaulted, the G-5 governments took practically no preventive action although many predicted the crisis.[51] They did not share equally the task of managing the crises country by country. They did not even accord equal priority to the national security aspects; among the G-5 foreign affairs ministries, only the United States State Department developed a strong technical cadre. Indeed, in the United States, where government and business are often adversaries, when managing debt crises the big banks have had close relations with the makers of foreign policy in their government.

System Maintenance and the Shift to Regional Hegemony

As a harbinger of change, the ILOLR is significant far beyond the banking system. It is part of a broader shift from U.S. global power[52] to a regional hegemony shared by the G-5 powers. Whether the shift continues depends on events outside international banking, but the way the G-5 countries manage the world's debt problems is nudging the world further toward regional blocs. A dip into history puts the originality of the ILOLR into perspective.

Innovations Introduced by the ILOLR

The novelty of the ILOLR today lies not in government involvement but in its tools. More than a hundred years ago, Ismail Pasha, the khedive of Egypt, overborrowed. He discovered that the major powers of the day, Great Britain and France, would send in troops and govern his country themselves pending repayment. In the 1980s, this is not an option for creditor governments. Nevertheless, they are still in-

51. For example, in June 1974, David Rockefeller, then the chairman of Chase Manhattan Bank, questioned the ability of the banks to lend massive amounts to developing countries. See C. Stabler, "Mideast Oil Money Proves Burdensome," *The Wall Street Journal*, June 6, 1974, p. 1. Much more recently, however, Diaz-Alejandro argued the crisis could not have been anticipated. Carlos F. Diaz-Alejandro, "Latin American Debt: I Don't Think We Are in Kansas Anymore," *Brookings Papers on Economic Activity*, 2:1984, p. 337.
52. See Robert O. Keohane, *After Hegemony: Cooperation and Discord in the World Political Economy* (Princeton, N.J.: Princeton University Press, 1984).

volved, but with other tools: instead of troops, they use their economic strength.

Unlike the practices in the earlier post–World War II era, government officials at the most senior levels, particularly in economic agencies such as finance ministries and central banks, take an active role. This antedates the country debt crises of late 1982, which raised few if any new issues for the home governments. Decisions had already moved from the technocratic level to that of high politics in January 1979,[53] when senior officials in the G-5 countries became actively involved in the effort to help Turkey. Turkey's crisis spawned the "Guadeloupe Four": the heads of government of France, Germany, the United Kingdom, and the United States met on the Caribbean island and discussed solutions to the crisis. Soon after, in 1980, Poland's debt problems involved Chancellor Schmidt and senior cabinet ministers, and quickly drew U.S. cabinet officers into debate about aid. The political dimension and the interests of the home governments had always been there; only the level of decision had changed.[54]

All five countries rely on economic tools to effect decisions of the ILOLR. All formally accord economic agencies much more importance than agencies responsible for security issues, the foreign affairs and defense ministries.[55] In each country, the finance ministry and central bank are largely if not entirely responsible for framing and

53. At least one source suggests that U.S. banks have turned to the State Department for help since the early days of the Eurocredit market. According to contemporary reports, "In early May 1975, Japanese bankers began to complain of pressures being exerted by the U.S. authorities on the Japanese government. According to these bankers, the U.S. wanted Japan to participate in a major aid package to Indonesia [whose oil company Pertamina had failed to service $10 billion in external debt]. . . . The U.S. was worried about the political situation deteriorating and, according to bankers in Tokyo, it told the Japanese government that it must give Indonesia all the assistance it could." *Euromoney*, June 1975, p. 3. Numerous interviews with U.S. bankers and government officials, however, have failed to confirm this story.

54. "Politicization" is not new; banks assessing risk before lending have long anticipated their home's interests in other countries. In their written country analyses, however, bankers could not necessarily include their reading of the borrowing country's strategic importance. If those analyses are considered evidence of prudence when dealing with regulators in the present or in future bad times, the author must avoid any hint of reliance on help from major governments.

55. I use *security* to encompass political and military policies as distinct from economic policy.

implementing policy. These agencies tend to work more through systemic means, influencing the macroeconomy, for example, or setting general regulations, than through direct means, such as lobbying or striking discrete deals with various players, as a foreign ministry would do.

All parties, the banks as well as the creditor and debtor governments, find it useful to resolve debt crises through market or standardized arrangements rather than directly. No party wants to be seen as the donor or recipient of "bailout" money. In a debt crisis, all prefer to channel aid through the debtor country rather than through the banks. Better still, the aid should result from macroeconomic policies. It makes sense that Walter Wriston, in his final years as chief executive officer of Citicorp, should try to get the Federal Reserve Board to adopt an easier monetary policy, which would take the pressure off the debtor countries. Market mechanisms, particularly when encouraged by the IMF, preserve an illusion of distance between the G-5 governments and the other players, banks and borrowers.

The Practical Limits of Market Mechanisms

Market solutions, though neat in technical terms, are inadequate to the task. In debt crises, the G-5 governments use their rule-making power to enforce, change, or bend the rules as necessary to help debtor countries or to force them to behave differently.

Rule bending is informal, and this type of contact has increased. In 1980, the German government took extraordinary steps to encourage the flow of funds to troubled countries in Eastern Europe. I have already described the German chancellor's intervention with the big German banks over Poland in that year.[56] Yugoslavia was also then verging on trouble. German law permitted the government to guarantee bank loans to the country only to secure raw materials for Germany or when a multilateral group was discussing rescheduling. The raw materials rationale was not available for Yugoslavia. At the

56. After West Germany's chancellor intervened in 1980, German banks agreed to lend a nearly bankrupt Poland DM 1.2 billion, of which the government guaranteed only 33 percent rather than the 50 percent sought by the banks. The banks did not, however, lend with less guarantee merely because it was in the German national interest to do so; they were deeply involved themselves. Indeed, they may have reached an understanding with the chancellor about future government help.

IMF meeting that year, the Germans therefore hastily convened a short meeting of officials from a few other governments (who were otherwise not committed to a rescheduling), informally discussed the Yugoslav debt, complied with the law, and guaranteed the credit. Only then would the German banks consider making the loan. All G-5 governments have informal contacts with their banks, of course. In April 1982 an under secretary of state held a conference about Yugoslavia with representatives of major U.S. banks. This does not seem to have been a unique event for the United States or the other G-5 governments.[57]

The G-5 governments have begun to use their banks for foreign policy objectives in countries with debt crises. The governments of the United States and the United Kingdom, at least, have acted directly. U.S. regulators required U.S. banks to put up reserves against loans to Poland even while Poland was current on interest and principal, declaring that such loans were "value impaired." The effect was to force U.S. banks to write off immediately even a new trade credit, which was not required of them in their lending to other troubled countries. The U.K. government acted in a similar vein. During the Falkland Islands War, British law stopped British banks from lending to Argentina.[58] During the same war, Brazil denied British planes the right to refuel and the British government retaliated in the rescheduling. The Thatcher government was reported in late 1983 to have refused to accommodate the demands of British banks and firms that the United Kingdom contribute new funds to Phase II of the Brazilian rescheduling.[59]

57. Bankers consistently report that State Department officials in embassies around the world encourage lending to their host country. For example, bankers and State Department officials have confirmed in interviews since the mid-1970s that in the early part of the decade the agency encouraged U.S. banks to lend in Zaire. Bankers elsewhere report the same: even in Japan, they describe meetings between senior officers of the major banks and the minister of foreign affairs, who encourages them to lend more to a South Korea. Interview, Tokyo, October 1982. Such exhortations seem common to all G-5 countries and are hardly noteworthy. They do not resemble the Dresdner Bank consultations in 1906, described in the Introduction.

58. Britain's action was not unique. For example, the U.S. Trading with the Enemy Act imposes a broader set of constraints on U.S. banks.

59. The Thatcher government later asserted that its November 1983 Paris club contribution to Brazil, through the Export Credit Guarantee Department, was twice the ECGD's exposure. Unpublished letter dated 5 December 1983

The Role of National Security Policymakers

The growing role of national security policymakers in the ILOLR system reflects their countries' regional responsibilities and interests under the new international regime. Nowhere is this more obvious than with the U.S. State Department. Although all G-5 national security agencies remain at one remove from the ILOLR, working instead through the economic agencies, not all are equally distant. Compared with other G-5 countries, the U.S. government has a foreign ministry better equipped to understand banks and the issues they raise, and more willing and able to talk to them and to officials of debtor countries. This is a response to the demands placed on the U.S. government as it took responsibility for Latin American loans, which far outweighed those of troubled debtors in other regions. The other G-5 countries have not yet had to develop a capacity similar to that of the U.S. State Department.

Without exaggerating the role of the U.S. State Department in matters that fall largely within the bailiwick of the Treasury Department and central bank, one can see a difference in organization among the G-5 that reflects the stronger interests of the U.S. government in the Latin American debt crisis. In comparing the roles of the ministries of foreign affairs, finance, commerce, and defense, I assume that each ministry represents its own competence. If the finance ministry is the sole spokesman for the government, one can conclude at least tentatively that the dominant and nearly exclusive focus of policy is financial.[60] We should learn something about the importance of issues that concern foreign political relations, commerce, and war by determining whether the other ministries play much or any role in formulating policy toward the banks.

Among the foreign ministries of the G-5 countries, only the U.S. State Department organized to represent with sophistication its interests on banking matters. Since the late 1970s, as the threat of debt

from Geoffrey Howe, Foreign Secretary, to Sir Robin Maxwell-Hyslop, M.P. In fact, however, too few data were released for other banks and governments even to form an official opinion of whether the British government had pulled its weight in the late-1983 package. The outsiders were forced to rely on the private assurances of Jacques Delarossiere, head of the IMF, that all parties had played their part.

60. *Financial* must be broadly defined, since most finance ministries are concerned with stability of the financial system at home and abroad, which requires sound economies.

crises grew, officers in the Bureau of Economic and Business Affairs unit of the U.S. State Department have tracked the international banks and interpreted their behavior to senior officers. Within the State Department, the unit's success varied with the economic skills and political affiliations of the top men; Secretary Haig, a former military officer, was less interested in debt issues than Secretary Shultz, a businessman and economist. The officers also represented State Department interests to other agencies, such as the Treasury Department and the comptroller of the currency, and interpreted U.S. policy to the banks. By 1983, fifteen officers in this division were involved in banking matters: six in the Office of Monetary Affairs had regional responsibilities; six in the Office of Development Assistance coordinated with multilateral institutions like the World Bank and with agencies like the Export-Import Bank and the Commodity Credit Corporation; and three staff economists gave the entire bureau in-house macroeconomic analysis.

Compared with the U.S. State Department, the foreign ministries of the other G-5 governments had a much more restricted role, if one considers the limited manpower. France and Germany had junior officers whose portfolio simply included bank lending.[61] Although the British had a more senior officer in the Foreign Office to track the debt problems as part of a broader portfolio, he rarely dealt directly with the banks, relying instead on the Bank of England. In Japan, Finance Ministry policy and bureaucratic politics prevented the Foreign Ministry from even having an officer responsible for banks and security issues.[62] Part of the issue is bureaucratic turf, of course. But the outcomes reflect priorities of substantive policy, domestic financial over national security. Of these countries, Japan has not had primary responsibility for problem countries. Even Germany, with Eastern Europe, had to manage countries whose total debt was far below that of Latin America and therefore posed less of a threat to national security. It is not surprising that the national security agencies in each country would play a smaller role than those in the United States.

61. That the German Foreign Affairs Ministry provides an officer in the country's delegation to the IMF does little to approach the staff of twelve to fifteen in the State Department.

62. That Japan's Finance Ministry is increasingly willing to discuss common issues with the Foreign Affairs Ministry does not mean the latter agency can contribute much to the discussion.

The formal organization and manpower reveal the relative importance each foreign ministry attaches to the banks. It is true that organization does not reveal the full extent of a ministry's involvement in an issue; informal contacts, particularly at the highest levels, are important. The size also will not reveal the quality of analysis, but will suggest whether a foreign ministry could think through an issue in advance rather than simply ad hoc during a crisis, or formulate its own position rather than rely on the finance ministry, or take part continuously at the technical level as policy evolves. In foreign ministries, the desk officer for each country is the focal point for policy toward that country. To the extent that the issues extend beyond one country, others on the staff must coordinate policy. Only the U.S. State Department has this capacity.

A Further Shift toward Regional Hegemony?

In accepting the role of an ILOLR as a means to help maintain the international system, the G-5 governments hold a common view that while all must share in the costs of the ILOLR, each is primarily responsible for certain regions of the world. This reflects the shift in power among the G-5 since World War II. As U.S. global power has declined, a regional hegemony has been replacing it at least in the area of international banking and debt. The shift is of major significance if it draws government agencies concerned with national security into the ILOLR more formally.

The problem with the use of economic actors and aggregate solutions is twofold. The distinction between foreign economic and political-security issues is often hard to draw. The two sets of issues may require contradictory solutions. The West German government's *Ostpolitik* entwined both economic and security concerns in the German banks' lending and rescheduling. Japan's interests in Southeast Asia included securing petroleum supplies from Indonesia with projects financed by Japanese banks. So far, the economic agencies have staved off the other agencies. Their ability to keep the political-security agencies at bay depends on two factors. First, their solutions cannot threaten vital security issues. Second, they must succeed.

In restructurings, the ILOLR must therefore accommodate G-5 national security interests. This would become a problem if the need for economic reform in the debtor countries came into conflict with the security interests of the ILOLR members. As mentioned above, debilitating corruption might be allowed to persist in a debtor country if to remove it would harm a governing elite whose continued existence was seen as essential to political stability. Mexico and, until 1986, the Philippines are examples of this thinking.

The conflict between economic adjustment and security imperatives may grow if the existing market-based system fails. Success is not entirely in the hands of the economic ministries administering the system of an ILOLR. If success eludes the parties, then national security agencies will assert themselves more directly. The move toward regional hegemony would then push further.

Conclusion

The lender of last resort, on either the national or the international level, is a way to manage a crisis. That crisis may be triggered by events outside the financial system, including such macroeconomic forces as a recession or collapse in commodity prices and such political forces as a sudden change in government. The world now employs a rudimentary lender of last resort *function* at the international level, but the institutions are national.

The ILOLR is built around alliances of banks and their home governments. These home alliances bring a durability that cannot be matched by other institutions today. International alliances exist, of course. The steering committees and such selling efforts as the 1983 world tour to promote the Brazilian debt rescheduling are recent examples. But they are transitory. The players know their deeper affiliations are at home.

The national organization of this ILOLR reflects and extends the changes taking place in the world's political economy. The effect of this decentralization is to focus attention even more than before on crisis management. We have abandoned responsibility for the long-term direction of the system. I now examine the implications of this.

8

The Buck Stops Here: Stabilizing an Uncertain Environment

How will the debt problem unfold? Will the debtors recover or will we see another crisis, even more serious than in 1982? In the longer run, how will the system evolve? Will any players take responsibility for its long-term direction, or will we continue simply to maintain a system that creates imbalances as serious as those it tries to solve?

The imbalances exist in part because the home country is of such great importance to banks in international credit markets. Although this truth is often lost in debates about lending, public policy, and crisis management, the case of Sicartsa demonstrates it. Financing was paramount to the buyer/borrower, therefore to sellers. The banks' lending depended on the success of their home customer, the seller, who in turn depended on the policy of the home government to win the bids.

Each G-5 home government yokes its banks' international lending to the country's manufactured exports. Most did so after the oil price shocks of the 1970s; all do so to a greater or lesser extent generally. National strategies are a useful way to understand these home policies. Indeed, the government policies that use the banks extend deep into the home economy and, during the 1970s, resulted in a very light hand in the regulation of the banks' international operations.

These big banks are not global institutions independent of any and all nations. Instead of treating their home country just as they treat other countries, they make it the centerpiece of their international lending strategy because its policies so deeply affect their cost structure, the terms they can offer customers, and the nature of their competition. This renders the liberal view of the overall relations between international banks and their home governments suspect. Also suspect, however, is the simple mercantilist view that governments direct their banks' lending. While each view loosely fits banks from some G-5 countries, neither recognizes that a bank's own corporate interests may lie in maintaining its home country links rather than in achieving global scale. Compared to the other G-5 countries, each home offers different costs and benefits to its banks.

The differences among the G-5 countries affect bank strategy by taking competition from the level playing field implicit in the liberal model. Evidence that this is so is found not only in trade-related finance but in Eurosyndication, so global a market that it would seem far removed from the home country's influence. Yet if, for example, a French bank leads, the syndication will—on average—differ from that led by a U.S. or Japanese bank, or one of another nationality.

Even if other factors like trade or regulation become less important, in the final analysis the home remains central to the banks' strategy because it steps in when debt crises loom, doing for its banks what they cannot do themselves and what others will not do for them. Many people have examined the general phenomenon of the lender of last resort. Missing so far has been an understanding of the precise mechanism of this institution in international lending, because who leads affects the course of each crisis.

The real international lender of last resort is a combination of the G-5 nations aided by their major banks. The criteria by which a G-5 nation assumes leadership in a particular crisis, and others follow, are their relative interests in the problem country. In the short run, during a crisis, this international lender of last resort protects itself, dealing with potential free riders by decentralizing from the global to the national level, where the home disciplines its own. In the long run, the international lender of last resort does not protect itself from free riders who, during the 1970s, appear to have anticipated the home's help. The public good this international lender of last resort thus serves is system maintenance: it preserves the political and economic status quo worldwide, at least in the short or medium term. It does not provide international financial stability, promote economic growth, or augment the power of any of the G-5 countries.

Economic nationalism, active as well as passive, encouraged the steady march of banks toward the debt crises of the early 1980s by promoting loans to countries especially vulnerable to external shocks and prone to domestic mismanagement. Private and official creditors believed that borrowers, with nowhere else to turn for finance, would have to continue to service their debt. Bankers understood that their institutions and the key borrowing countries were so important to the G-5 nations that if those borrowers could not service their debt by borrowing more or by increasing their trade surplus, the G-5 nations would step in as the international lender of last resort. This system encouraged banks to lend without adequate attention to the borrowing country's use of funds, as the Sicartsa case illustrates.

Unfortunately, no amount of external funds makes up for bad economic policy in the borrowing country. The story of Sicartsa illustrates how bad projects can be financed. It is not an isolated case, either in Mexico or elsewhere; bad economic policy extends far beyond individual projects. Chapter 6 describes the ill effects of macroeconomic policies, such as fiscal, monetary, or exchange rate policy. In its 1985 *Development Report*, the World Bank recognized that external finance allowed borrowing countries to maintain such ill-suited policies, damaging their economies in the long run, even though by historical standards the borrowing was not excessive.

Once funds are badly used, they can neither be recovered nor later earn a return. On a broad enough scale, this raises the question of whether the countries' debt problem is one of liquidity or solvency. If the problem is simply that Mexico, for example, lacks liquidity because the price of oil is temporarily low, then the solution is to provide bridge finance for a short period of time until the oil price rises. On the other hand, if the problem is that the underlying economy is increasingly unproductive, then until this problem is addressed external funds will only exacerbate the country's precarious position. The line between liquidity and solvency problems is usually not obvious, nor is every nation with debt problems insolvent. The distinction is, however, essential to G-5 policy toward the debtors. The G-5 should not treat as temporary the problems that resulted from years of bad economic policy.

The G-5 governments and their banks now have four choices. First, they could continue with the status quo. The story of Sicartsa explains how this works and shows its destabilizing effect. Second, they could struggle to free the market of government intervention so that economic forces could establish an efficient equilibrium. Even Sisyphus would blanch at this task. Third, banks and their governments could build better alliances at home, allocating costs and benefits to strengthen their own and the world economy. This is dangerous in the long run. Fourth, they could seek incremental change that would give long-term direction to the short- and medium-term policies we use to deal with the debt crisis.

In this chapter I consider these four options for the home governments. On the assumption that the status quo is most likely to persist, I then show how banks can use economic nationalism to resolve issues of business strategy (such as portfolio composition or product choice), country analysis (and therefore geographic markets), and competition in global industries.

Public Policy: Basic Options for Home Governments

Option 1. As Is: The Drawbacks of the Status Quo

A common refrain since the Mexican debt crisis was negotiated in 1982 has been that the system works. After all, there was no collapse. The debtors serviced their debt, for the most part. The serious tests facing major U.S. banks like Continental Illinois and Bank of America were domestic rather than international in origin. Banks were sufficiently burned by the international problems that they would not repeat their massive lending to third world borrowers. Indeed, banks drew back from syndicated lending and, with other intermediaries, turned to more liquid securities and to services that earned fees without placing assets at risk. Bond markets would finance the countries in the future. The third world debt crisis was of historical interest only.

This view may seem compelling. It suggests that home government policy should continue as is. It leads analysts to propose further action similar to that of the early Mexican rescheduling: reduce spreads and fees on reschedulings, reschedule loans due over several years rather than one, extend maturities, and provide new funds, for example.[1]

1. See C. Fred Bergsten, William R. Cline, and John Williamson, *Bank Lending to Developing Countries: The Policy Alternatives* (Washington, D.C.: Institute for International Economics, 1985). The IIE study identifies four major kinds of policies. First are innovations already made in one or more countries. These reduce the immediate pressure on the borrower (by lowering costs or extending maturities), shift some risk from banks to official or private agencies, or make credit more liquid. Second, some policies smooth payments of principal or, by capitalizing it, interest. The third type links a borrower's payments to its capacity

The problem with this view is its assumption of an economic and political environment in which the G-5 governments can continue to maintain the status quo. It assumes that the cost of providing debtors the necessary finance will be acceptable in the home countries. The performance of the world economy in the mid-1980s makes this assumption credible. Yet little change is required in the world economy to raise the cost of system maintenance to potentially unacceptable levels. We face a very uncertain future.

Scenarios are a vehicle to explore very uncertain futures.[2] We may assume that over the long run international lending has the cyclicality recorded by Kindleberger. Of pressing concern to today's policymaker is the curve of the current cycle: Will it be as manageable as others in the post–World War II period, or will there be an even larger challenge than the international lender of last resort has yet faced?

The critical numbers are the borrowing countries' need for foreign credit to service existing debt (in a sense, this is their basic demand) and their capacity to borrow for debt service (the supply).[3] In the period after the first oil shock, borrowing capacity outstripped need. Developing countries could borrow far more than they needed to service their debt; Brazil was able to borrow $12.9 billion, net, from 1974 to 1976, for example. Later, high interest rates on a high volume of debt led a more cautious banking community to slow the growth in lending, thus narrowing the gap between capacity and need. After

---

to pay, perhaps measured against export earnings. The last relieves the country from payment. The authors evaluate the ability of each option to address the persistent problems of developing country debt. The IIE study endorses proposals mainly in the first group, the existing innovations.

2. For a good look at how these scenarios can be used, see Pierre Wack, "Scenarios: Uncharted Waters Ahead" and "Scenarios: Shooting the Rapids," *Harvard Business Review*, September–October 1985, p. 73, and November–December 1985, p. 139. A favorable critique is found in David E. Bell, Stephen P. Bradley, and Varda T. Haimo, "Scenario Analysis," unpublished paper, Harvard University, May 1985, revised November 1985. For an example of scenario planning and industry analysis, see Michael E. Porter, *Competitive Advantage* (New York: Free Press, 1985), chap. 13. Stephen P. Bradley and Dwight B. Crane, *Management of Bank Portfolios* (New York: John Wiley, 1975) apply scenario analysis to banks' portfolios.

3. I assume, with Aliber, that the borrowing countries' willingness to service their debt depends in part on whether they can do so from new borrowing. See Robert Z. Aliber, *The International Money Game*, 2d ed. (New York: Basic Books, 1976).

the August 1982 crisis, the banks on balance drew back from the developing countries; they were net users of funds rather than net lenders. Debt capacity had fallen below the need. Figure 8-1 illustrates this change.

What will happen next? The World Bank has explored this question, publishing part of its analysis in its 1985 *World Development Report*. Alternative scenarios of recovery and deterioration in the world economy indicate two possibilities. In a recovery the financing capacity would exceed the need (the high case); in deterioration the needs would rise and capacity would remain low (the low case) (see Figure 8-2).[4]

To estimate the magnitude of the financing needs the international lender of last resort may reasonably face, and thus assess its continuing ability to manage international debt crises, I chose two groups whose members include the biggest debtor countries: major exporters of manufactures[5] and middle-income oil exporters.[6] I have postulated the outcomes in constant dollars for both cases, using medium- and long-term debt only (see Figure 8-3).[7]

My interest here is how the international lender of last resort performs in both cases. If economic and political conditions in the industrial countries lead to conditions resembling either case, will the international lender of last resort be able to manage? The short answer

---

4. World Bank, *World Development Report, 1985* (New York: Oxford University Press, 1985), chap. 10. The key macroeconomic variables in this example are the growth of exports and the rate of interest. The important policy variables are the extent of protection and the fiscal policy in the industrial countries. In the high case, export growth would exceed the interest rate. In the low case this is reversed. Both cases use internally consistent political and economic assumptions. Both assume that the developing countries "continue to implement policies required for structural adjustment." To 1990, these variables would affect various groups of developing countries in different ways. The World Bank held the oil price constant in both cases. Although a deep sustained drop in oil prices would affect oil exporting and importing debtor nations differently, the overall financing needs would still be immense in a low case that added oil prices as a variable.

5. Argentina, Brazil, Greece, Israel, Portugal, Yugoslavia, Hong Kong, South Korea, Philippines, Singapore, Thailand, and South Africa.

6. Mexico, Peru, Trinidad and Tobago, Venezuela, Iran, Iraq, Syria, Indonesia, Malaysia, Algeria, Angola, Cameroon, Congo (People's Republic), Egypt, Gabon, and Nigeria.

7. The data are the World Bank's, the presentation and interpretation, mine.

FIGURE 8–1. Non-oil-developing Countries' Debt-funding Capacity and Needs, 1973–1983

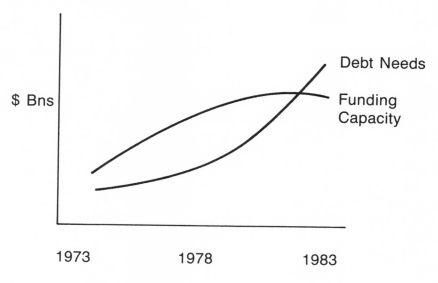

FIGURE 8–2. Hypothetical Debt Capacity and Need in the Future

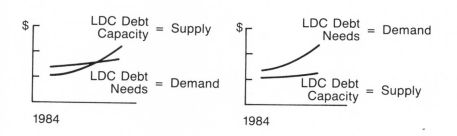

FIGURE 8–3. Two Scenarios for Funding Capacity and Need by 1990

High OECD Case   Low OECD Case

Major Exporters of Manufactures

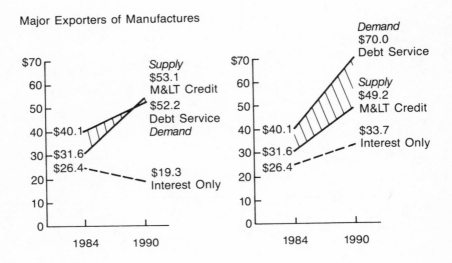

Middle-Income Oil Exporters

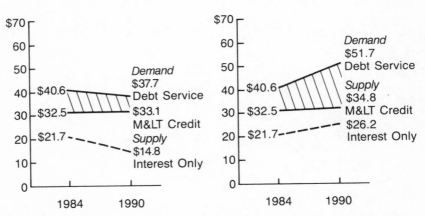

SOURCE: World Bank, *World Development Report, 1985* (New York: Oxford University Press, 1985), chap. 10.

M&LT credit is medium-term and long-term credit to the countries. Debt service is principal and interest on M&LT credit.

is that even in the high case, the benefit of stronger performance to 1990 is limited. Need continues to outstrip capacity for the oil exporters, though the gap has at least narrowed from $8.0 billion to $4.6 billion. Capacity exceeds need for the manufacturers, but barely, and not until just before 1990. As interest rates fall, the declining burden of interest payments relieves both groups. As confidence builds, most players see the value of staying in the game. Private lenders are net suppliers of funds by 1990 (see Figure 8-4). The system works. One foresees more of the same. Given time, banks might even devise a way, other than Eurosyndication, to lend substantial new funds to borrowers in many of the same borrowing countries. In the high case, as the gap slowly narrows, so does the burden to the home governments. The job of the international lender of last resort is to keep the players together during the years to 1990, or long enough for the recovery to catch on.

In the low case the gap between need and capacity widens for both groups of countries. For manufacturers, the $8.5 billion gap in 1984 reaches $20 billion by 1990. The oil exporters' shortfall of $8 billion rises to $17 billion. Much of the increase results from rising interest payments. If these scenarios had used different oil prices, a low price in this case would worsen the oil exporters' shortfall and improve that of the manufacturers. Even without this variable, the low case is serious.

In the low case the international lender of last resort confronts an unprecedented challenge. Groups of countries see their financing gap more than double, in real terms, to massive proportions by 1990. Who will pay for this? Only a few groups are contenders in the debtor and creditor countries.

By 1990, the debtor countries would find little left to squeeze in order to reduce the financing gap. The low case assumes that the borrowing countries continue to make "structural adjustments" that nevertheless prove inadequate. Further economic contraction would endanger political stability. In many of the debtor countries, capital flight had already allowed the rich to escape by the early 1980s; their wealth seems largely unreachable. In most countries, the poor offer little that would lower the financing gap. Their demand is already reduced; their ability to help the country earn foreign exchange, limited. Further reductions in imports will not only lower consumption but also force down production and employment even more as people import fewer intermediate goods.

FIGURE 8–4. Medium- and Long-Term Financing of the Current Account,
Net of Interest (1984 & 1990, $ billions)

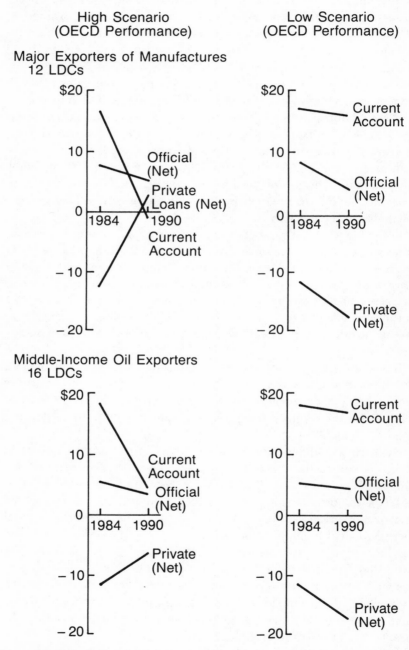

SOURCE: World Bank, *World Development Report, 1985* (New York: Oxford University
Press, 1985), chap. 10.

This means the gap must be financed by the creditors. At one level this is obvious. Less obvious—and quite important—is which groups among the creditors would make up the shortfall, the proportions each would bear, and the methods they would use. They could provide more funds, stretch out the loans, or accept losses. The two key groups among the creditors are those with equity in the banks (since even big uninsured depositors in big banks now appear protected) and those who finance the home governments, the taxpayers.

Between 1982 and 1985, the international lender of last resort used official finance to buy time for the borrowers and the banks to adjust. An ingenious mix of development aid, trade credit, and multilateral assistance allowed borrowing countries to introduce structural change at the same time the banks became net recipients of funds from those countries. The G-5 governments bore a large share of the cost of financing. They continue to do so in the low case: net official flows are always positive, net private flows increasingly negative (see Figure 8-4). As 1990 approaches, it would become more apparent that the G-5 governments were helping the borrowers bail out the banks, by ensuring that the banks' loans are serviced, rather than reducing the banks' exposure in nominal terms (see Chapter 7). In addition, the gross cost to the G-5 would rise. In the low case, the financing gap, in constant dollars, more than doubles for both manufacturers and oil exporters. If the main debtors were isolated, the increase would be even larger. If oil prices were a variable, the increase would be greater for the oil exporters than the manufacturers.

The international lender of last resort must confront the possibility that as its costs grow and the borrowers' problems worsen, the larger transfers will become politically unpalatable at home. This does not mean transfers will necessarily cease, but that some nationally acceptable reason must be found for them to continue. An obvious reason would be national security. In the United States, for example, a borrower like Mexico could well continue to receive financial assistance because of U.S. security interests in a bordering country. Another rationale for transfers to a country like Mexico would be to support existing trade, either vital imports or significant exports. If there is no clear home government interest, the political struggle over who pays in the home country will be between exposed banks and the spokesmen for taxpayers in industrial countries.

The low case assumes slower growth in industrial countries, employment problems, and rising protection. Those who articulate G-5 foreign economic policy would have to cater even more to these domestic interests. As debtor countries' problems grew, spokesmen for G-5 security interests would be likely to have greater weight in national councils than in the past. They are unlikely to want to force massive changes that would disturb the domestic political balance in important borrowing countries. The spokesmen are even less likely to support unimportant borrowers, which would languish further. Under such conditions, effective control of the international lender of last resort could slip from the finance ministries and central banks to others in the government, such as the foreign ministries.

Banks have the most to lose and therefore must look for ways to draw taxpayers into sharing these losses. Their task will be easier the more complex the issues and the longer negotiations drag on. Innumerable reschedulings, each assisted by official incentives in the form of official grants and soft loans, would be ideal. The taxpayer would become a major supporter of restructuring without a keen awareness of his or her special role. This is by far the best resolution a bank could expect as the system works today.

In short, the broader macroeconomic context will determine the course that players must steer through the debt crises of the mid-1980s. The precise causes of high and low scenarios are not at issue. Protection and low demand in the G-5 countries may not be the factors that generate the low case. Low prices for oil and other commodities over a prolonged period could create similar results. Nor is the likelihood of either scenario at issue. In 1985, when the World Bank prepared these, the high scenario seemed unlikely. In 1986, the low scenario seems less likely. The point is that we should not rely on the hope for a healthy macroeconomic environment to solve developing countries' debt problems. If all goes well, it may be possible to keep the status quo. If not, the borrowers are even weaker and the lenders still exposed. More radical action would be necessary. We should prepare now.

Playing the system is the *realpolitik* of internationl banking. It may be the most likely option to occur, but its potential costs now too far outweigh the benefits. Even the high case can be expected to precede another downswing, made more serious by the next wave of euphoric lending. In either the high or the low case, the human cost is immense. This alone would justify a better policy response than the status quo. Yet the G-5 governments face a profound dilemma. Somehow they must find a way to discourage lending that they themselves may at some time want to encourage. The United States, for example, would need to dampen euphoric lending to Mexico even though it may want Mexico to have access to credit that would promote American exports or keep the ruling party in power by funding growth or elites there. One proposal to solve this dilemma is to apply the undiluted discipline of the market.

Option 2. Global Market Discipline: The Liberal Solution

Market forces are supposed to bring equilibrium to the system. They would force banks and borrowers to bear the loss associated with bad loans rather than share that cost with G-5 governments through the indirect channel of aid to the borrowing country. Individual banks that were overexposed would then have to turn to their national central bank for help at penalty rates. The idea is that lenders and borrowers would be more prudent if they could not expect that in a crisis the major industrial countries would provide aid without substantial penalties.

For the market to enforce its discipline, the G-5 governments would have to withdraw from activity in many spheres. Most prominent is their recent active role in the debt crises. Many proposals to help resolve the crises rely on market mechanisms to impose costs. For example, banks could be required to mark down existing loans to or near market value. If banks in 1986 had to reduce the nominal value of their outstanding loans to, say, Mexico, by 40 percent or 50 percent to reflect their discounted value in secondary markets, banks in the future would be much more careful when lending to a country like Mexico. Other proposals place squarely on the banks the risk of high interest rates. These proposals would adjust loans with floating interest rates by setting interest at a fixed rate, capping it at the real interest rate, or indexing the principal to inflation. Unlike the existing loans, when interest rates crossed the agreed threshold the borrower would not be obliged to pay the additional amount. The impact on banks, which operate on very thin margins, would be severe.[8] The market would impose the needed discipline.

8. Less draconian are proposals that merely postpone agreed servicing costs to a time when the borrower could presumably afford them. These include capitalizing excessively high interest, capping interest rates around an average rate over time, or varying the maturity of the loans. Even the proposal that banks should shift part of the risk to private insurers looks to a market solution.

These proposals would have two effects. First, since they apply to existing loans, they could seriously hurt the big banks' income statements. Second, they should reduce the flow of external finance to many borrowing countries over the long run. Yet are the G-5 governments prepared to let either effect come about?

The evidence in this book shows the intensity of the governments' economic activism. Chances are slim that they will become appreciably less active. The G-5 governments used international credit to achieve national goals in the past. These goals are likely to persist in the future, scuttling efforts to impose market solutions. First, the G-5 governments will not accept the price of waiting for domestic market forces to find equilibrium in important borrowing countries. Second, the G-5 will not refrain from helping strategically important debtor nations. Third, the G-5 are not themselves ready to stop manipulating trade and capital flows. The trade credit wars persist in the mid-1980s, skewing credit allocation worldwide. The low scenario would make this worse. Particularly if growth slows, can one realistically expect these broader policies to change in order to move international lending to a free market? The specific proposals I listed that might move the world toward this goal are even now seen as too damaging to the banks.[9] As a general proposition, pursuing a free market in international banking is an elusive goal, given the multitude of state interests that use banks.

In short, the prospect is remote for international capital markets to become free of G-5 government activism. Perhaps it is time to acknowledge this activism and, by doing so, to force those who practice it to act in the interest of the broader community.

Option 3. Bank-Government Alliances: The Mercantilist Solution

Another way to bring long-term direction to the system would be to strengthen and rationalize the existing alliances between home government and big banks at the national level. Mutual interests in stability would help assure sound lending in the future. In this approach, the G-5 governments acknowledge their active role, recognize the benefits this confers on the banks, and impose acceptable, perhaps

9. See Bergsten, Cline, and Williamson, *Bank Lending to Developing Countries: The Policy Alternatives*.

nonfinancial costs on the banks to moderate lending during cyclical upswings. To this end, the banks would take a more immediate role in framing policy beyond regulation and a more explicit role implementing it. The key is cooperation at the time of lending.

Before dismissing this option out of hand, the reader should recall that precisely this type of cooperation existed between each G-5 government and its big banks during the major debt crises. The dilemma is how one extends such cooperation from the time of crisis to the earlier time of lending. A few proposals to deal with the debt problems aim in this direction by reinforcing the banks' ties to their home country. For example, one common suggestion is official insurance for new credit, which is more likely to be issued by a national agency than a multilateral one. This proposal carries the seed of a national effort to guide lending.

For this approach to succeed, each G-5 nation must address its own strategy and the structure of its decision making. Given strong state interests pushing credit for various uses, each G-5 country needs the will to ensure productive use of the loans and the capacity to formulate and implement such a policy. None has had the will to provide the necessary discipline. Several have the capacity.

To strengthen the bank-government alliance means creating a creditors' cartel even more effective than that now in existence. Its members must address basic economic mismanagement in the borrowing country. They must be prepared to reward productive policies, given the political damage of further recessionary policies in the borrowers' countries. The $29 billion proposed by the Baker Plan is just a beginning. The banks and their home governments could devise ways to repatriate the capital that has left the borrowing countries. New governments could be able to trace funds that were obtained by fraud or corruption at home and taken from the country. At present, these funds are out of reach in financial havens. Enormous practical difficulties (how does one prove a corrupt source, for example?) combine with ideology and self-interest in financial centers to thwart any such effort. Only a close alliance between home governments and their banks, and among the creditors as a group, would even begin to make such an effort feasible.

Four of the G-5 countries could build an alliance to ensure productive use of bank credit. To form an alliance, big banks and their home governments must recognize their mutual dependence and refrain from trying to win an advantage at the other's expense, today or tomorrow. Japan and France built an alliance, Germany had one at the political level though not at the technocratic level, and even the United Kingdom fashioned an alliance. In each nation, however, the alliance was formed to achieve a goal such as export promotion. Each country would have to temper such goals in order to ensure that bank loans were productive in the borrowing country, which may run against the original goal. Business-government relations in each of these four countries are more amenable to such an outcome than those in the United States. This is unfortunate because the United States is the biggest player in the weakest part of the borrowing world, Latin America.

The United States now lacks the institutions needed to formulate and implement such an alliance. As discussed in chapter 2, U.S. strategy subordinates long-term economic interest to national security interests and short-term pressures. U.S. policy is formulated in a fragmented process that undercuts long-run concerns. The effective way out of this dilemma requires changes in U.S. government policy and process that extend beyond the financial system.

The broader concern with this option is that it could fortify economic nationalism among the G-5. The capacity for a closer bank-government alliance is only part of the story. Each nation must be willing to adopt a strategy that promotes growth and stability in the world economy. The guiding principle is that all parties would acknowledge the activism of the G-5 governments and commit to responsible behavior in the future. This seems as unlikely today as the requirement of the liberal option that the major governments take a less active role in matters of trade, finance, and security.

Long-term direction to system through market mechanisms or coordinated action seems beyond the capacity of the major powers today. How, then, can the G-5 governments mitigate the effect of their broader policies on the banks' international lending? One is left with a set of small policy changes that, if they were allowed to take hold, could gradually shift lending practices to more stable, productive uses.

Option 4. Cost Sharing, Regulators, and National Strategy: Incremental Steps Toward Stability

The evidence in this book identifies lending for nonproductive purposes as a central cause of the debt crises. At the very least, then, public policy in the G-5 countries should seek to increase the productive use of funds in the future. This means addressing contrary behavior by each of the three major groups: the borrowing countries, the banks, and their home governments. Borrowers should be discouraged from taking funds for nonproductive uses. Banks should be discouraged from lending for those uses. The G-5 government themselves should be discouraged from abetting such loans. Since no central authority can play this role, one needs ways to have each player do so itself. The best way is to impose costs on each if they fail to do so, which means putting risk back into the system. Conversely, those that do accept this responsibility should be rewarded, or at least not penalized.

In the mid-1980s, mechanisms exist to discipline and reward borrowing countries. The International Monetary Fund and the World Bank are important buffers between borrowers and creditors. They must be able to channel funds and evaluate borrowers' performance and policies. Although a quantum increase in their authority and resources is not likely, some change is essential. The G-5 governments should tilt toward greater autonomy for both institutions, IMF policies that address longer-term problems, and World Bank policies that address the developing countries' macroeconomic performance. The hesitant steps already being taken in these directions should be encouraged. The enlightened regulator must fight within its own government to discourage actions that bypass these multilateral institutions, even though this fight cannot be won in all cases. The Mexican rescheduling in mid-1986 is an example of such a loss.

Public policy in the home governments should discourage their banks from lending for nonproductive purposes in the future. The best policy would be to make the banks bear the losses associated with such loans. Since the home governments have been unwilling to apply such a rule to the banks' existing loans, such a policy must be prospective. The rule must be so clear and simple that administrative interpretation will find it difficult to vitiate later. The rule must also be nondiscretionary in application. The best approach would be to place its enforcement outside even the regulator, perhaps in the market itself. Regulators might rule prospectively that when banks make medium-term sovereign loans, some part of each loan must be sufficiently negotiable to be traded on public markets. This would subject at least that part of the credit, and thus the lenders and borrowers, to some market discipline. It is true that even this prospective technique could be avoided. The story of the 10 percent rule in the United

States shows how legislative language can be interpreted to accommodate other state needs. Suppose the U.S. executive decided at some point in the future that banks should be encouraged to lend to third world borrowers again. One could imagine interpretive language permitting the small set of large banks to hold the negotiable portion of most loans; with this power, they could control the impact of market forces despite apparently contradictory legislative language. Nevertheless, such a rule would make it harder to disguise the other state interests.

Home government policy should rely on carrots as well as sticks. It can help the banks manage the losses. An example is the way the German government managed interest rates to help its banks recognize and provide for losses. Here some of the cost was borne by depositors and borrowers at home, while the two troubled banks and their shareholders also paid.

Home governments must address their own role in the euphoric lending and crises. It is easy but pointless to say they they should stop promoting unproductive trade or bailing out important borrowers and banks regardless of the wisdom of the credit. It is not practicable to try in advance to impose costs on government. Home policy should be encouraged to tilt more toward productive applications when the loans are being made. Some agencies within the home governments have supported such a stance; in the future, their voices should carry more weight when public policy toward banks is formulated. This means rethinking the role of regulation.

Looking back, one can see that regulation failed to address the scale of lending in optimistic times, despite the law's wide coverage in the G-5 countries whose banks were most active. U.S. regulators, for example, applied a "composite prudential rating" scheme to banks; asset quality is one of its five crucial elements.[10] The regulators evaluated country risk, grouped countries according to their capacity to repay external debt,[11] weighed U.S. banks' aggregate exposure abroad, reviewed the banks' own country analysis and exposure systems, and

10. Robert R. Bench, "International Lending Supervision," Office of the Comptroller of the Currency, 1984, pp. 4–18.

11. See, for example, the comptroller of the currency's announcement in July 1985 of the countries it considered to be in serious trouble. Monica Langley, "Regulator Lists Countries Whose Loans Require Special Reserves at Banks," *The Wall Street Journal*, July 24, 1985, p. 8.

could force banks to establish reserves against transfer risk. Yet even with such elaborate rules, U.S. regulators did not prevent euphoric lending to the developing countries.[12] One reason this supervision of U.S. banks' foreign assets did not succeed was that other U.S. governmental interests took priority. The G-5 governments are active players who influence the volume and direction of bank credit in the upswing.[13]

The traditional medicine for euphoric lending is related antidotes that assume a passive government. Rooted in the nineteenth-century rationale for the central bank as lender of last resort, the prescriptions have been modified recently to reflect the global economy but not the active governments of the late twentieth century. First, the regulator is to penalize those who draw on lender-of-last-resort facilities. Although the penalties should discourage more risk, such a policy is unwieldy when applied to international credit. Next, the regulator is to oversee the entire operations of its banks, including consolidating accounts, examination, supervision, and disclosure.[14] Third, the regulator must be able to coordinate its own actions; hence, for international lending, one needs a single international lender of last resort.[15] These prescriptions include no notion that the existing lender of last resort at the national level is part of a broader government that contributes to the euphoria in the first place.[16]

12. For a recent synopsis of bank supervision in each of the G-5 countries, see Board of Governors of the Federal Reserve System, "Report to Congress on Bank Supervision in the Group of Ten Nations and Switzerland," May 31, 1984, made pursuant to the International Lending Supervision Act of 1983.

13. Makin explains the debt crisis as a function of development needs, the industrial countries' needs for raw materials, and the U.S. response to external shocks. John H. Makin, *The Global Debt Crisis* (New York: Basic Books, 1984).

14. James W. Dean and Ian H. Giddy, *Averting International Banking Crises*, Monograph Series in Finance and Economics, 1981–1, Graduate School of Business Administration, New York University, pp. 23ff. Pecchioli says trends in this direction should continue. R. M. Pecchioli, *The Internationalization of Banking* (Paris: OECD, 1983), pp. 110–111.

15. Kindleberger, *Manias*, chap. 7.

16. Recent modifications of the regulatory system address some of the problems regulators face, but also fail to account for activist governments. To solve the information hiatus, regulators have provided banks with more data and even better analysis. Central banks and multilateral institutions like the Bank for International Settlements, the OECD, and the IMF circulate the data. Cofinancing, with agencies like the World Bank, may help to improve analysis.

291

Today, none of the G-5 regulatory systems offers a way to address government activism. On the contrary, apart from the asset regulation described above, some G-5 regulators abet the government activity that prompts overlending. Rather than say that the regulators were inept, however, one should ask whether it is appropriate to expect them to work against the national strategy.

Because of government activism, regulators cannot alone solve the problem of euphoric lending and may not even have an important part in the solution. Regulators are just part of the government picture: other actors include officials in trade and foreign ministries. Recall that the conventional medicine uses regulators to moderate the upswing. Implicit here is the idea that law can shape global macroeconomic effects on bank lending. I propose that we think differently about regulation and its role in at least this type of international economic activity. Such an alternate approach may seem somewhat bizarre, given the high profiles of people like Paul Volcker, chairman of the U.S. Federal Reserve Board, during the 1982–1983 crisis. Then, however, Volcker managed the crisis; the problem here is behavior over the long run. Still, who other than regulators can and should assess the banks' exposure? In such a regulated industry, the idea that the role of the law is minimal seems odd.

The standard reasons to regulate,[17] externalities and moral hazard, do not unambiguously justify regulation here.[18] How one treats externalities largely determines whether one concludes that regulators should have an important role in moderating euphoric lending. Most economists treat financial instability as a classic example of externalities or spillovers.[19] Others, however, caution that where externalities

17. *Regulation* is hard to define. "Efforts to distinguish intellectually between...governmental 'regulatory' action and the entire realm of governmental activity—are difficult and the subject of controversy." Stephen Breyer, *Regulation and Its Reform* (Cambridge, Mass.: Harvard University Press, 1982), p. 7. Here, I define *regulation* narrowly to exclude the government-as-player.

18. Breyer identifies several major and secondary reasons to regulate; those that seem at first glance to apply to the problem at hand do not stand scrutiny. Breyer's main reasons are to control monopolies, rents, or excess profits, or to compensate for excessive competition, inadequate information, or spillovers (externalities). His minor reasons are rationalization, paternalism, scarcity, and moral hazard. Ibid., chap. 1.

19. Dean and Giddy describe today's banking instability as a "situation in which risk has been increased...[by] two market-signal-blunting phenomena: domestic safety regulation without comparable offshore safety regulation, and aid

describe "commodities, the value of which is incapable of even rough monetary estimation—commodities such as justice, security, and so on—the 'spillover' notion is virtually useless....One is better off speaking directly of noneconomic reasons for and against taking a particular action rather than explicitly invoking the notion of 'spillover'."[20] In the debt crisis, the term *spillover* refers to the macroeconomic instability caused by euphoric lending. *Growth* and *employment* are economic terms, of course, but they are also values. In this second sense, they are social goals that reach far beyond the statistics that capture them. Many government agencies other than bank regulators help define these goals, then formulate and implement policies to achieve them. These agencies take the lead in periods of euphoria. One must look to them to help moderate the euphoria. Moral hazard is also used to justify regulation in dealing with euphoric lending. Defined as the circumstance when "someone other than a buyer pays for the buyer's purchase,"[21] moral hazard appears to arise in the policy problem at hand: the government pays for the bank's "purchase" of the loan asset, picking up some of the risk associated with the cross-border loan. Yet the government benefits. Its constituents gain markets, growth, and employment in exchange for the banks' assumption of some risk. This set of circumstances does not fit the classic notion of moral hazard.

By expecting regulation to reduce euphoric lending substantially, one asks too much of the law. In this global industry, the common reasons to rely on regulation to solve such problems are tenuous. Law is at best one part of the policy equation. This means, for example, that the grilling Congress gave U.S. regulators was inapposite. The regulators could not be expected to prevent, single-handedly or even largely by their own effort, the debt crises of the developing countries. Obviously, regulators must review individual banks to promote the safety and soundness of each. Regulators cannot change the environment in which the banks operate, however, particularly when other

---

or country lending (e.g., by the IMF) that allows deferral or avoidance of real internal adjustment." Dean and Giddy, *Averting Crises*, p. 24. I note different interventions. In my view, their IMF is shorthand for G-5 action and understates the extent of government involvement. Here is a center-of-the-universe issue. According to Dean and Giddy, financial institutions are at the center, the IMF and governments are epiphenomena. In my view, G-5 policies are at the center, bank lending is the epiphenomenon.

20. Breyer, *Regulation*, p. 26
21. Ibid., p. 33.

government agencies are actively shaping that environment. Do the regulators then have no systemic role in reducing euphoria? Experience shows that their role is in bureaucratic politics. They should try to sway government policy away from actions that fuel the euphoria.

In short, the G-5 governments use their banks now to accomplish a wide variety of national goals. Their various agencies must move toward more systematic and considered cooperation than in the past if the government is merely to take a less active role promoting euphoric lending. Regulators may have to take the lead. How they do so will vary by country. In the United States, more disclosure of the links between trade, national security, and finance would be an important first step. Senior executives in the world's biggest banks, if they are interested in more than their own banks' short-term advantage, should support policies that move in this direction. In the meantime, however, the banks must formulate their strategy in an environment that seeks to preserve the status quo.

Conclusion

People who set public policy need to give a direction to international credit that has been lacking so far. This requires them to address basic problems that led to the crisis. In brief, they must ensure that the costs are borne by all players: the debtor nations, the banks, and the creditor countries as well. So far, the governments and their people have borne the greatest costs. The main need for direction is to ensure not just temporary recovery but a world that is less inclined to play the system in the future. In part, this means adopting proposals to deal with the crisis in the short and medium term that are consistent with the longer-term direction. Such proposals must also be able to work in an environment of economic nationalism. In part, the G-5 governments must build toward a relation with their banks that is constructive rather than adversarial, one in which each recognizes their responsibility and shares the cost. An important step in this direction is to rethink the appropriate role of financial regulators in G-5 states with active governments.

The Choices for the Banks

Big banks face a set of choices similar to their official counterparts, and subject to similar external constraints. Banks could push for a free market or strengthen the alliance with their home government. On the other hand, they may decide to keep playing the system. In the mid-1980s, this means getting government help to resolve existing debt problems, while working to limit constraints on their operations during and beyond the crisis. Passing the buck is surely the easiest route and would probably succeed given the economic and political conditions of the high scenario. It would also continue to have a volatile effect, one that could put the banks in even worse trouble when the world economy next turns down.

The Limited Ability of Banks

Given the number of players, big banks alone cannot address the euphoria in international banking; some, indeed, profit from it. Given their political importance at home, the big banks can adjust their own behavior to stay afloat. They can also use their governments to competitive advantage. We cannot look to the big banks for the statesmanship to resolve the basic problems leading to instability.

A simple logic often compels the individual to act in ways that could lead to serious harm if others followed suit. Banking is no exception. The innovating bank creates a new product or taps a new geographic market that is profitable precisely because others do not yet compete in it. Other banks enter, not merely because of high profitability, but because by staying out they may cede to first entrants not only the new market but an existing position as well. In the early 1970s, while their competitors at home exploited the new Euromarkets, few individual banks would stand by for fear of losing customers in home markets to the innovator. One must add to this most banks' ignorance about the full extent of others' credit and their reading of the ILOLR. Thus euphoria sweeps the industry.

These sturdy truths guide banks in the late 1980s, as before. Not limited to lending to borrowers in developing countries, euphoria extends to many other activities. By reasserting the importance of the home country and its big banks, the international lender of last resort itself prompts the oligopolistic reaction that characterizes many home banking markets and that explains much herding.

In the mid-1980s, euphoria tinged the banks' shift to fee-earning services. All banks rushed to this line. Normally this shift should not involve credit risk, but to earn fees banks also create contingent exposure that may mature into unmatched obligations in the future. No one knows the extent of this practice. The impact could be serious. When banks sell others poor assets, such as notes issued by borrowers in countries with debt problems, selldown may be incomplete in that the bank retains a liability that is contingent on a future event and not necessarily reported on the balance sheet. The bank gambles that if the contingency should occur, any crisis would be managed at least as effectively as the developing countries' debt crises. On the other hand, if the assets sold are good, the bank in effect keeps its riskier assets and its portfolio worsens. This solution to the regulatory and shareholder pressure for more equity appears to weaken the banks' assets against the next downswing of the financial cycle.

Many of the biggest banks try to maintain their international role by greater lending in domestic currencies, a move that taken en masse could also be destabilizing. This move is healthy when the bank matches assets and liabilities in the local currency. Local regulation often prevents foreign banks from gaining direct access to local deposits, however. To the extent foreign banks rely instead on managed or volatile sources of domestic funds, such as central bank swaps or deposits from local banks, they may not have truly matched. These funding sources are common in the protected markets of many developing countries.

When general purpose lending becomes suspect, as in Latin America during the mid-1980s, many banks seek projects to finance. This can be destabilizing. It hobbles the buyer's ability to choose suppliers and thus undermines the credit: like aid tied to the purchase of goods from the donor's country, project finance of this sort specifies a package of goods that may not be optimal.

Contributing to the euphoria is the banks' frequent ignorance of others' exposure to a country or a borrower. This is willful ignorance. It is certainly destabilizing. With the support of their regulators, banks themselves seek opacity. In the United States, the country most inclined to disclose information, the Federal Reserve Board and comptroller of the currency discourage efforts for more disclosure by the Securities and Exchange Commission. Bank regulators in the other G-5 countries oppose disclosure even more.

That international banks would continue to play according to existing rules has some benefits. It reduces instability somewhat by increasing predictability, as does the banks' competitive response to the debt crises. Since international banks have shifted to G-5 territory, the major governments can manage credit growth more effectively than they could lending to developing countries. On the whole, however, betting the system still contributes to euphoria.

The alternatives to the status quo are greater regulation, a free market, or a better alliance of banks and government. Banks will not want their government to assert much greater control over them, a trend already under way. Since home governments are not likely to free up the market by pulling out, banks are left with the option of building or strengthening the alliance at home.

Banks and the Alliance at Home

Banks may decide to forge their alliance at home and maintain it as a strategic tool. Their ability to do so is more apparent at the level of individual transactions than at the systemic level. Their competitive advantage from such alliances is most visible in transactions like Sicartsa, in which banks can use the alliance to win deals abroad. When this help calls for no change in official policy, banks simply build on their ties at home. Otherwise, the bank's job is to shape policy more actively than in the past.

Alliance is imperative in the low scenario, less so in the high one. The low case would force banks to be more explicitly political. This means banks would have to develop their human resources with an eye to shaping and using policy made by a wide range of officials and legislators. The need runs to the top of the corporate chart. It varies by home country. For example, banks in France, Germany, Japan, and the United Kingdom have drawn their chief executive officers and other senior executives from the top ranks of government service. U.S. banks have done so much less. Events may force them to change.

Much more important than the individual transaction, however, is the broad systemic alliance. The banks' pattern of behavior is critical. Over the long run, they must curtail if not abandon the impulse to bet the system. What is being renounced? Not an agreed sharing of costs and benefits; this must take place. Alliance means accepting the costs associated with the benefits, rather than trying to pass the costs to the "ally." In the mid-1970s, it would have meant that banks adequately priced and provided reserves for loans according to the borrowers' risk. The banks must also ensure that their home government similarly abstains. Banks must be able to make their displeasure felt if their government benefits from banks' activity—such as petrodollar recycling—without acknowledging its own responsibility for the costs associated with that activity. Finally, big banks must be able to discipline the maverick, at least with the home government's help.

From these general principles one can define guidelines for banks, addressing a bank's overall strategy, choices about geographic markets, product lines and industries, asset management, and competitive analysis.

Overall Bank Strategy

How the individual bank strikes its alliance depends on its home country. *A bank must formulate its own strategy in light of the strategy of its home government and the broader process of business-government relations there.* A Japanese bank will position trade finance differently from a U.S. bank because of Japan's national strategy. A German bank will position trade finance differently from a Japanese bank because of the nature of business-government relations in Germany. To maintain this strategic tool, the bank's ongoing job is to monitor its home government's priorities, and the trends in performance, for the impact on the alliance.

Each bank evolves its own business strategy that is to some extent unique. To succeed, that strategy—whether formal or informal, explicit or implicit—must accurately reflect the system of international lending this book describes. The precise way in which it does so must vary by bank. The opportunities are legion. The home influences banks' costs at many points. Each offers a way to use the home alliance to competitive advantage.

An important guideline for banks venturing into international markets is that *in a competitive commodity business, the home alliance offers the best way for a bank to follow a successful strategy of differentiation.* Despite the voluminous literature about international banking, few texts examine the big banks' international strategies, which are at once complex and simple.[22] The complexity springs from the maze of regulations to which banks are subject and from the mushrooming number of securities, services, and markets. Complexity might be expected to offer banks chances to differentiate themselves from their competition. Yet differentiation is hard. Big banks readily duplicate others' new services and, in the absence of controls, easily match one

---

22. See, for example, Derek F. Channon, *British Banking Strategy and the International Challenge* (London: Macmillan, 1977).

another's institutional moves. As intermediaries, they add relatively little value. The many rivals in the industry do not treat it as a gentlemen's club. So a low-cost strategy is generally the key to above-average profitability. This conclusion is implicit in the few discussions of banks' strategic decisions.[23]

Nationality, however, is a ready and effective tool for a bank with a differentiation strategy. First, in any one country the number of big banks is small. Second, nationality is indivisible. Although a German bank may copy the latest yen-denominated zero bond or sterling note issuance facility, for example, it cannot make itself Japanese or British. In this basic sense, nationality creates the most defensible strategic groups. Third, nationality is demonstrably powerful, most evidently in the international lender of last resort. Banks continue to rely on the official umbrella when it rains, but they look to their home country rather than all the G-5 countries, because it is at home that they must strike their bargains during restructurings. The impact is pervasive.

Geographic Market Choice and Analysis

Where banks choose to lend must reflect the national strategies of its own home and those of the other G-5 countries. This should be both a major point for corporate strategy and a cardinal rule of country analysis. *A bank should distinguish among three markets: its own home, its major competitors' homes, and third countries, for which it should profile the strategic interests of the G-5 countries.* Since a big bank's own home offers the bank the greatest chance to differentiate itself from foreign banks, it follows that the home markets of other big banks are hard to enter. This holds even for U.S. markets, where non-U.S. banks find it a long, arduous process to establish a customer base outside their existing home clientele.[24] Foreign banks, however, have penetrated the home markets of their competitors to widely varying degrees.[25] A U.S. bank that makes a strategic shift to concentrate in its home market will not escape the thrusts of foreign banks as much as would a Japanese bank that shifted back home.

23. See Marcia L. Stigum and Rene O. Branch, Jr., *Managing Bank Assets and Liabilities* (Homewood, Ill.: Dow Jones-Irwin, 1983), chap. 11.

24. Interviews.

25. See chap. 2.

In contrast, many third-country markets seem accessible. In fact, the extent of a target country's ties with the G-5 nations is crucial for entry decisions. Bankers must ask: Where does Malaysia fit in Japan's strategy, Ivory Coast in France's, or Hungary in West Germany's? Similarly, they must consider where a Brazil or a Philippines fits in the U.S. strategy. If the national strategy in one of the G-5 countries changes, new opportunities as well as risks may arise. This affects the banks' operations in the upswing and downswing of the credit cycle.

As banks plan for the next upswing in the lending cycle after the mid-1980s, one might hope they have learned the dangers of excess. If so, the learning must have come late. Banks were "quite relaxed" as late as October 1981 "about country risk," in the words of a leading analyst at Morgan Guaranty Trust Company.[26] The banks' initial reaction to the 1982 crisis was another form of excess. They replaced their relaxed pose with a simple injunction: (a) do not lend cross border, (b) especially to most countries in Latin America, Africa, or Eastern Europe. This was a first-cut response to the working of the international lender of last resort. Shareholders, at least in the United States, did indeed lump all developing countries together and penalize the banks with large exposures there.[27] Yet the international lender of last resort actually transmitted a lesson that should lead the banks eventually to more sophisticated distinctions among borrowing countries. Over the longer run, bank lending should reflect new perceptions of risk in countries, depending on whether they received more or less protection from the ILOLR than expected before the 1982 crisis. This raises as an issue the techniques of country analysis.

Of the many guides to country analysis, few refer to the G-5 interests in the country and none accords them weight. Irving Friedman expressed the position common among U.S. bankers, in private as well as in public: "Private bank lenders should not assume the existence of a lender of last resort."[28] Those writers who do mention

26. Rimmer de Vries, "Perspective: Country Risk, a Banker's View," in Richard J. Herring, ed., *Managing International Risk* (Cambridge, England: Cambridge University Press, 1983), pp. 177, 178.

27. Steven C. Kyle and Jeffrey D. Sachs, "Developing Country Debt and the Market Value of Large Commercial Banks," Working Paper No. 1470, National Bureau of Economic Research, Cambridge, Mass., September 1984.

28. Irving S. Friedman, *The World Debt Dilemma: Managing Country Risk* (Philadelphia: Robert Morris Associates, 1983), pp. 301–302. See also Pancras Nagy, *Country Risk* (London: Euromoney Publications, 1984).

such interests relegate them to the end of long lists of variables, most having to do with the economy of the borrowing country. Concluding one list, the president of a U.S. regional bank tacks on a short paragraph about factors external to the country, in which he says, "Or a major power may have an economic or strategic interest in maintaining the political status quo in a developing country, evincing this through economic, military, or other aid."[29] The Group of Thirty, reviewing thirty-two variables used in eleven systems to assess country risk, found that only five systems looked at "external relations" of *any* sort.[30]

The true role of this sort of country risk analysis by banks, however, is not at all clear. Before the 1982 crisis, loan officers do not seem to have applied its techniques to lending decisions in a regular way. One study found that even the most careful country analysis yielded to growth imperatives in the banks.[31] In one view, a country analysis serves a different function. It exists to justify marketing decisions after the fact, if a loan goes bad. When it is actually used, country analysis helps banks decide country limits, but not evaluate portfolio quality or set prices.[32] One reason banks do not rely on country analysts is a residual skepticism about their science. The market may outperform the analysts. Another study found that rankings of countries by the spreads they pay, taken from the market, predict debt repayment problems better than models using economic statistics.[33] So one must be careful in accepting statements by country analysts as indicators of actual practice.

Pretense often serves a useful social purpose, and may be a factor in bankers' common denials that they consider a borrowing country's strategic importance to the G-5 countries. Certainly, it would be awkward to make such a calculus explicit if the regulators objected. On the other hand, perhaps it is time to be forthright. Candor suggests the following for future lending.

29. Alexander McW. Wolfe, Jr., "Country Risk," in F. John Mathis, ed., *Offshore Lending by U.S. Commercial Banks,* 2d ed. (Washington, D.C.: Bankers Association for Foreign Trade, 1981), pp. 43, 58.

30. *Risks in International Bank Lending* (New York: Group of Thirty, 1982), pp. 45–46.

31. "Multinational Strategies," Unpublished report, New York, 1983.

32. "A Survey of Country Evaluation Systems in Use," Policy Staff Analysis, U.S. Export-Import Bank, December 22, 1976, p. 21.

33. Monroe Haegle, cited in Chris C. Carvounis, "The LDC Debt Problem: Trends in Country Risk Analysis and Rescheduling Exercises," *Columbia Journal of World Business* (Spring 1982), pp. 15, 19.

The needs and concerns of the banks' home countries will help to determine the speed at which banks return to the hard-hit regions. The debtors' policies are very important. Home country interests are an additional factor. Among banks based in Europe and Japan, cross-border lending is especially likely to continue to follow trade. Among banks based in the United States, cross-border lending should grow as the stock market's concerns about developing countries lessen. When the home regulators and shareholders discourage cross-border lending, they push banks with international networks into other markets in the problem countries. The banks with large international networks respond to the logic of the system, their own mission, and sunk costs by trying to find alternatives to cross-border lending. One important option is lending in local currency in countries other than their home. The biggest banks can consider funding such loans in domestic currency markets because they have the stature to attract local funds.

As banks position themselves for the low case, they will prefer countries that have support from the G-5 nations. This means that in judging geographic markets, the bank must evaluate the political and economic importance of the borrowing country to at least one G-5 power. Other powers have demonstrated they are less reliable than the G-5 governments. Mother Russia's umbrella barely left the closet for Eastern Europe, and the Saudis abruptly left Egypt after the Camp David accords. Banks now cannot expect the leaders of other blocs to support allies.

Among the G-5 governments, all supported the biggest borrowers, to some extent. The difficult calls concerned which borrowing countries had clear, continuous strategic importance to the bank's home country. Nigeria should have had the United Kingdom's active support in rescheduling, but lost it in a diplomatic conflict. Because of the recent crisis, banks can now consider the deeds of their governments, not mere words. Rapid support for a country, such as Mexico, as it heads into a crisis is the best indicator of its strategic importance.

Product Lines and Industries

In their choice of product or service lines and their selection of industries in which to develop expertise, banks should build on the home alliance. *The more important a product line is to the home, the less is its risk and the greater its defensibility.* Anticipating the downswing in the credit cycle, banks must judge which operations are important to their home and so less risky than they would otherwise be.

Banks can categorize services according to the home's impact on them. Two important variables are whether the financing is related to trade or based on market relationships (see chapter 6). A proxy for the latter is the extent to which the transaction must be tailored to the parties' needs rather than standardized.[34] The more closely the operations are related to home trade and the more the transactions must be tailored to the parties' needs, the greater the home's impact (see Figure 8–5). One can classify the range of operations into three groups:

1. *Home impact is high*. Project finance is the best example of trade-related and specially negotiated debt. Such transactions are tied to the home in many ways: direct promotion (official export credit, aid, insurance), indirect promotion (industrial policies, exemptions from home credit standards, less control of cross-border than domestic loans), home support of reschedulings (through various industries), government support of big lead banks, and protected home financial markets (cost of capital, limited home currency lending).

2. *Home impact is moderate*. If financing supports activities that are less tied to trade or less negotiated, the home's involvement is moderate. It consists of selected promotion (such as aid to commodity exports or the help Japan gives resource imports) or general prudential rules.

3. *Home impact is small*. If the financing is both standardized and unrelated to trade, the home does not seek to shape foreign flows. It may, however, have an impact as a side effect of policies designed for other purposes (such as macroeconomic policy affecting the interbank market through monetary or fiscal means).

34. A common functional analysis of financial markets reveals that the more standard the terms of the instrument, the more easily it can be widely traded in broad public markets, where there is less opportunity for direct government intervention in individual transactions. On the other hand, the highly tailored transaction throws it from the broad public markets to banks or other intermediaries, such as venture capitalists.

FIGURE 8–5. The General Impact of Home Countries on Selected Cross-border Credit Operations

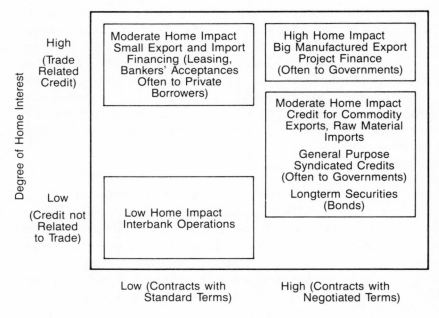

Bankers must consider these varied effects in selecting product lines. That they do so, at least in part, is seen in the banks' decision to offer specialized services in project finance, like those provided in the Si-cartsa financing. The ostensible reason banks prefer project finance is that it is linked to a cash flow they can calculate and, along with assets, perhaps even attach. One must discount this as a reason when borrowers are in the public sector. Most projects are not true projects, since the host government may play a formal or informal role if the project's performance is weak. But since in a crisis the host government will not give such projects priority over other government debtors, for all practical purposes this project financing bears just as much risk as other government debt. Yet banks prefer project finance of this sort. Their preference is reasonable, since the credit often visibly supports the home country's exports, sometimes even including the participation of the home government. The home gives a kind of security, more so in some G-5 countries than in others.

The home enhances a bank's ability to defend its market position in specific products. The clearest example is ex-im bank cofinancing. Although most countries now permit foreign banks to participate in cofinancing, the home country's banks defend their dominant role by virtue of their nationality. The existence of this sort of defensibility should affect decisions to enter product markets.

A second example of product defensibility based on nationality is Eurobond underwriting. The bank that tries to break into the underwriting of nondollar Eurobonds must allow for the potent force of national groups of banks—French for Eurofranc bonds and West German for Eurodeutschemark bonds—in this product line. Because these operations involve the long-term allocation of credit, they have remained important to the country of currency, France or Germany, whose impact remains high even as legal barriers fall.

Finally, banks from the same home that specialize in similar product lines, either by choice or by government fiat, form strategic groups that defend their turf. One example is the German banks' defense of their home markets against U.S. banks in the mid-1970s. A bank's analysis of its product lines must therefore include the impact of national groups.

A bank weighing risk and return in various industries should *identify the underlying strength of its home's major industries and the firms in them, and should evaluate the home's dynamic comparative advantage.* The standard methods of portfolio analysis, applied to international lending, leave a gap between microeconomic and macroeconomic variables. At the microeconomic level, many big banks analyze their portfolios in specific industries as those industries evolve. At the macroeconomic level, many test their portfolio's sensitivity to fluctuations in the economic cycle, and some use multiple scenarios to measure the resilience of their portfolio in hypothetical futures. But bankers lack a way to evaluate the impact of the national strategy on the evolution of industries in the world economy.

Until recently, it was not possible to carry out this evaluation in a comparative way with enough specificity for portfolio analysis. Recent research, however, is beginning to fill this gap. Research has documented the change in market share of each of the G-5 countries in up to fifty-seven product categories from the mid-1960s to the early 1980s. It reveals the distinct patterns of growth in the manufactured exports of the United States and Japan, and the less focused areas of growth for France, Germany, and the United Kingdom.[35]

Portfolio analysts can now put this new research and its approach to use in two ways: first, as an overview of the long-term performance of each country's industries in relation to those of the other G-5 countries and, second, as an indicator of future growth. To this end, the analyst combines the historical performance and the country's present national strategy. Today big U.S. banks set up industry specialists as line units, responsible for credit and fee-based services. For example, a U.S. bank has industry units in such sectors as energy, shipping, electronics, capital goods, and commodities. If the bank could have anticipated fifteen years ago the market strength and growth of U.S. exports of office machines, engines and turbines, agricultural chemicals, processed foods, beverages, and tobacco, it could have positioned itself in these industries early on. The existence and resources of such units should reflect each industry's prospects, which the analysis of national strategies can reveal.

Asset Management

The decision rule for asset management is clear: *Banks need to recognize the impact of the asymmetric cycle on credit markets.* To do so, they must be alert to the impact of the G-5 national strategies. The G-5 governments individually and as part of the international lender of last resort shape the financial cycle, cushioning the downswing and exacerbating the upswing. Since groups of depositors and borrowers respond differently at various points in this cycle, banks should explicitly incorporate the asymmetry of the cycle in managing their portfolios. There is an extensive literature on how banks manage their portfolios; I discuss here only the impact of the asymmetric cycle.[36]

The choice facing banks is whether or not to play in markets subject to waves of euphoria. The answer, not always negative, lies in the bank's timing and its alliances. The ideal position is that of the first

35. Bruce R. Scott and George C. Lodge, eds., *U.S. Competitiveness in the World Economy* (Boston: Harvard Business School Press, 1985), chap. 2, figs. 2–1 to 2–10.
36. See, for example, Stephen P. Bradley and Dwight B. Crane, *Management of Bank Portfolios* (New York: John Wiley, 1975).

mover who identifies the new market, wins high margins, then withdraws as other, slower banks enter and before the market crests. Few achieve the ideal. Those who do risk alienating other banks in markets that require mutual confidence. Those who do not must be able to recognize a first mover of this sort if they choose to play.

Alliances may appear to compel banks to take part in euphoric markets. The cost of not playing can be high. Banks stand to lose existing customers if they cannot offer services a competitor provides. To preclude this, they will enter markets offering minimal profitability. Banks that participated in syndicates to protect a branch in the borrowing country or a tie with a supplier to the borrower are examples. The decision to play under duress should meet high standards of proof. Will failure to play really matter to the ally? Does the return on the related business fully justify the risk? If not, do we have a clear agreement with all concerned parties about the quid pro quo? It would be easy to say that experienced senior officers will counsel reckless youth, but during the 1970s some of the most senior bankers in the industry set a rapid pace. Walter Wriston's 15 percent growth goal is a common example.

Alliances that seem to offer opportunities in euphoric markets demand rigorous scrutiny and constant tending. In certain conditions, the biggest banks' special position in their home market may not end up protecting shareholders or senior management. Continental Illinois Bank demonstrated this in the United States. The banks' historic roles in a region or a country can evaporate if home government strategy changes. British banks' role in Nigeria, for example, may erode if the banks do not serve needs defined by the Nigerian government or if the U.K. and Nigerian governments are caught in another diplomatic imbroglio. Each bank must understand accurately the value of the ties and must be prepared to lobby aggressively to preserve the conditions that permit the special relation.

Competitive Analysis

The strategic options of the world's biggest banks derive from events in the underlying political economy. The degree of rivalry and the direction of lending reflect more than just the banking industry's structure. National strategies touch all aspects of international banking (see Figure 8–6).[37] These industry forces, in turn, affect the broader context. The relations are complex and the lines of causality intricate.

The evidence in this book suggests a basic rule: *A bank should analyze its competitors in light of their home countries' strategies.* Alliances reinforce the competitive power of the biggest banks. If the international lender of last resort's commitment was vague before the debt crises, its actions during the crises showed again that the big banks receive special treatment. This reinforces their ability to take more risk, but the extent varies. Official willingness to protect depositors while letting shareholders bear loss means that a skeptical stock market undercuts

FIGURE 8–6. *National Strategies and Competition in International Banking*

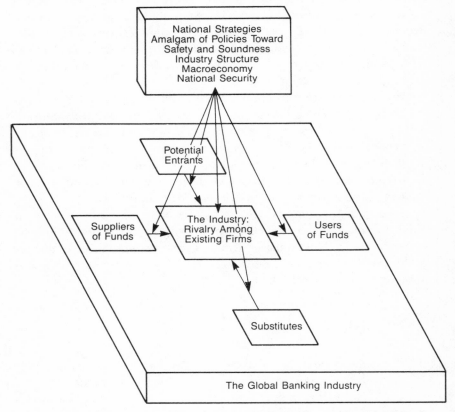

37. This figure draws on Porter's model of industry analysis. See Michael E. Porter, *Competitive Strategy* (New York: Free Press, 1980), p. 4.

the big banks' ability to take on more risk.[38] In general, however, the biggest banks remain aggressive competitors in international markets they select, helped by their home governments' role in the international lender of last resort.

Alliances also reinforce the strategic groups built of banks from the same home country. The debt crises threw banks that had ventured abroad back into their home countries, reinforcing the dynamic that groups banks by home even in the expansionary phase of the credit cycle.

The challenge for strategists in the big banks is now one of intelligence and analysis. Senior managements must learn to relate the national strategies of other home countries to their own competitive behavior; they must identify areas of long-term opportunity and risk. By answering the following questions, a banker can anticipate the moves of foreign competitors and understand the effect of the home government's strategy on the bank's competitive position.

How Will Home Foreign Trade and Investment Policies Affect Competitors?

First, the manager must determine the importance of trade to the home country, the likely performance of the trade account, and the government's probable response. For example, a government may call on banks to help reduce a growing current-account deficit, as France did during the mid-1970s. Of course, the French government's export credit facilities were available to all banks in France. A foreign bank could have taken advantage of such facilities. Some did read the French national strategy accurately and provided capital to exporters, but most did not.

Bankers must also keep their eyes on foreign investment policies. If the Japanese current account has a surplus, for example, the foreign banker can expect capital outflow through Japanese banks and downward pressure on spreads. Instead of withdrawing in reaction, however, a better response would be to ride out the swing in capital markets. When the Japanese current account goes back to a deficit, the bank can be almost certain that pressure on spreads will ease and it will have a new opportunity to lend in Japanese areas of influence.

---

38. The experience with Continental Illinois points toward willingness to protect depositors and let shareholders bear the loss.

How Will Home Macroeconomic Policies Affect Competitors?

Governments use various tools for macroeconomic management, as described in earlier chapters. To control the money supply, for example, the U.S. government manipulates bank deposits (liabilities), whereas the French have managed credit (assets). These policies have different competitive effects. Credit ceilings at home have encouraged French banks to lend abroad. Tight money policies in the United States have forced banks abroad to fund domestic loans. To anticipate macroeconomic policies, a bank must identify the home government's principal tools, anticipate their use, and then trace the implications for the banks.

For bankers, a knowledge of such policies will tell them more than whether credit demand will be strong or weak in France or West Germany. It will indicate the prospective intensity of competition from banks in those nations. If the government of France eases domestic restrictions on credit, French banks may return to home markets for growth and drop their aggressive stance abroad. Anticipating this change, a bank could take up the slack in markets that have been traditionally French.

How Will Home Income Policies Affect Competitors?

A bank must understand possible controls, anticipate change, and trace the impact on banks. Domestic price controls often affect the incomes of banks and their customers, inhibiting loan pricing or the payment of interest on deposits. U.S. bankers know well how Regulation Q encouraged their own foreign expansion. Other banks often face similar constraints: changes in price controls may affect their foreign activities.

How Will Home Structural Policies Affect Competitors?

The banks' prominence often makes them the target or tool of policies to bring about structural change at home, just as West German banks have recently become. Though still unlikely, big changes could reduce the banks' dominant role in the economy by shifting their ties with West German companies and the West German government. Foreign banks could then serve previously inaccessible West German companies in a closer relationship.

Regulatory change that narrows or expands the capacity of big banks to operate abroad can affect others. In earlier chapters I suggested that there are times when the trade component of national strategy takes precedence over regulation. Short of a crisis, bankers should not anticipate major new initiatives to constrain their foreign competitors. They must focus instead on reforming their own home's trade policies.

How Will Home Foreign Policies Affect Competitors?

Although few officials or bankers admit it, the home government's foreign policies involve the banks and can change their calculations of risk and return. A good example in the United States is the freeze of Iranian assets by the Carter administration. In West Germany, Chancellor Schmidt's call to the presidents of the three largest German banks to help Poland in August 1980 may have implicitly guaranteed the banks' Polish exposure.

The implications for bankers remain straightforward: in countries of strategic value to their home country, bankers can continue to expect the greatest official, if unvoiced, interest. It would take a strong political effort, however, to obtain any explicit recognition of these interests from most home governments. Elsewhere, bankers should play the game according to the rules of the country whose influence dominates the region. Efforts by banks to act against those rules, as U.S. banks attempted to do during the Polish debt rescheduling, generate hostility and yield little or no return.

How Should Banks Organize to Better Identify National Strategies and Analyze Them?

Big banks should find it fairly simple to coordinate the human and institutional resources already available to them. At least these banks have officers in several of the key home countries who examine the home countries' macroeconomic performance as part of a credit analysis. They could supply planners in the banks' headquarters with the data necessary to identify and respond to national strategies. My experience with bankers at their headquarters and abroad suggests, however, that few of the big banks use their resources in such a

311

systematic fashion, precisely because of their structure. The banks' regional organization separates line officers familiar with the key home countries (such as France or Britain) from line officers in third country markets (such as Asia or Latin America).

Banks other than the largest do not have officers in Japan, France, West Germany, and other major countries. Whether they should make or buy the necessary analysis is a serious question. Fortunately for analysts, only a small number of home countries—perhaps five or six—field banks that represent any significant market force.[39] Moreover, specialization in a product or a market may reduce the number of home countries whose banks are competitive threats. Smaller banks might place the necessary staff in their existing country analysis unit, but integrating staff analysis with line decisions will be a severe problem.

Bankers must not assume that a national strategy benefits only the home banks. The existence of clearly defined, relatively coherent strategies may permit competitors to spot opportunities the home banks cannot grasp. A national strategy ensures a certain consistency in the behavior of that country's banks and makes it possible to predict their competitive behavior. In France, the new Mitterrand government's shift to "recapture domestic markets" might have been expected, for example, to open third-country markets in French-speaking Africa that were once almost impenetrable. The less coherent strategy in the United States may hamper the predictions of competing banks about the behavior of American banks.

Banks must now define both their own home government's interests and the other G-5 nations' interests more rigorously than before. Even the home government's spokesman closest to the banks, the central bank, considers both public and private interests other than those of the banks. Often neither readily apparent nor simple to negotiate, these interests slow the government's decision-making process, increase uncertainty, and encourage a short-term perspective on solutions to crises. This affects the banks' ability to implement their international lending strategy, as Sicartsa showed.

Bankers must test the timing of critical moves against the interests of their own and competitors' home governments. They must gauge

---

39. Some of the newly industrializing countries, such as Brazil, India, Kuwait, Saudi Arabia, and South Korea, have launched banks that could eventually reach world scale and complicate competitive analysis.

the strength of alliances in other G-5 countries. More is at work in this environment than economic cycles and secular trends. Suppose a bank anticipates that competitors' home government policies may force them to withdraw from markets. The bank may decide to position itself early to take advantage of forthcoming opportunities. For example, in the early 1980s, the Japanese trust banks might have been restrained from international markets by their Finance Ministry, opening opportunities for foreign banks to enter ventures with them. Early ties with the trust banks could give a foreign bank an edge when the restriction took effect. Or a bank might deliberately build capital in periods of wide margins, anticipating narrow margins later as new foreign competitors enter a market previously denied them by their home government.

Conclusion

Banks that know how to use their governments as allies in international competition will be at an advantage. Those that do not will suffer. The decision rules just sketched flow logically from the preceding analyses. A free market ideology may well prompt one to object to conclusions such as these, but they are rational in the context of the existing international financial system. More generally, one may ask whether such behavior contributes to the stability of that system.

We have gradually abandoned responsibility for the long-term direction of the system. Over the last decade, the G-5 nations and their major banks engaged only in system management. We cannot return to a simple U.S. hegemony. The G-5 nations do seem to be evolving a shared hegemony with a distinctly regional cast. This probably cannot be improved on without a powerful supranational body, which is unlikely to evolve soon. For this reason, the public policy imperative is to recognize the importance of the G-5 home countries, to get all parties to share the cost of excessive lending in the past, and to discourage lending for nonproductive purposes in the future. This requires bank regulators to accept a broader vision of their role than they have had so far.

The system described has tremendous resilience. It fits well with the distribution of world political and economic power. It will surely persist in an environment such as that of the high case. That does not make it ideal. But banks and officials operating in such conditions must clearly understand the effect on their choices. If, however, the environment looks more like the low case, banks will face a new challenge. That does not mean the system will change dramatically; at least as likely is the prospect that the system's national character would become even more pronounced.

At the beginning of this book, I asked whether a bank's home country should be important in the calculations of three people: the bank strategist analyzing competing banks, the official in a borrowing country making portfolio choices about the mix of lenders, and the official in a major industrial nation weighing the external finances of a strategically important ally. The home country is important and will continue to be. Officials act on this knowledge to their country's gain. Banks that recognize it win a competitive advantage.

Appendix

To simplify the complex, diverse groups of intermediaries, I gathered data showing the sources and uses of funds on the balance sheets of all financial intermediaries in three G-5 countries at the end of 1980. The countries are Japan, Germany, and the United States; comparable data for France and the United Kingdom were not available.

Three groups of nonfinancial institutions supply funds to intermediaries: government, business, and households. The intermediaries then deploy these funds among many borrowers; some borrowers are the other financial intermediaries. All funds eventually reach the nonfinancial sector in the form of assets held by financial intermediaries.

Consider as an example a country with only two types of intermediaries: banks and pension funds (see Figure A–1). There are three steps.

(1) The savings are provided by government (10 percent), business (30 percent), and households (60 percent). Each is a segment of the intermediaries' market. Government places three-fifths of its savings with banks; this is 10 percent × 3/5, or 6 percent of all savings. Government places two-fifths with pensions, or 4 percent of all savings. Business and households also place their savings. As a result, banks hold 57 percent of all savings (6 percent + 15 percent + 36 percent) and pensions hold 43 percent.

(2) The intermediaries place 20 percent of their funds with each other. Banks place 4 percent with pensions and receive 16 percent from the pensions. Banks thus increase their holdings by 12 percent

FIGURE A–1. *Financial Intermediaries—Market Segments and Share Illustration*

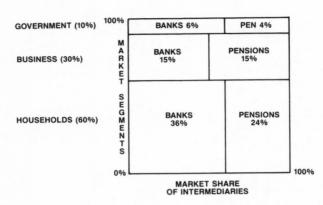

A. Three Groups of Savers (=100%)   PLACE THEIR FUNDS WITH THESE INSTITUTIONS (THE INTERMEDIARIES)

GOVERNMENT (10%)

BUSINESS (30%)

HOUSEHOLDS (60%)

MARKET SEGMENTS

100%

BANKS 6%   PEN 4%

BANKS 15%   PENSIONS 15%

BANKS 36%   PENSIONS 24%

0%   100%

MARKET SHARE OF INTERMEDIARIES

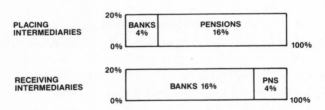

B. The Financial Institutions Place 20% of Their Funds With Other Intermediaries

PLACING INTERMEDIARIES

20%

BANKS 4%   PENSIONS 16%

0%   100%

RECEIVING INTERMEDIARIES

20%

BANKS 16%   PNS 4%

0%   100%

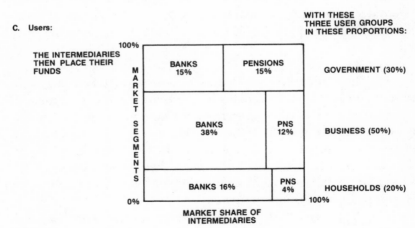

C. Users: WITH THESE THREE USER GROUPS IN THESE PROPORTIONS:

THE INTERMEDIARIES THEN PLACE THEIR FUNDS

MARKET SEGMENTS

100%

BANKS 15%   PENSIONS 15%   GOVERNMENT (30%)

BANKS 38%   PNS 12%   BUSINESS (50%)

BANKS 16%   PNS 4%   HOUSEHOLDS (20%)

0%   100%

MARKET SHARE OF INTERMEDIARIES

to 69 percent of all savings. Pensions' holdings fall to 31 percent. They must deploy these funds among nonfinancial institutions.

(3) The banks and pension funds place their assets with government (30 percent), business (50 percent), and households (20 percent). Banks have half of the market segment for government borrowing (or 15 percent of total investment by the intermediaries). Banks have over three-quarters of the business segment (or 38 percent of the total), and four-fifths of the households segment (or 16 percent of the total). This adds up to the 69 percent of the entire market, which equals the banks' share of savings.

One can also determine the intermediaries' market share and the net suppliers and users of funds. Government supplies only 10 percent and takes 30 percent, and is therefore a net user of 20 percent. Since business is also a net user by 20 percent, households must be—and are—net suppliers by 40 percent. In a sense, household savings are channeled largely through banks to business users and, secondarily, to government.

Apply this analysis to the United States, identifying each of the major groups of players and then giving their share in each major market segment: (1) ultimate sources of funds— government, business, and households; (2) financial intermediaries; and (3) ultimate users— also government, business, and households (Figure A–2).[1] Over 14,421 commercial banks (C), for example, held 35.5 percent of all sources of funds (3.0 percent was from government, 5.6 percent from business, and 26.9 percent from households). The stock of outstanding funds is the outcome of strategic decisions over time, so it is more useful than the flow. According to the evidence, the top ten banks in the United States command 22 percent of the assets of all commercial banks. This gives them only 8 percent of total assets of the intermediated system (22 percent of [9.9 percent plus 14.2 percent plus 12.2 percent]).

1. Note that assets and liabilities are not identical. The data in these charts, which report only domestic accounts when known, come from various sources. Careful judgments about the users of various instruments were needed to classify assets and liabilities, but not all could be assigned.

FIGURE A–2.   *U.S. Financial Intermediaries—Market Segments and Share (End-1980)*

A.   The Markets for Deposits and Other Savings (Total Liabilities $3,225.8 Billion)

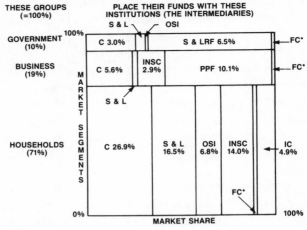

B.   The Intermediary Markets

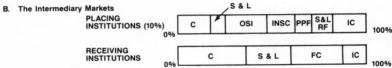

C.   The Markets for Loans and Other Uses (Total Assets $3,382.9 Billion)

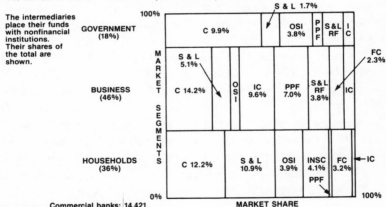

C	Commercial banks: 14,421
S & L	Savings and loans: 4,591
OSI	Other savings institutions: 17,806
INSC	Insurance companies: 4,895
PPF	Private pension funds
S & LRF	State and local retirement funds: minimums of 5 statewide systems per state: can go up to 100 in a few states like Massachusetts
FC	Finance companies: 2,775
IC	Investment companies: includes open-end investment funds, security brokers and dealers, real estate investment trusts, and money market mutual funds

SOURCE: Federal Reserve Board (September 1981).
*Less than 1%.

I have made every effort to include all players and to make the groups comparable. Any omissions are small. In the data for Japan (see Figure A–3), for example, I omitted two small groups: trading companies and insurance companies. The seven groups examined here are particularly important for business finance. The data for Germany are relatively straightforward (see Figure A–4).

Figure A–3. *Japanese Financial Intermediaries—Market Segments and Share (End-1980)*

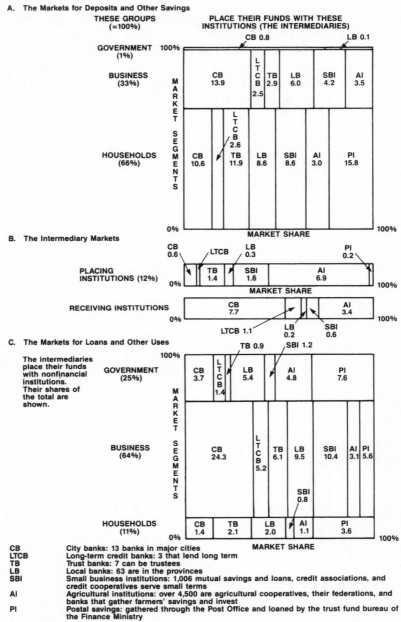

A. **The Markets for Deposits and Other Savings**

B. **The Intermediary Markets**

C. **The Markets for Loans and Other Uses**

CB	City banks: 13 banks in major cities
LTCB	Long-term credit banks: 3 that lend long term
TB	Trust banks: 7 can be trustees
LB	Local banks: 63 are in the provinces
SBI	Small business institutions: 1,006 mutual savings and loans, credit associations, and credit cooperatives serve small terms
AI	Agricultural institutions: over 4,500 are agricultural cooperatives, their federations, and banks that gather farmers' savings and invest
PI	Postal savings: gathered through the Post Office and loaned by the trust fund bureau of the Finance Ministry

Source: Bank of Japan *Economic Statistics Monthly* (May 1983).

FIGURE A–4. *German Financial Intermediaries—Market Segments and Share (End-1980)*

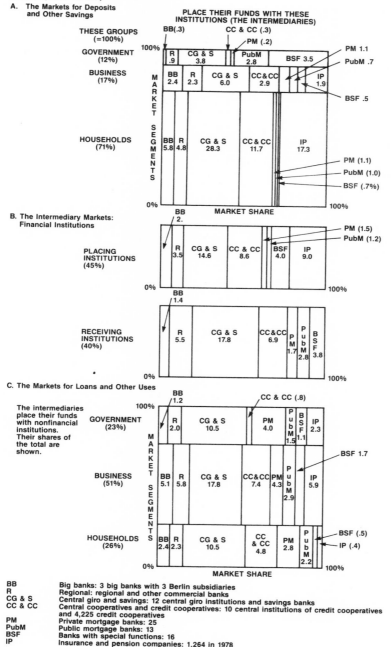

BB	Big banks: 3 big banks with 3 Berlin subsidiaries
R	Regional: regional and other commercial banks
CG & S	Central giro and savings: 12 central giro institutions and savings banks
CC & CC	Central cooperatives and credit cooperatives: 10 central institutions of credit cooperatives and 4,225 credit cooperatives
PM	Private mortgage banks: 25
PubM	Public mortgage banks: 13
BSF	Banks with special functions: 16
IP	Insurance and pension companies: 1,264 in 1978

SOURCE: ,,Zahlen Übersichten und Methodische Erläuterungen Zur Gesamtwirtschaftlichen,'' Finanzierungsrechnung der Deutschen Bundesbank, (1960 Bis 1982), pp. 30 & 40.

Index

Page references to figures or tables are in boldface. References to footnotes are denoted by the letter n following a page number.

Credit ceilings
  in France, 165
  and Japanese lead banks, 205n
  and portfolio diversification in G-5
    countries, 118–121
Credit Lyonnais, S.A., **173**
  credit strategies of, 218
  geographical focus of, 212, 218
  and loan reductions, 216
  and national strategy, 216
  pricing by, 212, **213**, 222
  and pure financial lending, 215
  and retrenchment, 216
  and syndication, 212, 214, 216
  and transnational grouping, 222
Creditor countries, and lender of last
    resort, 281–285. *See also* Group
    of Five countries
Credit paradigm, 125
Credit quality regulation. *See* Portfo-
    lio diversification
Credit subsidies, and regional trade
    balances, 61
Crisis management. *See also* Interna-
    tional lender of last resort
  and bank strategy guidelines, 250
  and international lender of last re-
    sort, 277–284
  and leadership by individual
    banks, 246–247
  national versus international forces
    in, 244
Cross-border lending, 167, 302. *See
    also* Banks; Foreign loans; Inter-
    national lending
Crum, M. Colyer, 96–97
Cudaback, David, 219–220
Currency. *See* Debt conversion; Dol-
    lar-lending; Domestic currency
Current-account deficits, 102, 112
Current-account surpluses, 94–95,
    143

D
Dai-Ichi Kangyo Bank Ltd., **173,
    204**, 205

Dale, Richard S., 118, 137, 140
Dam, Kenneth W., 63
Darity, William, Jr., 235
Davies, John, 94, 119
Davy Loewy, 19
Davy McKee (Sheffield), Ltd., 13,
    26–28, 36
Dean, James W., 116, 260, 291–292
Debt crisis. *See also* Crisis manage-
    ment; Rescheduling
  anticipation of, by banks, 238–240,
    265n
  and Argentina, 225
  causes of, 53–54, 226–230, 274
  costs of, 252–254
  and German banks, 196
  global leaders in, 246
  and interbank deposits, 111
  leadership in, 244–249
  and lending confidence, 230
  management of, and long-term
    goals, 273–294
  and role of G-5 governments, 53–
    54, 56, 265
Debtor countries. *See also* Developing
    countries
  bargaining power of, 253
  and capital flight, 281, 287
  in debt crisis, 226–228, 237–238
  and Eurosyndicates, 197–199
  and financing gap, 281–285
  government activity in, 5–6
  liquidity versus solvency problems
    in, 275
  mismanagement in, and G-5 public
    policy, 275
  and nation-based ILOLR, 260
  productive use of lending and, 289
  structural adjustments in, 281
  and uncertainty of bailout, 251
Debt relief. *See* Bailout
Decentralization to home country. *See
    also* Economic nationalism; Inter-
    national lender of last resort
  and focus on crisis management,
    272

London Interbank Offered Rate
(LIBOR), 41, 152–153
Lorain, Bernard, 220
Low case. *See* Deterioration, versus
recovery
Lurgi Chemie, 19

M
McFadden Act, 112
Makin, John H., 227–230, 291
Malaysia, 251
Mannesman Demag, 38–39, 50
Manufacturers Hanover, **173**, 188,
208, 209
Margins in Eurocurrency loans, 152–
153
Market choice, and national strate-
gies, 299–302. *See also* Country
analysis
Market mechanisms, and debt crises,
267–268, 285–286
Markets, administered, 75–77
Markets, capital. *See* Capital markets
Markets, domestic. *See* Home mar-
kets
Marsh, David, 215
Martin, Sarah, 246
Mathieson, Donald, 101
Mathis, F. John, 171, 301
Mattione, Richard P., 137, 140, 227–
230
Maturities, mismatched, and debt
crisis, 228
and German banks, 192–193
Maxwell-Hyslop, Sir Robin, 269
Mayoux, Jacques, 220–221
Means test. *See* Ten percent rule
Meerschwam, David M., 96–97
Melitz, 125
Mendelsohn, M. S., 136, 140, 179,
233–234
Mentre, Paul, 254
Mercantilist model, 6, 141–143, 145,
286–288
Mercantilist policies, in G-5 govern-
ments, 54–55
Mexican gas pipeline, 109n

Mexico. *See also* Sicartsa project
boom-bust cycles in economy of, 51
and borrowing by parastatals, 105
and debt crisis, 225, 230, 236–240,
255–256
euphoric lending to, 236, **239**
and illiquidity period before crisis,
227
and oil deal with Japan, 20–21, 24
opportunity for, in export credit
wars, 22–24
rescheduling in, and individual
bank stakes, 254–255
and steel industry, 13, **18**
and U.S. interests in, 236–240,
253n, 283
Midland Bank, **173**, 209, **210**, 211
Miller, Stephen W., 115
Mitsubishi Bank Ltd., **173**, 205n
allies in government of, 36
and Mitsubishi Shoji, 31
and Nippon Steel, 30
and passive strategy, 46
pricing, by year, **204**
and Sicartsa cofinancing, 42, 46
Mitsubishi Heavy Industries, 30–31
Mitsubishi Shoji, 30–33
Mitsui Bank, 120
Mitsui Bussan, 30–31
Mitsui Engineering and Shipbuild-
ing, 31
Mitterrand, François Maurice Marie
(French president), 34–35, 215,
220
Mixed credits. *See* Export credit
MNCs. *See* Multinational corpora-
tions
Modigliani, Franco, 125, 144
Moffitt, Michael, 139–140, 230
Mohammed, Azizali F., 175, 233–234
Monetary policy, national paradigms
for, 125
Montagnon, Peter, 258
Moral hazard, as reason for interna-
tional regulation, 292–293
Moran, Theodore H., 8, 48, 134–
135, 142